The Criminal Humanities

CRIMINAL HUMANITIES & FORENSIC SEMIOTICS

Michael Arntfield and Marcel Danesi
General Editors

Vol. 2

This book is a volume in a Peter Lang monograph series.
Every volume is peer reviewed and meets
the highest quality standards for content and production.

PETER LANG
New York • Bern • Frankfurt • Berlin
Brussels • Vienna • Oxford • Warsaw

The Criminal Humanities

An Introduction

EDITED BY Michael Arntfield
AND Marcel Danesi

PETER LANG
New York • Bern • Frankfurt • Berlin
Brussels • Vienna • Oxford • Warsaw

Library of Congress Cataloging-in-Publication Data

Names: Arntfield, Michael, editor. | Danesi, Marcel, editor.
Title: The criminal humanities: an introduction / edited by
Michael Arntfield, Marcel Danesi.
Description: New York: Peter Lang, [2016]
Series: Criminal humanities & forensic semiotics; vol. 2
ISSN 2378-7732 (print) | ISSN 2378-7740 (online)
Includes bibliographical references and index.
Identifiers: LCCN 2016001287 | ISBN 978-1-4331-3194-3 (hardcover: alk. paper)
ISBN 978-1-4539-1673-5 (e-book)
Subjects: LCSH: Criminology. | Crime in literature. | Crime in mass media.
Crime in popular culture. | Crime in art.
Classification: LCC HV6030 .C745 2016 | DDC 700/.4556—dc23
LC record available at http://lccn.loc.gov/2016001287

Bibliographic information published by **Die Deutsche Nationalbibliothek**.
Die Deutsche Nationalbibliothek lists this publication in the "Deutsche
Nationalbibliografie"; detailed bibliographic data are available
on the Internet at http://dnb.d-nb.de/.

"You see, but you do not observe. The distinction is clear."

—Sherlock Holmes, *A Scandal in Bohemia*

For our students—past, present, and future—
who both challenge and invigorate us.

Table of Contents

Acknowledgments xi

List of Contributors xiii

Introduction: Rise of the Criminal Humanist 1
MICHAEL ARNTFIELD & MARCEL DANESI

Part I. Language & Literary Studies

1. A "notable newe Italionisme": Providence, Plague, and the Final Words of the Criminally Condemned in The Unfortunate Traveller 11
JAMES JOHNSTON

2. Original Gangsta: Self-Conceptualization and Criminogenic Authenticity in Hip Hop Music 37
LEE MELLOR

3. Metonymy & Mass Murder: Diagnosing "Splitting" Through Automatic Text Analysis 61
YAIR NEUMAN, YOCHAI COHEN & JAMES KNOLL

Part II. Film & Media Studies

4. Psychopaths in Film: Are Portrayals Realistic and Does It Matter? 73
JOAN SWART

5. The Hammer and the Hummingbird: Spectating Crime Inside the Documentary Film 99
TREVOR GRANT

Part III. Religious & Cultural Studies

6. Looking Inside the Coffin: An Overview of Contemporary Human Vampirism and Its Relevance for Forensics Professionals 117
DJ WILLIAMS & JOHN EDGAR BROWNING

7. A Yiddishe *Cop: Jewish Identity, Police, and Prisoners in Contemporary Law Enforcement* 135
SONIA HALPERN

8. Killing for Slender Man: The Emergence of an Electronic Gospel 171
LEE MELLOR, VIVEK VENKATESH, JASON WALLIN & TIEJA THOMAS

Part IV. Visual Arts & Museum Studies

9. Crime as Curation: Understanding Crime Through the Lens of the Museum 199
VICTORIA BIGLIARDI

10. Crime and the Canvas: Depicting Criminals and Their Punishments in the Visual Arts, from Antiquity to Present 207
BETHANY K. WALTERS & ERIC W. HICKEY

Index 229

Acknowledgments

This anthology and the yawning chasm it fills with respect to the practical and *applied* study of crime—and at the same time the need for the humanities to undergo something of a makeover—did not come about by accident. The scholars assembled here represent a guild of globally recognized experts who, both individually and collectively, have been loosely joined at the forefront of a truly interdisciplinary approach to the scholarship of crime for some time now. They have done so by not only creating but also mobilizing knowledge through the lens of the humanities as the oldest and perhaps the most intuitive of academic traditions. They also all happen to share a common pedagogical tradition grounded in credible, consistent, and publicly responsible research—one that enmeshes the forensic and empirical with the comparative and philosophical. As this anthology will aptly demonstrate through a series of incisive and remarkable essays reflecting original research, these domains should not—and were never supposed to have been—mutually exclusive.

We're not sure to whom we owe the erroneous assumption, taken for granted in many circles, that the study of crime is relegated strictly to traditional "schools" of criminology as itself little more than an adjunct of sociology at its most pedantic and proscriptive. It tends to be those of equally pedantic and myopic scholarship, and with a dearth of relevant real-world experience, who most vigorously defend the existing model. It is one that, as the scholar-practitioners assembled here can attest, has been of little to no practical service to those actually working in the field.

In subsequently building this ambitious anthology from the ground up, we have sought out contributions from scholars who one might liken to criminological reformers. Not only reformers but pioneers—map makers who are etching out a *new* criminology while at the same time providing some degree of succession planning for the humanities. Thus, while we naturally recognize the contributions of those earnest colleagues, and in some cases prescient and stalwart students, who helped create this collection and whose bold work is contained herein, we also want to thank those who allowed us to get to this point—to achieve liftoff in the first place. In no particular order we would like to acknowledge Peter Lang Academic Publishing, and in particular Michelle Salyga and Christopher Myers, for recognizing the global importance of the larger literary series for which this title serves as the proof of concept. We would also like to thank the academic members, fellows, and students affiliated with the University of Toronto's Victoria College and its Centre for Research in Forensic Semiotics—in particular Mariana Bockarova—the members, past and present, of the Western University Cold Case Society, as well as the Northeastern University Collaborative and Listserv for Atypical Homicide, the American Investigative Society of Cold Cases, and the Murder Accountability Project for their support of this project as well as the collective tutelage and peer review provided by some truly extraordinary scholars, scientists, and investigators.

Between Canada and the United States, there are also a number of police officers, forensic practitioners, and specialized regulatory investigators—too many to inventory here, unfortunately—who have provided wonderful insights and who we know will make good use of this anthology. We know they will carry forward its message to the rank-and-file members of law enforcement and related professions who have all too often been let down by criminologists willfully eschewing practical engagement with their work.

With thanks,
Dr. Michael Arntfield & Dr. Marcel Danesi

Contributors

Michael Arntfield is associate professor in the Department of English and Writing Studies at Western University where he specializes in literary criminology and forensic writing. He is also a previous visiting Fulbright Chair at Vanderbilt University specializing in law and literature, is a fellow with the Centre for Research in Forensic Semiotics at the University of Toronto, and is co-editor of Peter Lang's criminal humanities and forensic semiotics collection. A former police officer with over fifteen years' experience across myriad areas of investigative specialization, he sits on both the law enforcement and academic committees of the American Investigative Society of Cold Cases, the Board of Directors for the Murder Accountability Project, and regularly serves an investigative consultant for government, industry, and media. His other related works include *Introduction to Forensic Writing*, a manual of style for criminal investigators authoring search warrants and wiretap affidavits; *Murder City*, a social history of serial homicide in a small Canadian city in the 1960s and 1970s; *Gothic Forensics*, a survey of key texts in Victorian horror and mystery that served as the literary progenitors to contemporary police investigative techniques; and *Practical Criminology*, an introductory textbook that advocates a major reform in the applied scholarship of crime.

Victoria Bigliardi is an intern curator and collections administrator at the Gardiner Museum in Toronto and an honors undergraduate student specializing in material culture at the University of Toronto's Victoria College. Her work has previously been published in the literary journal, *Acta Victoriana*, and she is the co-president of Metaform, the undergraduate society at the University of Toronto's Centre for Research in Forensic Semiotics.

John Edgar Browning is a Marion L. Brittain Postdoctoral Fellow at the Georgia Institute of Technology. He is internationally recognized for his horror, vampire, and Dracula scholarship, with over twelve published or forthcoming books that include *Speaking of Monsters: A Teratological Anthology*,

The Forgotten Writings of Bram Stoker, and *Zombie Talk: Culture, History, Politics*, as well as over sixty published or forthcoming articles, book chapters, and reviews on similar topics. He is widely regarded as a chief expert on real vampirism in the United States and abroad.

Yochai Cohen is a graduate of the mathematics program at the Hebrew University and currently works as a freelance software programmer and computer programming consultant.

Marcel Danesi is full professor of anthropological linguistics, cultural studies, and semiotics at the University of Toronto's Victoria College. The author of the 2013 monograph, *Signs of Crime*, he is considered the international pioneer of the now burgeoning field of forensic semiotics. The founder and director of the University of Toronto's Centre for Research in Forensic Semiotics, he is also co-editor of Peter Lang's criminal humanities and forensic semiotics collection, and series editor of Palgrave-Macmillan's semiotics in popular culture series. A prolific author and public intellectual, he has served as a visiting professor across Europe and his co-authored book, *Made Men: Mafia Culture & the Power of Symbols, Rituals & Myth* established him as a preeminent authority on the symbols and ciphers of transnational organized crime groups, street gangs, and serial offenders.

Trevor Grant is assistant professor in the School of Journalism at the University of Regina where he specializes in documentary film and television production and *cinéma véritée*. He is also a veteran documentarian and television producer whose twenty-year career has featured a number of internationally acclaimed docu-dramas that lay at the intersection of crime and narrative experience. As an acclaimed scholar, director, and raconteur, his work has won awards and nominations from the New York International Film Festival, the U.S. International Film & Video Festival, the Gemini Awards, and the Canadian Screen Awards.

Sonia Halpern is assistant professor in both the Department of Women's Studies and Feminist Research and the Department of English and Writing Studies at Western University. Her research focuses on gender history and on issues of Jewish identity. She is also a recognized art historian and poet whose most recent collection, *The Life and Times of Transition Girl (Revised and Expanded)*, was published in 2015. Halpern's most recent scholarship has appeared in *Women in Judaism: A Multidisciplinary Journal* and *Ontario History*, and her study on Jewish police has been profiled in *The Canadian Jewish News*.

Eric W. Hickey is core faculty with the Walden University forensic psychology graduate program and professor emeritus of criminology at California State University, Fresno. The author of numerous books and the current editor-in-chief for the *Journal of Police and Forensic Psychology*, he is an internationally recognized and court-certified expert in crimes of violence, including serial and mass murder, stalking, and sexual assault. He frequently works on serious and serial cases with law enforcement around the world and has previously served as an investigative consultant on a number of high profile committees and task forces. These include the FBI's Threat Assessment Regional Evaluation Team, the UNABOMB task force, and the California's Peace Officer Service Training program. His monograph, *Serial Murderers and Their Victims*—now in its seventh edition—is widely regarded as the definitive academic treatise on serial and mass murder.

James Johnston is assistant professor of English and Writing Studies at Western University where he specializes in Shakespeare and non-dramatic literature from the Early Modern Period. He also teaches courses on contemporary healthcare writing, organizational and interpersonal professional communication, as well as style and rhetoric. His areas of research interest include sixteenth century health narratives, early modern crime writing, and martyrological literature, including the connection between writing instruction and confessional identity in early modern England. He is the co-author of the textbook, *Healthcare Writing: A Practical Guide to Professional Success.*

James Knoll is an internationally noted forensic psychiatrist and the director of the forensic psychiatry program in the Department of Psychiatry at the Upstate Medical University, SUNY New York. He is a clinician-scholar-practitioner who has worked extensively with American law enforcement, as well as offenders, and is a leading subject matter expert on civilian mass murder.

Lee Mellor is a lecturer in criminology and sociology at Concordia University and a doctoral candidate specializing in violence as communicative identity. Originally a true crime author, Mellor penned the definitive books on the history of multiple murder in Canada, *Cold North Killers: Canadian Serial Murder* and *Rampage: Canadian Mass Murder and Spree Killing*. He is the Chair of the academic advising committee with the American Society of Cold Cases, the editor-in-chief of *Serial Killer Quarterly*, and has analyzed and drafted behavioral profiles for law enforcement agencies in both the United States and Canada. He is also the lead editor of two recent scholar-practitioner anthologies, *Understanding Necrophilia: A Global Multidisciplinary Perspective* and *Homicide: A Forensic Psychology Casebook.*

Yair Neuman is full professor in the Department of Education at Ben-Gurion University of the Negev in Israel and a previous visiting professor at both Oxford University and the Weizmann Institute of Science. An internationally acclaimed scholar-practitioner, his work rests at the crossroads of forensic psychology philosophy, and cognition. Having served as a chief algorithm designer for the Intelligence Advanced Research Projects Activity (IARPA), and as a recognized authority on the writings of school shooters, he has published several books that blend scholarship in forensic semiotics and language coding with criminal and intelligence analysis, including the forthcoming *Shakespeare for the Intelligence Agent: Towards Understanding Real Personalities.*

Joan Swart is a scholar-practitioner and forensic psychologist in private practice in South Africa. She is also affiliated with the Apsche Institute where she specializes in mode deactivation therapy and psychopathology among youth. She has served on the editorial board for the American Psychological Association's *International Journal of Behavioral Consultation and Therapy*, is the current editor-in-chief for the *Journal of Cold Case Review*, and is a behavioral scientist with the American Investigative Society of Cold Cases. She has published several books and journal articles focusing on psychopaths and sex offenders, and is routinely retained as a consultant and expert by law enforcement in both her native South Africa and the United States.

Tieja Thomas is a research associate in the Department of Technology & Innovation at The Conference Board of Canada. She holds a Ph.D. in education from Concordia University where her research program explored the intersections of citizenship education and educational technology. Specifically, she investigated how socio-political phenomena such as hate, violence, and oppression resulting from perceived cultural differences are manifested in online environments. Her doctoral research received several accolades and her current research agenda was recently lauded at the 2015 annual meeting of the Canadian Society for the Study of Education. She currently holds a research grant funded by Public Safety and Emergency Preparedness Canada and is Director of Communication for the Canadian Association for the Study of Women and Education.

Vivek Venkatesh is associate professor in the Department of Education at Concordia University. He is also the former Associate Dean for Academic Programs and Development at the School of Graduate Studies, and former Director of the Graduate Certificate in University Teaching. Venkatesh is an interdisciplinary and applied learning scientist, investigating the psychological, cultural, and cognitive factors impacting the design, development, and inclusive adoption of digital media in educational and social contexts. He is especially interested in developing digital media applications to sensitize and prevent online hate speech amongst the general public, and curating live artistic performances which promote resilience to online violence.

Jason Wallin is associate professor in the Faculty of Education at the University of Alberta where he specializes in media and youth culture. He has authored or co-authored several key interdisciplinary works in this same area, including *A Deleuzian Approach to Curriculum: Essays on a Pedagogical Life*, *Arts-Based Research: A Critique and Proposal*, and *Deleuze, Guattari, Politics and Education*. He is also assistant editor for the *Journal of Curriculum and Pedagogy* and a reviews editor for the journal, *Deleuze Studies*.

Bethany K. Walters is a doctoral student in clinical forensic psychology at the California School of Forensic Studies. Her research and publications are focused on the assessment of psychopathy in violent predatory offenders. She also holds a degree in art history and criticism, with a specialization in Western art from the Early Christian to the Late Renaissance periods.

DJ Williams is Director of Research at the Center for Positive Sexuality in Los Angeles and associate professor of sociology, social work, and criminology at Idaho State University. In addition to his current work as a critical social scientist, he has conducted hundreds of psychosocial forensics assessments in correctional settings and is a world-recognized scholar in deviance and leisure, including vampire culture and real vampirism. He has published extensively in a variety of academic fields, including leisure sciences, social work, sexology, and criminology.

Introduction: Rise of the Criminal Humanist

MICHAEL ARNTFIELD & MARCEL DANESI

In the fall of 2009, New York's Metropolitan Museum of Art became an unlikely crime scene. More accurately, it became *several* crime scenes, with some of the most seasoned and decorated detectives with the New York Police Department (NYPD) descending on the gallery to ply their trade and vigorously scan for clues. It was not, however, some elaborate art theft as one might have suspected upon seeing cops pile into the unlikely location. The crimes under investigation were, in fact, slightly more obscure—the quintessence of cold cases. For starters, there was the robbery depicted in the 1599 oil on canvas painting, *The Calling of St. Matthew* to be solved—new leads to be gleaned from the brush strokes as seen through the jaundiced eye of the grizzled police veteran, rather than the art historian. Other NYPD investigators tried their hand at conducting a psychological profile of John Singer Sargeant's eponymous *Madame X* based on his 1884 portrait of the infamous Paris socialite. Murders, burglaries, and sexual assaults depicted in paintings dating to the sixteenth-century rounded out the other crime scenes for examination, all of which were scoured for new investigative leads—insights previously overlooked into the origins and motives of the malevolent entities and actions captured on canvass over the centuries.

After being placed into "surveillance teams" and assigned a particular work of art to analyze, the officers at the Met were participants in a groundbreaking program spearheaded by Manhattan art historian Amy Herman. The project required that criminal investigators use paintings produced during the Renaissance and onward as narratives that could instruct the police in new ways of approaching evidence and making probative investigative connections—the visual arts as loci for historicizing and contextualizing the antecedents of contemporary criminal investigation techniques. The exhibits were additionally used as training materials to help abate what is frequently derided as police "tunnel vision," or a subjective and unilateral approach to processing visual information, and to instead teach cops to see what is *not* necessarily in front of them—how their instincts, and even their experience, can sometimes betray them. The exercise was more than just academic navel gazing; to get the NYPD to participate in such an initiative and see such an enthusiastic turnout meant that there had to be some demonstrable value to such a radical initiative. Indeed there was.

Feedback later provided by officers hailing from a wide array of precincts and an equally wide array of operational units—from vice and narcotics to homicide and uniformed patrol—suggested that the art analysis program improved both their ability to scan for and process complex and sometimes contradictory information, as well as how to cogently articulate and communicate these same findings to their peers (Hirschfeld, 2009). The NYPD officers who participated in Herman's trial initiative likely were not aware of it, but they were possibly the first law enforcement iteration of a much larger interdisciplinary movement towards narrative—literature, poetry, prose, painting—as a teaching tool in what has historically been a "closed" profession not generally amenable to academic collaboration. Several blocks from Herman's exhibit at the Met, however, on the campus of Columbia University, that same idea had taken hold years earlier with the founding of America's flagship program in narrative-based medicine—an area of study and specialization that has since become synonymous with what is known as the medical humanities.

Now a well-established and respected pedagogical philosophy and paradigm for ongoing professional development, the medical humanities appropriately describe the intersection of medicine—both the practice of medicine and medical education—and the humanities as broadly defined. This includes how texts across myriad media—written works of fiction, literary non-fiction, theatre, art, film, folklore and so forth—can be used as didactic narratives to teach current and aspiring physicians and clinicians about life, death, disease, and the human experience of illness not told in any conventional textbook. There are a proliferating number of monographs, conferences, and journals committed to this very subject, the public face of the movement being Dr. Rita Charon (2008) and her graduate program in narrative medicine at Columbia University, and with her work building on an earlier anthology edited by Greenlagh and Hurwitz (1999) titled *Narrative Based Medicine*. Yet, few if any professions outside of medicine have sought to engage with the humanities and embrace historical texts with the same prescience as those in healthcare have. With the NYPD as the early adopters—and subsequent advocates—of using artwork for the purposes of criminal investigative analysis, it is law enforcement and the discipline of criminology that are—as much if not more so than medicine—actually best suited for such a marriage with the humanities. Remarkably, however, until now, no such covenant has been proposed. With this anthology, the criminal humanities is officially conceived. With this anthology, the criminal humanist now emerges as a scholar-practitioner who epitomizes the burgeoning global relevance of interdisciplinarity.

Just as the medical humanities conjoin medicine with literature as a progressive interdisciplinary pairing, it is the criminal humanities—the overlaying of literature and narrative on to the study of criminals and their victims, the evolution of the criminal justice system, and the epistemology of punishment and deterrence—that concerns this book as the first serious treatise on the matter. The criminal humanities, like the medical humanities, also naturally require the participation of practitioners and the contributions of those with field experience as a matter of credibility—they cannot be deployed from the sterilized confines of the ivory tower alone. This is also, somewhat regrettably, in part what has led the criminal humanities—an umbrella term that this anthology will collectively propose is an adjunct of what Arntfield (2016) calls *literary criminology*—to having thus far failed to launch. There are a few reasons why; there are a few reasons why the value of recognizing texts and salient works of narrative literature, regardless of medium, in moderating broader socio-legal, cultural, and even legislative debates about crime, deviance, punishment, and deterrence have heretofore gone unnoticed.

For instance, a generalization might defensibly be made about a number of professions that fall within the spectrum of the criminal justice system, criminalistics, and law enforcement. The nature of these generalizations is such that, due to the management styles and subcultures inherent to many of these professions, they are naturally incongruous and incompatible with not only literary criminology but also anything earnestly literary. Unlike their peers in medicine and healthcare, for example, there is comparatively little creative license or non-linear thinking that is permissible within vocations like policing, forensic investigative work, and corrections—all of them defined, for the most part, by occupational subcultures whose zeitgeists are still awkwardly rooted in a nineteenth-century working class paramilitarism and anti-intellectualism. Thus, while the physician or the clinician has historically proven able and willing—and is in fact expected in many cases—to double as an educator, whether public intellectual and author or by holding a professorial appointment at a medical school, and is thus empowered to independently spearhead initiatives that amount to disruptive innovation within their field, criminological occupations have cultures and management regimes that deter or in some cases outright prohibit such secondary activities. In many cases, the organizational regimentation and punitive structure of police and correctional organizations actually deters innovation, imagination, and critical thinking altogether. This often includes the imposition of elaborate disincentives in the way of disguised discipline to help ensure that engagement with the humanities and looking to the intelligentsia for outside perspectives is officially verboten.

With few exceptions, municipal policing in the United States, Canada, and the United Kingdom represents the oldest unchanged institutional model in the Western world, dating to Sir Robert Peel's *Metropolitan Police Act* of 1829. This includes a centralized command and control structure that enables police managers to monitor the activities of subordinates outside of the workplace, as well as restrict their leisure and social activities (Emsley & Shpayer-Makov, 2006). Given that officers with the Los Angeles Police Department (LAPD) and countless other law enforcement agencies were actually forbidden, whether by official policy or vernacular custom, to live in unmarried, common-law relationships until the late 1950s (Buntin, 2010), it should come as no surprise that there has historically been little appetite to take more radical steps to reinvent the wheel and challenge institutional traditions, both written and unwritten. Thus, it goes without saying that such environments are not generally conducive to independent scholarship or innovation—that the conditions have been less than optimal for the value of the criminal humanities to be appropriately recognized and taught.

But this is in part what made Amy Herman's collaboration with the NYPD so groundbreaking, and why a sea change is currently underway in terms of how scholarship on crime and violence is defined and executed. Suffice it to say, it has been a long and circuitous road to get to where we are now. It is a time and place where the criminal humanist conjoins theory and practice and, in simultaneously straddling both the criminal justice system and the humanities, restores overdue confidence in and relevance to both. As seen with the reluctant but later responsive participation of the NYPD—the largest police department in North America—in the initiative at the Met, the creative engine for interdisciplinarity in criminal investigative work therefore needs to come from the outside-in, and along a horizontal as opposed to a vertical axis. It is in part the objective of this book to do just that: to simultaneously educate and to disrupt.

The criminal humanities quite simply establish the humanities as a kaleidoscope of scholarly traditions, disciplines, theories, and methods that, in whole or in part, are the most cogent inroad to the critical study of criminal offending, criminal investigation, deviance, and penology, as well as how humans have defined justice over our history. The criminal humanities question how using artistic, literary, and multimedia texts, situations, and other products of the strictly non-investigative world as vehicles for exploring long-standing social and procedural issues of interest to both academia and the general public can allow for increased collaboration not only between the discrete humanities disciplines, but also between academics and practitioners. Positioned at the crossroads of the forensic and the artistic, the literal and the literary, the criminal humanities principally encompass the role of narrative, critical thought, and other comparative methods as the decoder rings with which to contextualize the study of crime. This includes a critical exploration of the connection between writing, painting, film and television production, music, folklore, religious symbols and rites, architecture and comparative literature, traditional electronic media, the Internet, and other domains of popular culture, and how they have influenced both perceptions and definitions of criminality. The synergy that exists between real crime and imagined criminality as manifesting itself through these mediated representations and interconnections ensures that, as one part cultural hermeneutics and one part literary criticism, the criminal humanities now rest at the center of academe's increasingly focused and collective movement towards interdisciplinary collaboration, public engagement, and, most importantly, knowledge mobilization.

This anthology is the first compendium of essays committed exclusively to the study of the criminal humanities, as well as the first book in an ongoing series of titles committed exclusively to the study of the criminal humanities and what Danesi (2013) calls forensic semiotics—the deciphering of archetypal symbols with respect to criminal activity and criminal organizations. Offered here are a total of ten original works reflecting a breadth of methods and styles and of varying length, all of which will to varying degrees appeal to an equally wide breadth of readers. These include readers at the undergraduate, graduate, and post-graduate levels, as well as faculty members, practitioners working in the field, and general interest readers. These essays are authored by a wide array of scholar-practitioners who represent the vanguard of new applied pedagogies and publicly relevant research methodologies alike. Some of these scholars are new and emerging experts, others are prolific contributors to academic life and globally recognized leaders in their fields. Some of these essays are replete with secondary source materials and build on what is already innovative and polemical scholarship, while others represent the equally polemical breaking of new ground and reflect primary source original research and critical thought. While special consideration has been given to preserving the interdisciplinary spirit of the criminal humanities and not limiting the chapters herein to any specific or exclusive area of study, for the purposes of illustrating the manner with which "traditional" humanities disciplines can be seamlessly overlaid on to the scholarship and investigation of crime this anthology has been organized into four discrete modules. Each of these modules, or parts, is labeled, largely for ease of navigation and quick reference, according to those existing humanities disciplines or topics are most explicitly engaged by the chapters contained therein.

Part I of this anthology, containing chapters one through three, is comprised of original essays that examine crime and deviance through the lens of language and literary studies. James Johnston's essay conducts a discourse analysis of the last words of the criminally condemned in Thomas Nashe's *The Unfortunate Traveller*—an iconic text for which the preferred reading has, until now, seldom if ever been criminological in nature. It also offers contemporary scholars of crime and language alike a window into representations and popular understandings of criminality during the Early Modern Period. Lee Mellor's essay examines how criminal authenticity is reified through the use of specific lyrical structures in hip hop music, specifically "gangsta rap" from its origins in the mid-1980s. This includes an overview of how lyrical content can be disaggregated into overtures that reflect symbolic and non-symbolic victimization, as well as depictions of crime victims as both "canvasses" and "soapboxes" that form part of a larger discourse system and urban patois. Yair Neuman, Yochai Cohen, and James Knoll's essay, combining corpus linguistics and more empirical methods with the type of discourse analysis and comparative methods used in the first two essays, posits clear forensic applications of the criminal humanities by examining a psychological phenomenon known as "splitting" in mass murders and how diagnostic criteria can be gleaned through the written communiqués of killers.

Part II of this anthology will appeal predominantly to scholars of film, television, and communication studies, as well as practitioners working in these areas. This module features two lengthy and incisive essays that engage media texts as vehicles for not only disseminating information—and misinformation—with respect to criminal offending, but also as mechanisms for calibrating public responses to specific crimes and popular representations of criminals. Joan Swart's essay examines the accuracy of depictions of psychopaths in film and television by overlaying detailed analyses of well-known villains and antagonists in popular culture on to the accredited clinic and forensic literature. Trevor Grant's essay examines crime as a phenomenon experienced by documentary filmmakers through the camera's ken, including the role of the true crime documentarian as both a culture maker and raconteur who must, when negotiating between the expository and performative categories of documentary, balance both creative and moral obligations.

Part III, containing chapters six through eight, broadly engages a disparity of humanities disciplines, and can be best summarized as a module that is geared towards scholarship in cultural and religious studies. While the former is frequently drawn on during interdisciplinary discussions on the nature of crime, the latter is seldom taught in the context of criminal offending, deviance, and criminogenesis despite sharing some rather salient points of historical convergence. The essay by Sonia Halpern, for instance, examines through both religious and ethnographic lenses the seldom discussed intersection of Judaism and criminal offending from two discrete sociohistorical viewpoints. The chapter also includes a candid look at the experience of Jewish police officers on one hand, and the experience of Jewish offenders and prison inmates on the other—an essay that should be of particular interest not only to scholars of religion, but also to law enforcement recruiters and penitentiary officials alike. The second essay in this module, authored by both DJ Williams and John Edgar Browning, examines how forensic professionals can benefit from scholarship in vampire studies, including how cultural responses to the vampire mythos dating back to Stoker's original 1897 *Dracula* through to more recent iterations have engendered a movement in real vampirism. The emergence of the *real* vampire and its implications with respect to criminal investigative analysis and behavioral profiling represents one of the more practical applications of literary criminology and traditional ethnographic work, with both authors having spent considerable in the field learning the customs of this microculture. The last essay in this module is authored by Lee Mellor, Vivek Venkatesh, Jason Wallin and Tieja Thomas and examines the hysteria surrounding the Internet meme known only as Slender Man—a digitally created ghoul that has been interpreted by some as a real entity borne of the Web and who has apparently inspired at least one act of sacrificial violence. The essay, which broadly connects corpus linguistics, hermeneutics, and forensic psychology with both metaphysics and ontology raises timely and probative questions about how the criminal justice system will respond to codifying sanity as new angels and demons emerge from the only reality many people know—social media.

Lastly, Part IV of this anthology will appeal to a wide range of scholars, practitioners, and general interest lay readers who will find two essays that stake new territory for the study of criminal offending, the criminal mind, and the aesthetic treatments of criminality in both the visual arts and museum studies. The penultimate chapter in this anthology by Victoria Bigliardi postulates the existence of an innate "curator mind" among criminal investigators—the ability to apply narrative, metaphor, and forensic semiotics the intepretation of crime scenes in much the same way the museum curator assembles collections to (re)create tableaus of historic events. Lastly, this module—and the anthology proper—is punctuated with an essay by Bethany Walters and Eric Hickey which meticulously details the evolution of artistic representations of crime, punishment, violence, and victims in the visual arts, from sculpture to painting and all points in between.

There are a number of advantages to using a multi-authored text to establish a beachhead for such a new and notable branch of both criminology and the humanities—the first and defintive text to wed the study of crime with the expansive array of conceptual and comparative-based disciplines covered here. These advantages are both strategic and pedagogical. For one, it would be nearly impossible for a single author to speak credibly to the extensive spectrum of subject matters discussed with great expertise here. Second, in order to provide a realistic and equitable preview of what future scholarship in the criminal humanities might hold, a disparity of voices reflecting varying years of experience have been consolidated in one place—the pages of this text—to provide a varied and balanced overview of what the criminal humanities mean to them. After reviewing the contents of this anthology, whether in whole or in part based on areas of interest, the reader will no doubt have developed his or her own definition—and accompanying expectations—of what the criminal humanities are or are not. And so here it begins, for better or worse.

References

Arntfield, Michael. *Gothic Forensics: Criminal Investigative Procedure in Victorian Horror & Mystery*. New York: Palgrave-Macmillan. 2016.

Buntin, John. *L. A. Noir: The Struggle for the Soul of America's Most Seductive City*. New York: Broadway Books. 2010.

Charon, Rita. *Narrative Medicine: Honoring the Stories of Illness*. New York: Oxford University Press. 2008.

Danesi, Marcel. *Signs of Crime: Introducing Forensic Semiotics*. Berlin: De-Gruyter. 2013.

Emsley, Clive & Haia Shpayer-Makov (Eds.) *Police Detectives in History, 1750–1950*. Burlington, VT: Ashgate. 2006.

Greenlagh, Trisha & Hurwitz, Brian (Eds.) *Narrative Based Medicine: Dialogue & Discourse in Clinical Practice*. London: BMJ Books. 1998.

Hirschfeld, Neil. "Teaching Cops to See." *Smithsonian Magazine*. Online edition. October 2009. http://www.smithsonianmag.com/arts-culture/teaching-cops-to-see-138500635/.

Part I

Language & Literary Studies

1. *A "notable newe Italionisme": Providence, Plague, and the Final Words of the Criminally Condemned in* The Unfortunate Traveller

James Johnston

Introduction

A crucially important but still relatively under-explored progenitor of modern prose fiction, Thomas Nashe's (1594) *The Unfortunate Traveller* is almost gleefully preoccupied with representations of violence, both criminal and judicial. There are few early modern works so well-suited to the criminal humanities and to a mode of reading that can provide a critically productive inroad to reconsidering our historical understanding of criminality and the legal responses to it in more nuanced and provocative ways. Jack Wilton, *Unfortunate Traveller's* narrator and titular protagonist, employs "but a word and a *blowe*" to sum up his experience of a pseudo-historical, plague-besieged 1522 Rome. Wilton's phrase is charged with a depth of meaning that goes well beyond both its reference to the accompanying liturgical refrain "Lord have mercie upon us," which speaks of a need for collective prayer in the face of widespread suffering, and its punning invocation of *plague*'s Latin etymology (*plaga*: stroke). In this essay, I contend that such a depth of meaning is enabled and informed by the fact of Rome's being the geographical location of the plague in Nashe's text—more precisely, by the operative metonymic exchanges between threats of spiritual and of bodily infection that Rome encourages as both a real and imagined space of cultural, confessional, and criminal otherness. What follows aims to read the violent death scenes that punctuate Wilton's Roman narrative with a broader view to just how it is they constitute "a word and a blowe" model of affliction. Specifically, this essay aims to read these scenes of criminal and judicial violence in terms of how they depict a problematized mode of linguistic agency effected in the face of punitive suffering. To wit, the ritualized final words of those about to die raise important questions as to the limits and coherence of a prevailing early modern discourse of providentialism that understood both spiritual and legal threats to the social order as being equally and necessarily subject to state-endorsed (capital) punishment.

As Jonathan Dollimore (2004) describes it in *Radical Tragedy*, a landmark cultural materialist reassessment of early modern drama, the primary governmental function of "establishment providentialism" in late sixteenth-century England was "ratification of the existing social order. God encoded the natural and social world with a system of regulative (and self-regulating) law. The existing order, give or take a few aberrations, is the legitimate one." Providentialism "was reinforced in [Elizabethan England] by the idea of specific intervention … usually, though not always, involving a punitive action by God or one of his agents" (87). At the time, of course, criminal behavior of any stripe represented at once a threat to social order and a sinful influence from which frequently violent punishment by the state provided the means of deliverance. As such, the exercise of criminal justice in early modern England was conceived of as curative and at least potentially as an indicator of divine favor: a re-assertion of Protestant England's status as God's chosen (Gaskill 2000, 290). This last was particularly the case when, in the wake of *Regnans in Excelsis*, Pope Pius V's 1570 bull labeling Elizabeth I a heretic and negating her authority as a ruler, the crime being punished was treason and the perpetrator was Catholic.[1]

Due to its being understood as another recurrent threat to the social order (and to life) similarly subject to the explanatory narratives of providentialism, the all-too-common experience of plague infection tended, especially in the later sixteenth-century imagination, to shade almost indistinguishably into the discourse of crime and punishment. Whether religious or secular in nature, texts of the era insistently depicted a sinful, criminally diseased morality and a physically diseased body as inextricably linked. Thus, not surprisingly, in *Unfortunate Traveller*, plague infection elides seamlessly with the judicial violence enacted by the state on criminals, Catholic traitors specifically. More to the point, it elides with the scene of execution that represents the state's final, most seemingly complete enactment of criminal justice. Consequently, the onus for articulating the providential significance of suffering, as a result of either crime or of disease, gets put on the rhetorical performance of the last dying speech. Of the several such depictions of punitive violence in Wilton's Italian narrative, really only the final scene of the revenger Cutwolfe's ghastly torture and death is characterized by an actual speech uttered by a condemned criminal on a scaffold as precursor to a state execution. Other scenes, though, offer versions of such speeches that are just as readily discernible as dying speeches—solicited final words, by the standards of contemporary capital punishment—with respect to both form and function. Certainly, it seems significant that Nashe so insistently opens up spaces in the text for engaging the explanatory providential rhetoric of dying speeches, and for considering the nature of those speeches as ritualized discursive performances. The query that ensues is what might be at stake in such repeated turns to the last dying speech as a model for agency?

Mihoko Suzuki (1984), among other critics, has noted that the redemptive, salutary potential of Christian providence is, in the end, wholly inaccessible throughout Wilton's various accounts of suffering (368). And it is to a recognition of the ultimate absence of certainty with respect to the end of affliction that Wilton seems to speak in the wistful assessment by way of which he begins to draw his narrative to a close: "Unsearchable is the booke of our destinies" (Nashe 1594, 2.327). There is a radical providential uncertainty inherent in dying speeches due to their characteristic inability to articulate any sort of stable, positive *telos* of suffering in an unproblematized way. That uncertainty affords Nashe an opportunity to re-imagine the limits and (in) efficacies of language offered in the face of persecution and to rehearse the anxiety and instability that informs the early modern providentialist understanding of criminal justice. The sensationalized, murderous violence that proliferates in Wilton's Rome resists association with any sort of positive end. Providential assurance of justice in the form of punitive affliction wrought by the hand of God gets insistently called into question by human agents who, to quote Suzuki (1984), misleadingly "arrogate to themselves the power of being [providence's] instrument" in persecuting and pursuing the execution of others, or even of themselves. The characters who populate Wilton's narrative demonstrate an abiding desire to assert control over the violence and disorder of their world by way of insistently invoking providence (368). Those attempts to ascribe some fixed meaning, however, are undercut by the very nature of their experience as a function of punitive personal agendas and desires for retributive justice that belie the presence of any guiding moral authority and dispute the potential for spiritual deliverance or societal redemption.

Such misplaced articulations of providential justice appropriate not only the form of the ritualized last dying speech but also the uncertainty of its impelling interpretive challenges. As played out most prominently in the Elizabethan state's scaffold confrontations with convicted Catholic traitors, "the privilege attaching to words delivered in the face of death" became the focus of a heated cross-confessional struggle to make apparent the positive spiritual significance of an execution or, conversely, to negate such significance (Lake and Questier 1996, 75). Narratives of providential deliverance from affliction were by no means solely the domain of establishment Protestantism in later sixteenth-century England. The preoccupation with ascribing providential significance to suffering was equally characteristic of both sides of the primary Elizabethan confessional divide. Both Catholics and Protestants tried insistently to identify wherever they could in political and legal events "explanations … and (eschatologically charged) vindications of their eventual, inevitable triumph" (Lake and Questier 2002, 322). Appropriating and expropriating interpretive control of the last words of the condemned was one very important component of this polemical desire to fix meaning.

It is with a view to such fraught moments of cross-confessional confrontation that I now turn to a reading of *Unfortunate Traveller*, specifically with a view to the many sites of contact and exchange those moments reveal between the closely related discourses of plague infection and criminal prosecution—or rather persecution. And indeed, since the subjects of legal power in the narrative are Catholic or have circumstances informing their executions that invoke the familiar enough scene of a Catholic traitor being put to death by the Elizabethan state, prosecution and persecution may be justly considered interchangeable terms going forward. My starting point is a reading of Rome as it was usually imagined in early modern England—Nashe's Rome (and Wilton's)—as the primary geographical locus for the junction of these discourses. The purchase of that reading is, in large part, a recognition of ways in which representations of Italy at the time were bound up in the task of (re) producing narratives of cultural pathology: of dangerous, contagious foreign otherness; of subversive, criminal infiltration; and of the need to purge the disordering and debilitating disease of Romish influence from the body of the state. With such narratives in mind, I want first to look at some works whose concerns are much more overtly political than Nashe's in order to map out the key sites at which plague, prosecution/persecution, and linguistic agency intersect. Identifying such points of contact entails tracing out the recurrent image of Elizabethan England as both subject to and source of a contamination of which it must rid itself—as a community besieged, like Rome in *Unfortunate Traveller*, by its own conflicted nature as at once infected and infecting as well as by the conflicting, troubled nature of the resultant attempts to apply some model of providential justice to explain and justify the experience of punitive suffering.

The "art of poysoning": Pathology and Persecution

One key to imagining an idealized Protestant English identity in the late sixteenth-century was maintaining a sense of the nation as a body free from infection or injury. Other than during times of plague outbreak in early modern England, threats of physical infection were mainly conceived of as the province of other lands and cultures: dangers to be negotiated by travelers on the continent and elsewhere. At the same time, the Protestant community of Elizabethan England was also invariably depicted as highly susceptible to infiltration by carriers of continental diseases, be they physical, moral, or spiritual. Dangerous foreign agents of infection could be readily understood to infiltrate England by various means, threatening dissolution of its spiritual and national community from within. And for the obvious reasons associated with its being the center of Catholicism, as well as for the perhaps less immediate reasons of its pervasive influence on European fashion, manners, and political thought, Italy proved the most popular site from which to figure a variety of infections as emanating. It was the country that many in England considered "the pinnacle of southern debauchery and spiritual corruption" (Scavuzzo Wheeler 1998, 59).

In *Unfortunate Traveller*, Nashe acknowledges the prevalence of such attitudes, reproducing common fears and widely held negative beliefs about Italy when he has Wilton encounter a banished English earl, a traveler in Rome more by necessity than choice, who launches into a diatribe warning against journeys to the continent. Notable among his descriptions is the assertion that Italy will make any young English traveler "to kis his hand like an ape, cringe his necke like a starveling. ... From thence he brings the art of atheisme, the art of epicurising, the art of whoring, the art of poysoning" (2.301). Though he references in this last the actual means of committing murder silently and from a distance, his mention of the Italian "art of poysoning" resonates unavoidably with significance to a narrative of cultural pathology and the threat of England's "ingesting" harmful agents. According to his description, the culture and thought of Italy effect a negative transformation that can be conceived of as much in physical terms as it can be in those spiritual or psychological. "It is nowe a privie note amongst the better sort of men," the earl explains, "when they would set a singular marke or brand on a notorious villaine, to say, he hath beene in Italy" (2.301). The harmful influences of Italy are so obvious and well known in the mind of Nashe *qua* Wilton that they are fodder for one's ready classification. They mark a person as being culturally infected and, strikingly, are even imagined as capable of being rendered visible on the skin as a "brand" that marks one's depravity and criminal nature—a type of physiological stigma. The act of branding and the raw, puffy wound produced together provide an apt figure both for how subversive cultural influences impress themselves upon one from outside, as well as for how those influences, once internalized, come readily and unavoidably back to the surface in noticeable ways.

In *Foreign Bodies and the Body Politic*, Jonathan Gil Harris (1998) discusses the "growth in the popular pathological vocabulary" over the latter part of the sixteenth and early part of the seventeenth century (55), concerning himself with the ways in which that vocabulary functions figuratively to inform "organic political analogy" (1). He locates the basis for conceiving of English contamination by foreign Catholic agents in the relatively new medical paradigms of the physicians Fracastoro and Paracelsus, which saw disease as the product of unseen forces external to the body: tiny, invading "seeds" of infection taken in through one's pores or orifices (25). Certainly, the reference made to "the art of poysoning" by Nashe's banished earl speaks to such a conception of foreign disease as the transformative agent at stake takes effect only after it is unknowingly ingested. Harris identifies as corollary to the expansion of our understanding of political disease to accommodate the threat of Catholic infection an abiding question: what course of treatment might such a mode of social pathology demand, if any treatment could be efficacious? What could be done to rid Protestant England's body of the infectious foreign "seeds" infiltrating it?

The answer to such queries, at least as Roger Ascham (1570) has it in *The Scholemaster*, a treatise on education famously concerned in part with the disordering and disruptive influence at court of "An English man Italianated" (229), is chiefly "to discover the sore to others," though Ascham readily accedes that he possesses "no authoritie to amend the sore my selfe" (230). The first step towards dealing with the Catholic infection at hand is fostering awareness of it, and of its points of entry. Such thinking is illustrative of an anxious conception of the body politic that gets more and more frequently reproduced in the late sixteenth and early seventeenth centuries. Harris (1998) asserts it to be a model indicative of "a crucial shift in the articulation of organic political metaphor," in that it depicts "less the harmonious concord of the diverse members [of the state body], than the vigilant surveillance of the body's limits in the face of political infiltration" (44). And it is in this way of figuring the state's susceptibility to spiritual and cultural infection, at this point of metaphorical recognition of a need for greater preoccupation with the various sites at which infiltration might occur, that the discourse of pathology intersects with the discourses of persecution and of providence as well.

That Rome served as a seed-bed from which spread criminal behaviors and subversive ideas and modes of spiritual experience, and that Catholicism was to be readily imagined as a sort of exogenous infection besieging the Protestant community were notions foundational to the Elizabethan state's precarious sense of its own spiritual identity. We need look no further for evidence than William Cecil's (1583) *The Execution of Justice in England*, the foundational articulation of the Elizabethan government's ostensible interest in punishing Catholics only for treason—which is to say, for criminal transgressions only, not for spiritual ones. Cecil, Lord Treasurer of England and Elizabeth's chief advisor, offers a passage early on that draws rather heavy-handedly upon a literal translation of the Latin root *semina* in depicting Jesuit seminaries as producers of infectious "seedmen" who infiltrate the "realms of England … under secret masks" and engage in the "tillage of sedition" (6). What made the products of Jesuit seminaries so dangerous and threatening in the Protestant imagination was the covert and unseen nature of their machinations in England. They entered the country undetected and undercover, traveled abroad in disguise, and they published and disseminated their writings by secretive means. Cecil's primary focus is the way in which Jesuit infiltration manifests itself as criminal behavior, namely treasonable plotting. As a result, his desire for the surveillance and exposure of infectious agents is virtually indistinguishable from his desire to enact the full judicial power of the state in the form of execution. In the very title of his work (*The Execution of Justice*) is a punning advertisement of Cecil's inability or unwillingness to separate the general task of pursuing justice from that pursuit's most negative and visceral end result. At least in theory, however, the cure for Catholic "infection" once it had been exposed was the repentance and (re)conversion of those afflicted, usually under considerable duress, with the tacit assumption that such open renunciation would also foreclose the possibility of one's further susceptibility to seditious continental influences.

There are several late sixteenth-century tracts whose ostensible purpose is to deter the spread of spiritual disease by demonstrating to potential Catholic readers the errors of their ways, and to do so with a view to changing their confessional positions as opposed to pointing them automatically towards the scaffold. Thomas Bell's (1593) *Motives, Concerning Romish faith and religion* constitutes a prime example, especially considering its author was a captured seminary priest who had recanted his vows in 1592. Invoking the standard pathological political analogy, Bell defines his purpose as one of stark, necessary, diagnostic revelation. Asserting first that "none will or can in deed provide a remedy for that sore, whereof he hath no feeling or intelligence," he expresses hope "that all papists who shall seriously peruse this my briefe discourse; may with all facilitie perceive such to be grievous diseases of the soule, as heretofore they deemed to be none" (sig.¶¶2v). For Bell, Catholicism has so thoroughly infiltrated and infected the spiritual lives of many English citizens (as it had his own) that its inherent dangers remain effectively hidden in plain sight, unrecognized, and in need of being brought to light so that those bearing witness by reading his text may be "perfectly cured." The language of pathology and the image of bodily disease would undoubtedly have come easily to Bell, writing as he is against the cultural backdrop of plague infection in 1592–93 England that also preoccupies Nashe in *Unfortunate Traveller*. His text is presented as the means by which those taken with "diseases of the soule" that "exceed the diseases of the body"—the seriousness of which the vast numbers of plague dead no doubt provided daily reminders—will be forced to confront the threatening nature of their affliction (sig.¶¶2v).

To that end, Bell urges his imagined infected readership to "make due triall" of their submission to popery (sig.¶¶2v). He refers not to the processes of criminal justice, of trying and executing Catholic traitors though, but rather to something akin to the revelatory, curative nature of those processes: the internal course of action of coming to terms with the fact of one's spiritual sickness. Ultimately, what Bell offers is a version of rooting out sites of England's self-sustaining spiritual infection informed by the processes of revelation and forced examination. As such, it mirrors the model of criminal justice pursued by the Elizabethan state against himself and other priests and carefully defended by Cecil. The intended end result of both is the same: a purging of the political body and the reassertion or restoration of social order. That *quid pro quo*—compulsory purge in exchange for restoration—is why narratives of providential deliverance and divine justice are so readily attached to the revelation of infectious political and ideological agents as ways of explaining what is at stake for the Elizabethan state in persecutory processes. As noted earlier, the systematic, regulatory processes whereby the state rooted out threats to social order were invariably understood teleologically: the manifestation of God's salutary hand administering special, curative providence in effecting conversion and/or execution. From a broad providentialist perspective, then, such processes were inextricably bound to the eschatological narratives of loss and promised recovery invoked so pervasively in times of widespread disease.

Bell suggests that it is as a divine agent he offers his project of curing "diseases of the soule," and consequently of the (political) body, by way of encouraging repentance. He suggests at the outset of his tract that the efficacy of his "wishing thy christian conversion" is a direct function of the particular "small talent, which God ... hath bestowed on me" (sig.¶¶ 2^{v}). Likewise, Cecil (1583) implies that the project of the Elizabethan state's judicial self-definition is so crucial because it amounts to the necessary exercise of divinely ordained justice. "God's goodness,"

> he explains, hath otherwise given to Her Majesty, as to His handmaid ... the spirit of wisdom and power, whereby she hath caused some of these seditious seedmen and sowers of rebellion to be discovered ... not being dealt withal upon questions of religion, but justly by order of laws, openly condemned as traitors. (7)

In its reference to God's influence on "His handmaid" Elizabeth, such an assertion casts in providential terms the governmental task of rooting out infectious agents by means of the revelation and purging of Catholic traitors. The common providential and pathological terms these tracts employ in articulating the associated models of conversion and execution point to how the state project of (re)asserting order in the political and spiritual community readily aligns itself with the notion of divinely-ordained plague infestation. The hand of God manifests itself to England's ideologically besieged Protestants as a (chiefly foreign) Catholic affliction and, ultimately, as respite from that affliction's self-sustaining nature. Conversely, to condemned Catholic subjects of the state's powers of discovery and punishment, the hand of God takes the form of an extended process of forced physical and legal suffering that culminates in a redemptive and exemplary death.

From either perspective, what is at stake is a particular spiritual community's ostensibly inevitable (re)assertion: the divinely-effected reconstitution of an ideologically besieged collectivity. In the conversion and execution of infecting agents of Roman Catholicism, the Elizabethan state defined the final part of a foundational narrative of the English Protestant community's deliverance from dangerous, foreign subversion. Likewise, in their dying speeches missionary priests convicted of treason foregrounded for those attending their executions a positive teleological understanding of their demise as contributing to an ever-growing heavenly community of Catholic martyrs, as well as to the consolidation of a persecuted earthly community of faith. The scaffold was thus the site of cross-confessional competition between enactments of interpretive agency in the form of opposing discourses of curative providential deliverance. Some public reiteration of its fundamental rightness—whether legal, ideological, or both—in pursuing its course of justice is what was always at stake for the state in attempting to assert control over the privileged last words of the condemned (Sharpe 1985, 150).

At the point of execution, the Elizabethan government's representatives would usually push for a public conversion or recantation, which, as the examples of the reformed seminarian Bell and of his *Motives* demonstrate, could function in place of execution as a means of purging political and spiritual infection from the body of the state. The Catholic polemicist William Allen (1582) describes how the state was ever conscious of asking missionary priests convicted as traitors to "relent any little in religion, and they should live" (sig. bvii^{r}). Such coercive rhetorical performances, of course, created inevitably beneficial situations for the government, as the ensuing refusal of a public conversion was a necessary precondition for execution, the final and most visceral elimination of infectious agents from the state body. More subtly manifested, the same desire to urge Catholics to effect agency on the scaffold in offering proof of their conversion also impelled the formalized request that condemned priests pray with the Protestant ministers in attendance. Richard Challoner's (1741) *Memoirs of Missionary Priests* includes an account of such a request in Everard Hanse's being asked by "the Ministers" at his 1581 execution "to pray with them, and to desire the People to assist him" (sig. D^{r}). Similarly, it offers a description of how, on the scaffold in 1582, the Jesuit John Paine was "often called upon by the Ministers to join with them in the Lord's Prayer" (sig. F6^{r}).

Customarily, these requests were met with resistance in the form of a mode of linguistic agency that advertised itself as uniquely Catholic and underscored for the state the subversive, foreign otherness of the condemned: the offering of Latin prayers. As Challoner has it, Paine answers the request to recite in English the Lord's Prayer by stating dismissively "That he had [already] prayed in a Tongue which he well understood" (sig. F6^{r}), establishing by way of his dying speech an unambiguous marker of the defining spiritual/ideological distinction between himself and his persecutors. Such an exclusionary mode of speaking reiterates the condemned's participation in and representation of a unified and distinct community of sufferers; indeed, the utterance of Latin prayers at the scaffold was presented as something of a group exercise in publicly (re)asserting suffering spiritual identity. At his state execution, for instance, Edmund Campion responded to one Protestant minister "willing him to say some prayer with him" by pointing out that "You and I are not one in Religion," then turning to the crowd of onlookers to request "them of the Household of Faith to pray with me and in my Agony to say one Creed" (sig. E3^{v}). In a slightly different version of the same type of rhetorical performance, Hanse made clear the fact "That he might not pray with Heretics; but desired humbly all Catholics to pray for him and with him" (sig. D^{r}). These examples go to Michel Foucault's ([1977] 1985) position that those attending public executions "never felt closer to those who paid the penalty than in those rituals intended to show … the invincibility of power," here the ideological and legal rightness of the English state. As Foucault suggests, "out of the ceremony of the public execution ... it was this solidarity much more than the sovereign power that was likely to emerge with redoubled strength" (63).

Furthering in a similar way the public (re)assertion of English Catholics' communal identity as sufferers, perhaps the most common Latin prayer spoken at the scaffold foregrounds the familiar understanding of affliction as somehow associated with the chastening, special providential hand of God. *In manus tuas, Domine, commendo spiritum meum* at once recalls both Psalm 31:5—"Into thine hand, I commend my spirit: for thou hast redemed me, o Lord God"—and Luke's version of the same in his account of Christ's last words: "Father, into thine hands I commend my spirit" (23:46). This last is perhaps the exemplary Christian instance of linguistic agency enacted in the face of persecution and death. In its conscious emulation, Catholics invoked publicly the same teleology of faithful suffering and trust in deliverance that Luke reinforces in his Passion narrative's use of the Psalm. Being uttered just prior to the onset of physical suffering preceding death, the *In manus tuas* prayer is also tellingly ambivalent: the hand of God to which the condemned willingly gives over him- or herself refers as much to the means of immediate affliction awaiting the body as to the means of eventual redemption awaiting the soul. As such, the suffering of the condemned reveals its analogous reliance upon the same imaginative material as the providential loss and recovery narrative by way of which those threatened by plague infection seek meaning for their suffering. In such a narrative, divinely-ordained infection necessarily always assumes a dual role, at once the engine of death and the vehicle of divine deliverance from the fallen, sinful state that necessitates God's punishment in the first place.

My intent in developing this section of my discussion the way I have has been to map out the Rome of the Elizabethan imagination as site of origin for the multiply intersecting strands of an anxious narrative of sixteenth-century cultural pathology: Catholic infiltration, besieged and subverted spiritual community, self-sustaining physical and ideological infection, the curing of the political body by conversion or execution. I use the term "anxious" here because such a narrative was of course subject to resistance, to (re)interpretations, and (re)appropriations across the confessional divide. Indeed, its interpretive instability finds apt representation in the image of the scaffold, wherein competition between opposing notions of curative providence played out variously in the desire for public conversion or the execution of Catholics, and in the public utterance of Latin prayers or the assertion of an unjustly suffering Catholic community by way of the last dying speech. At stake in all cases is the invocation of a narrative of deliverance and providential justice that lends meaning to punitive affliction: of Protestants due to the subversive nature of Catholic infection, of Catholics due to Protestant persecution. The site and event of a Catholic's execution (or perhaps conversion) thus always provided at once a crucial opportunity for the articulation of a positive, salutary *telos* of suffering as well as for the repudiation of that articulation. The last dying speech coming by way of response to persecutory state violence constitutes a discursive mode whose inherent uncertainty and instability neccessarily problematizes its providential efficacy. It is with this fact in mind that I now turn to *Unfortunate Traveller* and its portrayals of the violence that defines the experience of suffering in plague-infected Rome.

"There is no heaven but revenge": Dying Speeches and Providential Uncertainty

Philip Schwyzer (1994) identifies in Wilton's Roman narrative, and in *Unfortunate Traveller* as a whole, a prevailing "hopelessness of appealing to the divine will"—a foreclosure of any potential for deliverance from suffering by the hand of God. In fact, he argues, the workings of the divine in Wilton's account are "so shrouded from human view … that even to have the idea of divine authority is to usurp it" (602). Such a statement speaks to the fact that, time and again in the plague-infested Rome described, narratives of spiritual deliverance and divine retribution are—somewhat predictably—invoked to mitigate and/or explain the experience of physical suffering. Those narrative attempts, however, invariably articulate instead the point at which a teleological model of affliction breaks down. They thus foreground the absence of providential certainty, or at least the deferral of providential meaning's articulation. The first such rhetorical performance is put in the mouth of the Roman matron Heraclide, whose rape rehearses the terms of a subversive transposition of the punitive hand of man for that of God—of the anxious and interpretively unstable discourse of persecutory violence for the more stable discourse of divine punishment.

The scene of her defilement provides the primary illustration of how the elisions of physical, political, and spiritual that are encouraged by Rome as an imagined site of infection seem to register in *Unfortunate Traveller*. Such elisions have as their corollaries the exchanges of execution and linguistic agency with notions of purgation and the restoration of community. Immediately after Wilton's uncharacteristically poignant turn to a survey of Rome's misery in the grip of divinely-ordained infection—he describes how "one grave was the sepulchre of seven score, one bed was the alter wheron whole families were offered" (1594, 2.286)—the narrative focus abruptly shifts to a human agent of desolation: "one Esdras of Granado, a notable Bandetto" (2.287). Esdras is depicted as being an extension of the terrible "visitation" afflicting the city, and his close association with the threat of infection works on a number of levels (2.287). He is, for one thing, a 'visitor' himself; he is Spanish, and that foreign otherness would mark him as immediately culturally subversive. This would seem especially so to a reading audience for whom, five years after the first Armada scare, Spain remained perhaps the most palpable political and spiritual threat, despite (or perhaps in keeping with) entrenched anxiety over the continued infiltration of England by Catholic agents from Rome. Of note, Esdras commits violence only by cover of darkness, and only, we are told, "where the plague had most rained" (2.287). His human path of destruction thus follows the path already laid out by God; "if there were none but the mistres and maide left alive," Wilton explains, Esdras would "ravish them both, & bring awaie all the wealth [he] could fasten on. In an hundred chiefe citizens houses where the hand of God had bene, [he] put this outrage in ure" (2.287).

The "chast" Heraclide immediately recognizes her attacker as a version of the divine plague besieging the city, asking of him "art thou ordaind to be a worse plague to me than the plague it selfe? Have I escapt the hands of God to fal into the hands of man?" (2.288). Yet despite being figuratively associated with the plague, as Heraclide's distinction between the "hands of God" and the "hands of man" seems to suggest, Esdras inflicts a type of individual suffering dislocated in the narrative from the communal suffering that requests providential explanation. She recognizes the scene of her impending defilement as the site of a potential shift in the experience of suffering from a salutary, divinely-ordained infection raging outside the walls of her home to the human violence and degradation inside. Indeed, Esdras is a "worse plague" because he denies his victims the possibility of a heavenly recompense from affliction and condemns them to physical and spiritual defilement without the saving release of death. Heraclide quickly comes to the realization of this, moving suddenly from her initial demand of Esdras to "send me to heaven with my husband" into the horrified recognition that "it is the spoil of my honour thou seekest" (2.288). At least in her estimation, that particular spoil negates any positive teleological potential obtaining in suffering. Her desperate prayers for death over dishonor suggest that spiritual redemption is predicated on her body remaining chaste: "my soule is my saviours ... Jesu, Jesu, spare mee undefiled for thy spouse" (2.288). Heraclide conceives of her rape as a comprehensive act of criminal violence that degrades body and soul in one fell swoop (Baines 2003, 121). Certainly, lending support to such a notion is Wilton's subsequent description of her "after she was deflowred" as being like "a reprobate soule rising to the day of judgement" (2.293).

It is this last judgment that Heraclide fears has already taken place. In abject despair in the wake of her defilement, she struggles with a desperate attempt to reclaim the providential narrative denied her when her pleas for salvation go unanswered (Andersen 2004, 54). Recalling first the abiding mercy of God before reversing course and convincing herself that she is necessarily damned—"grace is never denied to them that aske. It may be denied; I maie be a vessel ordained to dishonor" (Nashe 1594, 2.294)—she chooses to end her own life in the fleeting hope that freedom from her degraded state will warrant spiritual redemption, and the death of her body will "spurre forth my soule to mount poste to heaven" (2.295). There is an irresolvable tension underpinning her thinking. The concept of providence was perhaps more indicative than any other theological construct of the fundamental hope characterizing Christianity, while self-murder was the ultimate "expression of despair, the very antithesis" of that hope (MacDonald and Murphy 1990, 31). So much in conflict with teleological notions of spiritual deliverance was suicide in early modern England that self-murderers were as a matter of course denied proper Christian burials, and all things suggestive of the possibility of their heavenly after-life were eschewed: "No prayers for the dead were repeated; the minister did not attend" (15). With this in mind, we can discern in Heraclide's words the impossibility of attaching a positive end to her suffering—to "the horror of minde I endure" and from which, she announces, "my hand and my knife shall manumit mee" (Nashe 1594, 2.294). At the very least, the fate of the soul once freed from the afflicted body is in this instance left something of an open question (Schwyzer 1990, 603).

Heraclide's desperate attempt to rationalize self-murder is actually the last in a series of (mis)judgments about providence she articulates. Her initial response to being confronted by Esdras is one of confidence that God will save her from further suffering, but it is short-lived. She is silenced when she falls "in a sowne" after crying out unsuccessfully for the manifestation of special providence: "Heare me, Jehovah, & be merciful in ending my miserie. ... Jesu, Jesu, never faile those that put their trust in thee" (2.288). Upon her revival, she then takes the tack of warning Esdras about the seeming certainty of divine retribution for his deeds: "How thinkest thou, is there a power above thy power? if there be, he is here present in punishment, and on thee will take present punishment if thou persisteth in thy enterprise" (2.289). Retribution, however, does not come, or at least not immediately, and its mere possibility is certainly not enough to dissuade Esdras from his course of action. In invoking and re-invoking a redemptive teleology that is left unrealized, the speeches Heraclide offers in the face of her affliction establish a pattern for the failure of her metaphorical last dying speech.

The providential inefficacy characteristic of her repeated attempts to effect linguistic agency may be read as the symptom of her literal and figurative dislocation from the salutary communal experience of the plague. Wilton explains at the outset of his account of the rape how, while "al [were] snatcht up by sicknes" at the home of Heraclide, that "good wife" remained uninfected (2.287). Shut up in her house away from the "stinking exhalations" outside, she has, at least by her own estimation, "escaped the hands of God" that have even touched her husband, who lies lifeless on the floor beside her (2.286; 288). Part of her empty rhetoric of divine retribution is based on the threat of infection she should pose to Esdras, but does not. She urges him to

> thinke the anger of God apparently visioned or showne unto thee in the knitting of my browes. A hundred have I buried out of my house, at all whose departures I have been present: a hundreds infection is mixed with my breath: loe, now I breath upon thee, a hundred deaths come uppon thee. (2.289)

The fact that she remains uninfected, however, entirely undercuts her self-representation as the providential vehicle through which divine punishment operates at the same time that it effectively enables a non-salutary mode of suffering by failing to deter Esdras in his advances. In physically defiling Heraclide in her home as he does, Esdras, the profane version of the divine "visitation" afflicting Rome, interposes himself problematically in place of the salutary suffering experience from which she has been sheltered and wholly excluded.

We can see illustrated in the exchange of punitive visitations the sort of ready slippage between infection and execution I have identified with contemporary narratives of Roman Catholic invasion. The sheer length of Heraclide's final speech, though, and its rhetorical self-consciousness in attempting to fix an interpretation of her plight departs from the sort of directness and concision of the prayer and supplication most appropriate to the plague and exemplified by the brief liturgical fragment Wilton cites in his initial description of plague-besieged Rome: "Lord have mercie upon us." Heraclide offers an extensive, calculated rhetorical performance that is in many ways seemingly much better suited to the scaffold, hence my classification of it here as a version of a dying speech.

Further encouraging such a connection, Wilton imagines her infection by Esdras to be also an act of persecution. We are told, for example, that in "assail[ing] her with rough meanes," Esdras gets Heraclide "under shrift"

(2.288), a description that casts auricular confession and prayer as functions of physical coercion. J. B. Steane (1985) suggests that, considering its context, the use of "shrift" here seems to invoke in particular the "period for prayer and confession [occurring] before execution" (332n278). And certainly, Heraclide's rape is presented as being analogous to her execution. Wilton details how Esdras

> slipt his sacriligius hand from her lilly lawne skinned necke, and inscarft it in her long silver lockes, which with struggling were unrould. Backward he dragd her … and then, like a traitor that is drawen to execution on a hurdle, he traileth her up and down the chamber by those untwisted braids. … (Nashe 1594, 2.291)

At this point in her torment, death as on the scaffold presents itself to Heraclide as a viable possibility. She begs Esdras to "stifle me in my haire, hang me up by it on a beame, and so let me die" (2.291), invoking a grisly process of torture and hanging that further calls to mind the enactment of punitive, persecutory Elizabethan state power on the body of a convicted (Catholic) traitor. To be sure, there is much in Esdras' depiction that encodes him as the fitting agent of such punitive authority. Specifically, he is "authorised by the pope" in his actions. He tells Heraclide "how many execrable murthers with impunitie he had executed" as a result (2.288) and how he has come from Spain with an imagined "charter above scripture" to inflict violence and punishment with an impunity that, considering his association with the Pope, seems at once spiritual and legal (2.288–9).

At the same time, Esdras can also be seen to manifest a fraught, ambivalent relationship with the discourse of persecution. The same political "authority" that brings him to Rome to inflict violence on its citizens also associates him with the ostensibly traitorous targets of the English state's enactment of criminal justice. As a Spanish infiltrator licensed by the Pope and free to act without danger of repercussions due to his all-encompassing "charter," Esdras "presents a crude parody of a Spanish Jesuit" (Andersen 2004, 57). Both out of a need for protection and a desire to defend the foundational, identifying institutions of the Catholic Church, the Jesuits had indeed always closely associated themselves with the Papacy (O'Malley 1993, 296–7). In any case, my point is that the image of one's being dragged to the scaffold on a hurdle unavoidably has potentially multiple resonances in the scene of Heraclide's rape; "like a traitor that is drawen to execution" is a modifier that, to employ Barbara J. Baines' (2003) phrase, "dangles quite significantly" in how it at once refers to the victim's current circumstance and offers an imagined projection of a fate that might just as easily befall the perpetrator as a suitable punishment for his crimes or for his ostensibly subversive religious/political leanings (122). And when next we hear of Esdras in Wilton's narrative, such a fate has moved from imagination to reality.

Associated both with plague infection and with the violence of execution, represented as both the agent of persecution and the object (at least potentially), Esdras manifests not only the exchanges that occur *between* the discourses of pathology and persecution, but also those occurring *within* the discourse of persecution. By these last I refer to the reversal of roles, as across the confessional divide, wherein those who inflict punitive suffering may be understood to be the victims of a salutary affliction—per the rhetoric of the Elizabethan state's purging its infected body by way of execution—or to be the perpetrators of persecutory violence. The particular experience of suffering with which he is associated is depicted as at once tied to and dislocated from a divinely-ordained model of affliction conducive to providential explanation. And when Esdras himself provides the next instance in Wilton's narrative wherein the privileged nature of the condemned's words gets undercut by the seeming failure of those words to articulate a positive *telos* of suffering, that instance is presented as a function of the slippage he manifests between the role of persecutor and persecuted.

In a passage whose punning association of Tiber and Tyburn once again foregrounds the operative linkage of plague-infested Rome to the main site of public execution in England, Wilton describes how he departs with his courtesan for Bologna. "Oares nor winde could not stirre nor blow faster, than we toyled out of Tiber," he begins; "a number of good fellowes would give size ace and the dice, that with as little toyle they could leave Tyburne behinde them" (Nashe 1594, 2.318). Tyburn, and the human violence of the scaffold it calls to mind, are never really left behind at all though, as the scene subsequently shifts to the public execution of the murderer Cutwolfe. From there, virtually all of the remaining narrative comes in the form of a recollection of Cutwolfe's scaffold oratory—"a glose upon the text" is Wilton's phrase (2.320). In other words, Wilton's tale itself takes on the form and substance of a dying speech, albeit a providentially ineffective one. Glibly explaining how the "occasion of my comming hether … is to have a few of my bones broken (as we are all borne to die) for being the death of the Emperour of homicides, Esdras of Granado," Cutwolfe details at length his pursuit of Esdras to avenge the death of his brother (2.320). In Cutwolfe's narrative, the erstwhile persecutor of Heraclide and the vehicle of her suffering becomes himself the target of persecution, of degradation, and the object of punitive violence.

In fact, in facing death at the hands of man—specifically, the barrel of Cutwolfe's pistol—Esdras takes up the very same desperate rhetoric earlier adopted by Heraclide upon realizing her impending defilement at his hands.

As part of the attempt to dissuade her attacker with the threat of a divine punishment ultimately unrealized, Heraclide warned of how "Gods hand like a huge stone hangs inevitably over thy head," and how "the anger of God [is] apparently visioned or showne unto thee in the knitting of my browes" (2. 289). Echoing those sentiments closely, Esdras tells his persecutor that "Thy over-hanging sword hides heaven from my sight ... Ay mee, alreadie I see my life buried in the wrinckles of thy browes" (2. 322). This self-conscious though inexact rehashing of his former victim's attempts to invoke the topos of God's hand as the instrument of divine punishment is, in Jennifer L. Andersen's (2004) words, akin to "an actor trying to reconstruct memorially a theatrical player's lines and persona" (58). It produces an end product that fails to capture convincingly the tenor or intent of the original discursive construction. With false sincerity, Esdras suggests that his thoughts have turned to Heraclide's suffering, but in trying outwardly to adopt her suffering "persona" he reproduces only the emptiness and inefficacy of its providential rhetoric and not its genuine (though ultimately misplaced and unrealized) desire to appeal to the persecutor's conscience.

Esdras laments and foregrounds the absence of any positive *telos* of suffering in his situation by means of logic similar to that informing Heraclide's yoking of the body's degradation to the soul's. "[M]y bodie & soule both shalt thou cast awaie quite," he pleads to Cutwolfe, "if thou doest at this instant what thou maist. Spare me, spare me, I beseech thee ... seeke not my souls utter perdition" (Nashe 1594, 2.324). Heraclide's concern that a defilement she considered spiritual as well as physical precluded her from special providence ultimately impelled a desperate attempt to re-invoke by way of her self-murder an alternate narrative of providence. By contrast, Esdras ends up eschewing any desire for spiritual deliverance entirely. Indeed, he quickly abandons his concern for the fate of his degraded soul and offers instead to "sweare and forsweare, renounce my baptisme, and all the interest I have in any other sacrament" (2.325). And in so doing, he provides something of a parodic reversal of the rhetoric of conversion that is so closely tied to the providential potential of the scaffold in Elizabethan England. He offers to advertise publicly the way in which his experience of persecution precludes any possibility of divine deliverance or spiritual salvation. He gets to the point of writing in blood "a full obligation of his soule to the divell," and praying "more earnestly ... unto God never to forgive his soule, than many Christians do to save their soules" (2.326).

As the vehicle of punitive authority in the scenario, Cutwolfe sees in this perverse take on a scaffold conversion the opportunity to expropriate from his victim any claim to a narrative of providential suffering, and appropriate such a claim for himself by way of ascribing meaning to his impending retributive act of execution. Esdras's version of a dying speech prompts Cutwolfe to go off "in quest of some notable newe Italionisme" (2.325), by which he refers to a treacherous plan he devises to ensure the utter resistance of Esdras' suffering to any sort of positive interpretation. His plan is realized first by playing out to a grotesque degree the offer of a damning conversion, coercing Esdras into a series of "blasphemous abjurations" (2.326). It is realized second by the symbolically-charged act of then shooting him in his open mouth: "made I no more ado," Cutwolfe describes, "but shot him full into the throat with my pistol: no more spake he after; so did I shoot him that he might never speake after, or repent him" (2. 326). This last insight into his motive speaks to Cutwolfe's abiding awareness of the rhetorical power obtaining in the privileged words a condemned person utters in the face of death. And it speaks also to his desire to subvert the positive meaning-making potential of the last dying speech by rendering the experience of suffering it describes devoid of providential significance, then fixing that meaning with violent finality. It constitutes, that is, another provocative moment within Wilton's narrative wherein the punitive hand of man supplants the hand of God, enacting a violent final justice on the condemned that tries to prevent his persecution, suffering, and execution from being read by anyone bearing witness to it as in any way salutary or exemplary.

Just as Heraclide did prior to her self-murder, after executing Esdras by the vicious means of his "notable newe Italionisme," Cutwolfe tries (entirely ineffectually) to pass himself off as the instrument of divine providence in his last dying speech. For him, "There is no heaven but revenge" (2. 324). Cutwolfe here articulates the immediately recognizable perspective of a common protagonist from popular dramatic literature of the late sixteenth century: the wronged, single- (and bloody-)minded revenger. For the myriad early modern stage revengers with whom Cutwolfe is wholly in line, the drive to carry out some act(s) of retributive violence is everything: the power that impels their narratives, the telos of their actions, their *raison d'etre*. For revengers, the only means to justice—the only way to restore the sense of personal and/or social equilibrium lost when (like Cutwolfe) their loved ones were murdered—is inflicting further violence upon those who have wronged them. In the terms of sociologist Rene Girard's ([1972] 1979) classic study *Violence and the Sacred*, retributive violence is purgative but also purifying in its intent. Reflecting such a notion, as Cutwolfe frames it, his violent execution of Esdras gets equated with heaven, the site and goal of the redemptive spiritual elevation that is the final, definitive manifestation of providence. As such, the atheistic 'conversion' of Esdras and his subsequent murder are evidence of the intervening Hand of God in operation to justify persecutorial violence. That parodic conversion thus finds an apt real-world analogue in the process of conversion or public execution by which the Elizabethan state rid itself of infecting, treasonous Catholic agents.

Cutwolfe's scaffold rhetoric of revenge, wherein he figures himself a worthy, justified scourge of God, presents another troubling parody of state execution ritual. This time, the focus of the parody is the unifying call to prayer by which convicted Catholics could attempt to (re)assert a positive teleology of affliction in (re)asserting their place within a larger community of sufferers. The audience to whom Cutwolfe appeals in exhorting those attending his execution to reaffirm through him the nature of their collective experience consists of the "true Italians" who will "imitate me in revenging constantly and dying valiantly" (Nashe 1594, 2.326). He invokes a rhetoric of exemplary suffering, trying to cast his demise in the very terms Wilton employs in describing it to the reader: a "spectacle that will adde to your faith." But Cutwolfe falls far short of adequately explaining the experience of persecution at the hands of the state as so readily indicative of providence. Whereas the examples of Elizabethan state executions often showed to be at stake for the persecuted a reassertion of the language of divine intervention and special providence—the *In manus tuas* prayer, for instance—Cutwolfe's words at his execution are characterized by a marked turn towards privileging the hand of man. He ascribes the meaning of his impending suffering and death directly to the human need for vengeance. For him, "Revenge is the glorie of armes, & the highest performance of valure: revenge is whatsoever we call law or justice" (2.326).

Things are reversed in his adaptation of the Biblical notion that God's hand supersedes human justice: "Vengeance belongeth unto me: I wil recompense, saith the Lord" (Heb. 10:30). According to Cutwolfe, only through the punitive violence people pursue against others can one even begin to access the shaping influence of the divine. "The farther we wade in revenge," goes his argument, "the nearer come we to the throne of the almightie. To his scepter it is properly ascribed; his scepter he lends unto man, when he lets one man scourge an other" (Nashe 1594, 2.326). Especially when it comes to inform the representation of revenge narratives, the early modern English understanding of providence takes for granted the Calvinist notion that "human wickedness [can be] part of the divine scheme." As a result, depraved, immoral, and/or violent people may sometimes be the necessary instruments of God's judgment (Sinfield 1983, 107). It seems apparent, though, that at stake in the scene of Cutwolfe's demise is a rather grievous misapprehension of the nature and presence of divine will.

Cutwolfe's attempt to define for and among those bearing witness to his death a privileged community of "true Italians" for whom such a narrative of retributive justice exemplified by his "notable newe Italionisme" is foundational to their experience meets with serious resistance. His desire to have the grounds of his own suffering imitated "in revenging constantly" elicits a collective response from the spectators that is, in the end, wholly negative for him and for his tenuous conception of providence: "all the people (outrageously incensed) with one conjoined outcrie yelled mainely, Awaie with him, away with him. Executioner, torture him, teare him ..." (Nashe 1594, 2.327). The onlookers' immediate, literal reaction to and interpretation of the proffered account of a necessary cycle of human retribution results in Cutwolfe's being subjected to a horrific, state-endorsed punishment. The gleefully detailed description of his torment eliminates from consideration virtually any suggestion of salutary or redemptive potential. Writing about the ways in which revenge tragedy is informed by an intractable tension between the ostensible appropriateness of repaying a violent deed in kind and a seeming inappropriateness of or inequality in the level of retributive violence usually employed, Katharine Eisaman Maus (1995) concludes that, "[i]n so far as revenge contributes to a spiral of violence, its horrors exacerbate the agony it attempts to alleviate" (x). Certainly, this can be deemed the case for Cutwolfe's murderous act of "Italionisme," the goal of which is to ensure that body and soul are condemned together, thereby answering by way of reproducing it the non-redemptive affliction brought upon Heraclide at the defiling hand of Esdras (even though Cutwolfe ostensibly acts in the name of his brother). That particularly "blasphemous" method of revenge gets paid back in the excessive, mimetic cruelty of the Italian state (Hilliard 1986, 166). At the urging of those with whom the executed imagines a collective identity, the exacerbating "spiral of violence" continues on into an indefinite future. As Wilton sums it all up, "One murder begetteth another" (Nashe 1594, 2.327).

After having inflicted upon him a litany of horrors that includes the "jarring" of his bones "quaveringly with [a] hammer" and (in a moment that recalls his final silencing of Esdras) the pulling out of his tongue, Cutwolfe is left with "no lim ... but was lingeringly splintered in shivers." He is then made to lie "in this horror on the wheele," Wilton tells us, "as in hell" (2.327). It seems a fitting mode of exit for someone who had earlier declared, "of hell doe I esteeme better than heaven, if it afford me revenge" (2.324). To be sure, Cutwolfe has been afforded his revenge, but the extreme violence he inflicts in the process of vengeance has been in turn inflicted upon him, with its end depicted as a version of damnation. The image of him in the wake of his affliction "as in hell" speaks powerfully to the ultimate failure of his dying speech to affix a providential interpretation to his situation. His explanatory narrative of human revenge becomes merely a public call for continued persecution that, as his own example suggests, threatens to condemn the soul along with the body. In that sense, his experience of persecutorial suffering realizes the fear of the soul's demise along with the body's that the metaphorical dying speeches of both Heraclide and Esdras had tried to articulate. In presumptuously replacing God's hand with his own he has, it seems, ultimately made a fatal misjudgment about the manifestation of special providence, one that undercuts his rhetorical performance on the scaffold and belies its attempt at making forced suffering a viable site of interpretive agency.

In spite of his damaging misjudgment, because Cutwolfe willingly submits to his death on the scaffold—he tells his executioner that he is "readie for the utmost of thy rigor" (2.327)—he might be understood as an overwhelmingly positive figure in Wilton's narrative. He is someone who "reclaims and redefines martyrdom" for Elizabethan Protestants in that "he sacrifices his life in the general public interest to rid Christian society of a pernicious sociopath" (Andersen 2004, 62), a sociopath with close ties to the threat of Jesuit subversion no less.[2] Yet a consideration of the Italian setting of Wilton's narrative seems to render much less convincing such an ameliorative reading of Cutwolfe's death as being somehow the re-affirmation of conformist English Protestant values and politics. Cutwolfe's "creed" of an only ambiguously divinely-ordained revenge is certainly less a function of an orthodox perspective on the elimination of social/political disorder than the function of a punitive personal agenda. As one of the preeminent sites of Elizabethan cultural subversion, of the potential undermining of English religious and political identity, Italy here again realizes a palpable threat to and undermining of legal and moral norms. For Protestants in Elizabethan England, revenge was supposed to be the domain of God and/or the legal system. By the end of Wilton's narrative, however, it has instead turned into "something that will be honoured by all 'true Italians'" (Bate 1996, 70); as such, it is something to which no self-respecting Protestant English reader should give credence.

Moreover, it has become dangerously de-centered and disordered in being (re)located in the violent hands of man. For the Tudor state, "judicial murder" conducted on the scaffold was (at least in theory) cast providentially as a means of deliverance from affliction—a movement towards purgation of the infected body politic (Andersen, 2004, 62). For the infected and infecting Italian state in Wilton's account, execution realizes instead only the propagation of further meaningless violence, and therein constitutes only the continued dissolution and dismemberment of the political body *ad infinitum.*

The divinely ordained plague infection that, in the words of Heraclide, "dispearseth [Death's] quiver into ten thousande hands at once," thereby threatening the dissolution of Rome from within at the beginning of Wilton's Italian narrative, has been transformed by that narrative's end into a mimetic, persecutory process of "revenging constantly" through which dissolution is actually realized (Nashe 1594, 2.289; 326). It has turned into an endless regression of retributive violence with no positive *telos*, one that has effectively given the lie to the narrative's initial representation of punitive suffering as bearing a salutary potential that might be accessed through the enactment of providential language. "Lord have mercie upon us," indeed.

Conclusion

Unfortunate Traveller is effectively unrivalled in the period with respect to the comprehensive depiction of criminal behavior in its varied forms and degrees. Like most prose fiction of the era, Nashe's text is generically mixed and derivative. In its luridly sensationalist depictions of criminal and judicial violence, however, it draws as much from the popular true crime writing of the period—cheap, hastily-produced accounts of murders called chapbooks—as it does more conventional literary analogues such as continental European prose romances and chronicle histories. Akin to the tabloids of today, chapbooks were designed for mass consumption and generally pandered to a less elite readership. Unlike modern tabloid reporting though, chapbook accounts of violent crime frequently contained didactic passages that offered cautionary, moralizing commentary and invoked the standard Christian providential narrative to assign meaning and import to circumstances surrounding the criminal's discovery and invariably violent demise (MacMillan 2015).

Despite a general indebtedness to chapbook literature, as I have demonstrated, *Unfortunate Traveller* introduces in shifting its setting to Rome considerable ambiguity with respect to the efficacy of providentialism as it applies to the task of assigning meaning to scenes of murder and of (judicial) persecution. Reading such scenes through the standard lens of an establishment providential narrative becomes substantially more difficult over the course of Wilton's Italian narrative and a matter of much less certainty—both for us as readers and for those to whom attempts at providential meaning-making are directed in the text. Ultimately, Wilton himself comes to articulate the radical position in sixteenth-century England that any decisive interpretation of divine will or clear discernment of God's hand in human affairs is an impossibility—especially so when it comes to matters of criminal and judicial violence.

To cast things more broadly, in exposing the inherent insufficiency of providentialism as a means of accounting for and understanding both criminal violence and the legal and personal responses to it, *Unfortunate Traveller* highlights some important, abiding questions with respect to crime and (capital) punishment. Just what, if anything, separates judicial violence from criminal? Is there any distinction between violence applied to the cause of retribution—of restoring just order—and violence enacted as revenge? Can judicial murder ever actually be morally or socially restorative? How is the enactment of judicial violence impelled by a desire to contain those who are socially or culturally "other"? In what ways can the symbolic and rhetorical power that obtains in the spectacle of an execution be mobilized politically? Certainly, all of these resonate with the familiar moral and legal concerns of the modern debate over death penalties. And that fact bespeaks the reality that, at least with respect to the cultural and political anxieties that continue to inform our fraught understanding and application of criminal justice, we are perhaps not quite so far removed from Nashe's England—or Wilton's Rome—as we might wish.

Notes

1. Elizabeth's government staunchly refused to recognize Catholic defendants in legal proceedings as anything other than secular subjects of judicial power. Because with *Regnans* Rome had issued an unambiguous challenge to the English monarchy, it followed that anyone carrying out the duties of the Roman church was a potential traitor whose actions would define him or her as such according to the language of the existing English Treason Acts. Notoriously difficult to get at in any demonstrable way and render visible to the public eye, confessional truth—the private truth of an individual's faith, something that had been a primary state concern in England's recent past—was self-consciously avoided by Elizabeth's government, barred from recognition in the legal domain marked out by torture chamber, courtroom, and scaffold.
2. Sociopathy as it is currently understood, a personality disorder historically closely related to but still distinct from psychopathy (Arntfield 2015, 18), was not conceived of similarly in the early modern period in terms of any particular sort of coherent, defining set of behaviours and characteristics. Early modern sociopaths were really only be discernible as legal subjects charged with individual offences. And the impulsive criminal behaviors that may have been functions of someone's sociopathy would have fallen in each instance into and across any number of recognized early modern legal categories. These range from lesser social crimes (such as poaching, rioting, and public disturbance) to felonies (such as larceny, pickpocketing, or sexual offences such as sodomy—itself a problematic, imprecise, catch-all legal category) to capital crimes, namely murder (Goldberg, 1992; Sharpe, 1999; MacMillan, 2015). Notable about *Unfortunate Traveller* with respect to this last point about categories of early modern criminal behaviour is the sheer number and wide range of crimes discussed and depicted throughout the narrative. Perhaps no other work of early modern literature catalogues so comprehensively the various levels and possible forms of criminality at the time.

References

Allen, William. 1582. *A Briefe Historie of the Glorious Martyrdom of XII Reverend Priests.* Rheims.

Andersen, Jennifer L. 2004. "Anti-Puritanism, Anti-Popery, and Gallows Rhetoric in Thomas Nashe's *The Unfortunate Traveller.*" *Sixteenth Century Journal* 35: 43–63.

Ascham, Roger. (1570) 1970. *The Scholemaster.* In *English Works*, ed. William Aldis Wright, 171–302. Cambridge: Cambridge University Press.

Arntfield, Michael. 2015. *Murder City: The Untold Story of Canada's Serial Killer Capital, 1959–1984.* Victoria, BC: Friesen Press.

Baines, Barbara J. 2003. *Representing Rape in the English Early Modern Period.* Lewiston: Edwin Mellen.

Bate, Jonathan. 1996. "The Elizabethans in Italy." In *Travel and Drama in Shakespeare's Time*, ed. Jean-Pierre Maquerlot and Michèle Willems, 55–74. Cambridge: Cambridge University Press.

Bell, Thomas. 1593. *Motives, Concerning Romish faith and religion.* London.

Cecil, William, Lord Burghley. (1583) 1965. *The Execution of Justice in England.* In *Folger Documents of Tudor and Stuart Civilization*, ed. Robert M. Kingdon, 53–268. Ithaca: Cornell University Press.

Challoner, Richard. 1741. *Memoirs of Missionary Priests.* Vol.1. London.

Dollimore, Jonathan. (1984) 2004. *Radical Tragedy: Religion, Ideology and Power in the Drama of Shakespeare and his Contemporaries.* New York: Palgrave Macmillan.

Foucault, Michel. (1977) 1995. *Discipline and Punish.* Translated by Alan Sheridan. New York: Vintage.

Gaskill, Malcolm. 2000. *Crime and Mentalities in Early Modern England.* Cambridge: Cambridge University Press.

Girard, Rene. (1972) 1979. *Violence and the Sacred.* Translated by Patrick Gregory. Baltimore: Johns Hopkins University Press.

Goldberg, Jonathan. 1992. *Sodometries: Renaissance Texts, Modern Sexualities.* Stanford: Stanford University Press.

Harris, Jonathan Gil. 1998. *Foreign Bodies and the Body Politic: Discourses of Social Pathology in Early Modern England.* Cambridge: Cambridge University Press.

Hilliard, Stephen S. 1986. *The Singularity of Thomas Nashe.* Lincoln: University of Nebraska Press.

Lake, Peter, and Michael Questier. 1996. "Agency, Appropriation and Rhetoric Under the Gallows: Puritans, Romanists and the State in Early Modern England." *Past and Present* 153: 65–107.

Lake, Peter, with Michael Questier. 2002. *The Antichrist's Lewd Hat: Protestants, Papists and Players in Post-Reformation England.* New Haven: Yale University Press.

MacDonald, Michael, and Terence R. Murphy. 1990. *Sleepless Souls: Suicide in Early Modern England.* Oxford: Clarendon.

MacMillan, Ken, ed. 2015. *Stories of True Crime in Tudor and Stuart England*. New York: Routledge.

Maus, Katharine Eisaman, ed. 1995. *Four Revenge Tragedies*. Oxford: Oxford University Press.

Nashe, Thomas. (1594) 1958. *The Unfortunate Traveller*. In *The Works of Thomas Nashe* Vol. 2, ed. Ronald B. McKerrow, 200–328. Oxford: Basil Blackwell.

O'Malley, John W. 1993. *The First Jesuits*. Cambridge, MA: Harvard University Press.

Scavuzzo Wheeler, Laura. 1998. "The Development of an Englishman: Thomas Nashe's *The Unfortunate Traveller*." In *Christian Encounters with the Other*, ed. John C. Hawley, 56–73. New York: New York University Press.

Schwyzer, Philip. 1994. "Summer Fruit and Autumn Leaves: Thomas Nashe in 1593." *English Literary Renaissance* 24: 583–619.

Sharpe, J. A. (1984) 1999. *Crime in Early Modern England, 1550–1750*. Harlow, Essex: Addison Wesley Longman.

———. 1985. "'Last Dying Speeches': Religion, Ideology and Public Execution in Seventeenth-century England." *Past and Present* 107: 144–67.

Sinfield, Alan. 1983. *Literature in Protestant England, 1560–1660*. London: Croom Helm.

Steane, J. B., ed. 1985. *The Unfortunate Traveller and Other Works*. London: Penguin.

Suzuki, Mihoko. 1984. "'Signorie over the Pages': The Crisis of Authority in Nashe's *The Unfortunate Traveller*." *Studies in Philology* 81: 348–71.

2. *Original Gangsta: Self-Conceptualization and Criminogenic Authenticity in Hip Hop Music*

LEE MELLOR

Introduction

Sociologist Robert Merton (1938) vigorously argued that the American dream was demonstrably false, observing that certain social groups and individuals are excluded from the opportunity to obtain wealth and upward social mobility (the "cultural symbols of success") through circumstances that are beyond their control. Racism—both systemic and cultural—along with the accompanying poverty and lack of formal education in urban communities compels many members of these populations to adapt to their situation through either Innovation, Ritualism, Retreatism, or Rebellion.

In this essay, which builds on Merton's seminal work, it is first argued that hip hop artists have observed each of these same modes of adaptation in urban ghettos, and have sought to relay the "truth" of such experiences through lyricism in a wider cultural discourse. The second section briefly looks at the sub-genre of "gangsta rap" which corresponds with Merton's Innovation mode of adaptation, and, to a large extent, has permeated hip hop as a whole for the past 25 years. In order not to be expelled from the sub-genre, the gangsta rapper must always present what Athens (1997) refers to as an *incipiently violent* or *violent* self-image in his music, which as his research shows, can result in acts of violence in itself.

An important corollary discussed is that the traditions of "braggadocio" and "battle rapping" in hip hop music may lead to feuding, either intentionally or as a result of communication dysfunctions between artists which, in some cases, may evoke deep seated animosity. These feuds occur principally through literary warfare in much the same way that Athens (1997) has found that acts of physical violence originate. More specifically, when one or more people form a *defensive*, *frustrative*, *frustrative-malefic*, or *malefic* interpretation of a rapper's words and/or actions they respond in kind with an attack, usually verbal, but occasionally physical vis-à-vis Merton's modes of adaptation. Typically, these verbal attacks centre around the public identification of an opponent's stigmatizing attributes. Symbolic interactionism, cemented in the concept of the individual adopting the view of the *generalized other* to determine how he is expected to act and to anticipate the consequences of non-compliance, thus provides a bridge between an individual's "deviant" identity and the Mertonian social structure from which that same identity—or at least the self-conceptualization of identity—is derived.

When an author addresses a criminogenic trend, accurately or inaccurately, in any art form, it is generally assumed that they are condemning, calling for a ban of, or openly disapproving of said art form. This is not the intent of this chapter. In keeping with the discipline of literary criminology, this chapter has been written to reveal the causation of violence through a literary medium so that entertainers, music industry professionals, law enforcement, the criminal justice system, ethnomusicologists, and cultural historians may better understand the complexity and idiosyncrasies of this particular phenomenon.

Merton's Strain Theory and the Geography of Hip Hop Culture

Though debates regarding the authenticity of a given artist occur with irritating frequency over a number of musical genres, the necessity of calling into question or asserting authenticity by making threats of violence towards other artists or their friends and families is commonplace only in hip hop. This cannot be attributed in a general sense to the violent content of hip hop lyrics, especially considering that, by comparison, "death metal" groups have arguably surpassed hip hop in the prevalence of and level of graphic depictions of violence in their genre (Venkatesh et al., in press). Rather, to understand the relative abundance of actual, often fatal violence occurring in the hip hop community, we must first look at the geo-cultural areas where the genre first took root: urban ghettos.

In the twenty-first century, hip hop has become increasingly mainstream, often veering into Billboard Hot 100 and even Top 40 territory. However, it was originally more akin to inner-city folk music. Like the skiffle groups that arose in the late-Fifties and early-Sixties in Britain while the country was recovering from the economic devastation of the Second World War, the Blacks and Latinos inhabiting the urban ghettos of late-Seventies and Eighties America were forced to create improvisational instruments and novel methods of vocal expression in order to pursue music. In the documentary *Something From Nothing: The Art of Rap*, Lord Jamar (Lorenzo Dechalus) of the hip hop ensemble Brand Nubian, elaborates on the situation: "It was at a time when they were taking instruments and shit out of the schools ... So what did we do? We took the fucking record player, the only thing that's playing music in our fucking crib and turned it into an instrument" (Ice-T 2012).

Urban enclaves of the Seventies and Eighties such as Harlem, the Bronx, and Compton are illustrative of Merton's (1938) strain theory of deviance. In the contemporary United States, the acquisition of wealth, fame, and status is the dominant cultural goal. However, the manner and method in which American citizens are permitted to legally and ethically pursue these objectives—what Merton calls "the institutionalized means"—are often unavailable to the typically African-American and Hispanic inhabitants of these ghettoized areas. At a microscopic sociological level, an individual learns what the "cultural goals" and "institutionalized means" of his society are by doing what Mead (1934/1967) refers to as "taking the attitudes of the generalized other" (154). Mead similarly defines the *generalized other* as "the organized community or social group which gives to the individual his unity of self" (154). Essentially, the individual is able to look at himself as an *object to himself* by taking the perspective of the *generalized other* in order to determine the social conduct that is expected of him. This does not necessarily mean that he will conform to this social conduct. For instance, Merton (1938) proposed that when an individual is unable to recognize "cultural goals" through the "institutionalized means" they will often adapt to their situation by choosing one of four modes: Ritualism, Retreatism, Rebellion or Innovation.

In the *Ritualism* mode of adaptation, the individual resigns himself to the fact that he will never attain his cultural goal but continues to perform the tasks associated with the institutionalized means because he is afraid of the consequences of deviating from them. The protagonist of Grandmaster Flash and the Furious Five's classic "The Message" acts as a mouthpiece for this mode of adaptation:

> "Broken glass everywhere/People pissing on the stairs, you know they just don't care/I can't take the smell, can't take the noise/*got no money to move on guess I got no choice .../I tried to get away but I couldn't get far/*'Cause a man with a tow truck repossessed my car ...

> The bill collectors, they ring my phone/And scare my wife when I'm not home/ Got a bum education, double-digit inflation/Can't take the train to the job, there's a strike at the station ..." (Fletcher et al. 1982)

Retreatism is the category Merton uses to describe a mode of adaptation in which the individual not only rejects the cultural goal, but also the institutionalized means, effectively dropping out of society through homelessness, substance abuse, and/or mental illnesses—social problems all too prevalent in the areas where hip hop originated. Once again in "The Message" the protagonist speaks about the number of people in his neighbourhood who have chosen Retreatism:

> "*Junkies in the alley with the baseball bat ... Crazy lady, living in a bag/Eating out of garbage pails*, used to be a fag hag .../ *She went to the city and got Social Security*/She had to get a pimp, she couldn't make it on her own ..." (Fletcher et al. 1982)

Rebellion refers to when the individual rejects the "cultural goals" and "institutionalized means" and seeks to replace them with new ones. Peruvian-born, Harlem-resident Immortal Technique (Felipe Andres Coronel), named his first two politically charged albums *Revolutionary Volume I* and *Revolutionary Volume II* respectively. In the song "The 4th Branch" he accuses the American government of hypocritically waging a war on "terrorism" even though he claims that the United States has a history of sponsoring such acts when it serves their purpose. The artist also lambasts organized religion, and addresses the media's culpability in disseminating false information and propaganda in order to create patriotic compliance among the poor and uneducated. Immortal Technique expresses his wish to (perhaps allegorically) execute the American president George W. Bush along with the princes and sheiks who rule over the Middle Eastern oil states:

> "Corporate America, dancin' offbeat to the rhythm/You really think this country never sponsored terrorism?/Human rights violations, we continue the saga/ El Savador and the contras in Nicaragua/And on top of that, you still wanna take me to prison/*Just cause I won't trade humanity for patriotism* .../And the world doesn't believe that you fightin' for freedom/Cause you fucked the Middle East, and gave birth to a demon/It's open season with the CIA, bugging my crib/ Trapped in a ghetto region like a Palestinian kid/Where nobody gives a fuck whether you die or you live/*I'm tryin' to give the truth, and I know the price is my life/But when I'm gone they'll sing a song about Immortal Technique/Who beheaded the President, and the princes and sheiks* ..." (Coronel 2003)

Finally there is adaptation through *Innovation*, where an individual continues to accept and pursue the "cultural goals", but rejects the prescribed "institutionalized means" in his attempts to attain them. The most common manifestation of this mode of adaptation is to seek wealth and status through criminal enterprise. This accounts for the historically high crime rates in urban ghettos, which is articulated in the rapper Ice-T's (Tracy Marrow) 1991 recording "New Jack Hustler" (particularly relevant lines have been placed in *italics*):

> "*I got nothin to lose, much to gain/ In my brain, I got a capitalist migraine/*I gotta get paid tonight, you muthafuckin right/Pickin' my grip, check my bitch, keep my game tight/So many hoes on my jock, think I'm a movie star/ *Nineteen, I got a fifty thousand dollar car* .../All I can think about is keys and Gs/ *imagine that, me working at Mickey D's* [laughter]/ *That's a joke cos I'm never gonna be broke/* when I die there'll be bullets and gunsmoke .../I care nothing about you and that's evident/all I love is my dope and dead presidents/sounds crazy? Well it isn't/ *The ends justifies the means, that's the system/*I learned that in school then I dropped out/Hit the streets, checked a grip, and now I got clout/ *I had nothing, and I wanted it/You had everything, and you flaunted it/Turned the needy into the greedy/With cocaine, my success came speedy/*Got me twisted, jammed into a paradox/Every dollar I get, another brother drops .../ *Cool out and watch my new Benz gleam/ Is this a nightmare? Or the American dream?*" (Henderson & Marrow 1991)

Given MC Lord Jamar's aforementioned observations, rap itself could be regarded as an *Innovation*-based mode of adaptation to economic inopportunity. With these shared roots, it is no wonder that a dominant message of the music so closely parallels its medium. As hip hop artists generally hail from these strained Mertonian urban enclaves where "infringement of social codes constitutes a 'normal response'" (Merton 1938, 38), many rappers have violent and/or criminal pasts. Since the influence of gangsta rap, this is, in fact, often an expectation and a signifier of authenticity. Industry censors and moral crusaders alike may protest the thematic saturation of crime in hip hop culture, but it is inseparable from the lived experiences of the many rappers who inhabit or have inhabited these ghettoized environments. To provide some context for the pervasiveness of violence in African-American communities, Cooper & Smith (2011)—statisticians with the Bureau of Justice Statistics—noted that in their study on homicide in the United States from 1980–2010, Blacks (27.8 per 100,000) were 6 times more likely than Whites (4.5 per 100,000) to be homicide victims. Similarly, there were nearly 8 times the amount of black homicide perpetrators (34.4 per 100,000) compared to white offenders (4.5 per 100,000). Ninety percent of homicide offenders were male, with males also comprising 77% of homicide victims.

The daily reality of violence in transitional urban areas involving young black males has been acknowledged by nearly every major African-American hip hop artist. Given this social pattern, many rappers' associates are convicted felons, and this association with the artist may actually induce the associate to perpetrate violent criminal acts. As Ice-T explains: "Fifty percent of your crew is made up of homeboys that just came home from jail ... They do not have any other way of showing the rapper that they [are the rapper's] man than busting somebody in they head ..." (Spirer 2003).

The topics of hip hop songs reflect the social experiences that the artist has observed in his own community, thereby revealing to us the modes of adaptation which Merton posited inevitably occur in a disenfranchised society. Taking the attitude of the *generalized other* (Mead, 1934/1967), many of the inhabitants of these urban areas realize that they are expected to pursue wealth, fame, and status through legal conduct, but that these goals are not achievable in the prescribed manner. Many respond by rejecting the cultural goals, institutionalized means, or both. Even when a hip hop artist may rise from an urban ghetto to fame and fortune, his own and his associates' criminal socialization mean that violent responses to problems are still very real possibilities.

Gangsta Rap, Authenticity, and Violent Self-Image

Given that hip hop was originally a form of urban folk music, it is not surprising that artists working in this medium began to address the dire political and social issues that they experienced and observed in their communities. Perhaps the most successful and recognizable of these early attempts was "The Message" by Grandmaster Flash and the Furious Five in which MC Melle Mel (Melvin Glover) paints a lyrical portrait of a stark and polluted urban landscape plagued by crimes ranging from public urination to drug abuse, theft, and murder. While the protagonist of the song wishes to escape his situation, he has "no money to move on" (Fletcher et al. 1982) and therefore must remain in his environment. He is unable to "walk through the park/because it's crazy after dark" (Fletcher et al. 1982) making the carrying of a firearm for protection a necessity. Though he wishes his community was devoid of violent criminals like the "junkies in the alley with a baseball bat" (Fletcher et al. 1982), he understands why so many of his neighbors and peers turn to crime and is able to sympathize with those not as resilient. These individuals choose criminality (Merton's Innovation mode of adaptation) as a means of socioeconomic advancement because it is the only feasible option. However, Melle Mel sees what can ultimately happen to those who take this path: they are almost inevitably caught and sentenced to prison where they may be subject to repeated rapes and assaults, some even committing suicide. With no way to escape his circumstances, Melle Mel warns the listener not to push him because "he's close to the edge" (Fletcher et al. 1982) of doing something extreme, and is trying to maintain his moral sanity through Ritualism.

In 1982, at this stage in the evolution of commercially successful hip hop music, the protagonist is not displaying a violent self-image (Athens 1997), nor does he wish to resort to or be exposed to violence. Rather, he is using lyricism to explain what can be legitimately referred to as literary criminology by drawing attention to the multitudinous social ailments that he observes daily in his community and explaining why such an environment is criminogenic. The song itself is not criminogenic, in fact it discourages criminality and implies that a solution is necessary.

An important shift occurred in hip hop music in the mid-Eighties, when artists, in contrast to Melle Mel's protagonist and man of restraint, began to adopt the voice of the criminal. Interestingly, and perhaps coincidentally, this occurred roughly around the time that crack cocaine began to plague urban America, and just months after the most violent year in New York City history. Most notable and successful among this new breed of MC was Ice-T, who grew up in gang-ridden South Central Los Angeles. With the 1987 release of his debut album "Rhyme Pays" he introduced the world to what is generally considered to be the first gangsta rap song, entitled "6 N the Mornin'". Unlike the narrator of "The Message" who is trying his best to remain law abiding in the face of extraordinary provocation, the protagonist of "6 N the Mornin'" unabashedly surrenders to the lures of criminal behaviour (in **bold**) and revels in a grandiosely violent self-image (in *italics*):

> "6'n the mornin' **police at my door**/Fresh Adidas squeak across the bathroom floor/Out the back window I make my escape/Didn't even get a chance to grab my old school tape/Mad with no music but happy 'cause [I'm] free/And the streets to a player is the place to be/**Gotta knot in my pocket weighin' at least a grand**/Gold on my neck, my pistols close at hand/*I'm a self-made monster of the city streets*/Remotely controlled by hard hip hop beats .../*Posse* to the corner where the fly girls chill/Threw action at some freaks until one bitch got ill/She started actin' stupid simply would not quit/Called us all punk pussies said we all weren't shit/As we walked over to her, ho continued to speak/**So we beat the bitch down in the god damn street ...**/Sean-e-sean was the driver, known to give freaks hell/Had a beeper goin' off like a high school bell/Looked in the mirror, what did we see?/Fuckin' blue lights: L.A.P.D./**Pigs searched our car, their day was made/Found an Uzi,. 44 and a hand grenade**/Threw us in the county high power block/No freaks to see, no beats to rock/Didn't want trouble but the shit must fly/**Squabbled this sucker shanked him in the eye**/." (Marrow & Glenn 1987)

Criminality, violent actions, and violent self-image would become the defining elements of gangsta rap, and would culminate in the 1996 murder of

2Pac (Tupac Shakur) and the equally dramatic slaying of the The Notorious B.I.G. (Christopher Wallace), the following year. When considered superficially, it seems nonsensical that an artist who has managed to ascend from rags to riches would jeopardize his improved social status and situation by committing acts of violence, either directly or through his criminal associates. However, upon deeper reflection it is apparent that every human being—regardless of the nuances of their socialization—draws upon their past experiences to make sense of their world and, consequently, to *interpret* and *judge* how to respond to social phenomena (Athens 1997). Athens (1994) refers to those interlocutors from our past whom we cognitively replicate and whose perspective we carry with us mentally (ie. family members, former lovers, friends, enemies) as *phantom others*. When we consider their opinion of us as a conglomerate, Athens labels them our *phantom community*.

There is also a social experience unique to public figures which cannot be accounted for by the *generalized other*, *phantom other* or *phantom community*. It is the realization that, as a public figure, one has a body of advocates, supporters, and people who may live vicariously through you, many of whom are not even known to you. Nevertheless, there are conventions and expectations of conduct attached to public presentations within a particular field which a public figure must be aware of in order to be successful, and by which they are expected to abide (Goffman 1959). When a public figure refers to the conventions and expectations of a body of supporters, advocates, or potential supporters/advocates in order to make a social *judgment* (Athens 1997), this is considered taking the attitude of his or her *fandom community*. Print magazines, television programs, documentaries, and radio shows related to rap music, can also be considered part of the *fandom community* as they reflect, reinforce, accentuate, and (to a lesser degree) create the values and trends of hip hop culture.

As many hip hop artists hale from Merton's strained communities where the Innovation mode of adaptation, and thus criminality, are widespread, the likelihood that these artists will have a *mitigated* or *unmitigated* violent *phantom community* (Athens 1997) is particularly high when compared with those in other musical genres. If an individual's *phantom community* is of an "unmitigated violent" nature it gives them "pronounced and categorical support for acting violently"; if "mitigated violent" it "provides them with pronounced but limited categorical support for acting violently" (Athens 1997, 138–139). Similarly, the hip hop *fandom community* values street smarts, ghetto authenticity, loyalty to one's faction, lack of cooperation with police, unwavering confidence, heterosexuality, aggressive masculinity, and a willingness to embrace confrontation. Therefore, even if a rapper does not have a violent and/or criminal background, or a *mitigated* or *unmitigated* violent *phantom community*, the attitude of his *fandom community* may pressure him to take confrontational, aggressive, and threatening stances towards other hip hop artists.

Bringing this all into perspective, following the death of Tupac Shakur, journalist Kevin Powell who had interviewed the rapper numerous times over his six year career, stated that "Sometimes people will put on the [outlaw] persona. A lot of times Pac wasn't the person he was rapping about; he became it" (Scott 2014, Kindle Locations 2966–2967). Evidence seems to indicate that Shakur adopted and increasingly embraced his "thug" self-image in accordance with changes to the values of his *phantom* and *fandom* communities. Consistent with Powell's observation, Goffman (1959) noted that "At one extreme, one finds that the performer can be fully taken in by his own act; he can be sincerely convinced that the impression of the reality which he stages is the real reality" (17).

Links between the violent acts and violent self-conceptualization of Shakur will now be presented. Athens' study of violent felons relied upon the offenders' own oral testimony of who they were at various stages of their lives (self-image), then listed any acts of physical violence that occurred during each phase. He concluded that generally a person will have either an *escalating*, *stable*, or *de-escalating* violent career based upon changes in their self-image. Shakur evidenced a violent career that was *escalating*. A limitation to our methodology is that Athens interviewed each of his subjects in person, but as Shakur is deceased, this is an impossibility. Fortunately, there are video interviews with the artist (both formal and informal), testimony of third parties who were close to him, and information regarding the symbolic content of his tattoos. Drawing from these sources, a reasonably accurate appraisal of Shakur's self-image at three different stages of his short life can be formulated.

Case Study: 2Pac (Tupac Shakur, June 16, 1971–September 13, 1996)

Age 0–17: Nonviolent Self-Image

Describing himself as a child in a 1995 interview with MTV, Shakur claimed "I was the total opposite of what I am right now. I was quiet, withdrawn. I read a lot. Wrote poetry" (Tupac Amaru Shakur Unofficial Channel April 29, 2012). Shakur wrote his first rap on gun control while attending a school for the performing arts in Baltimore (Spirer 2002). Footage of a 17-year-old

Shakur as an aspiring actor reveals a young man who goes out of his way to distance himself from violence. He speaks about having started an anti-violence movement in Baltimore as a teen, and having come "to California to escape that violence …" (UHATIn uni April 24, 2012).

Age 0–17: Negligibly Violent Period

There are no accounts or history of arrests for violent or potentially violent offences during this period of Shakur's life. Reflecting back on the days before his music career, Shakur would remark, "Before I made a record, I never had a record" (Scott 2014, Kindle Locations 1851–1852).

Age 18–19: Incipiently Violent Self-Image

Following his move to Oakland, California at the age of 18, Shakur began to adopt violence into his self-image. Commenting on Oakland, he would say "When I got to Oakland that's where I learned the [thug] game … somebody just woke it up inside me like a religion. I saw it living in Oakland and I saw it thriving in Oakland …" (Xirix Seven July 9, 2014). Still, he seems not to have fully committed to the violent gangsta image until the beginning of his career as a recording arist. MC Shock G of the band Digital Underground who Shakur performed with at this early stage, said that in 1990 (aged 19) Shakur's lyrics were "hip hop fantasy … or political. It wasn't thugged out yet" (Spirer 2002).

Age 18–19: Unsubstantially Violent Period

Only two violent incidents stand out during this period. The first is a mild physical fight Shakur had with a friend (Russell 2000). This act of violence was *unsubstantial* and defensive. In the second, Shakur thought the audio technician was ruining a Digital Underground show that he was performing at, and "tried [unsuccessfully] to beat up the soundman" (Spirer 2002). No physical contact was made, and ultimately this can be considered an *unsubstantial* violent act, though indicative of a person with an *incipiently violent* self-image.

Age 20–25: Violent Self-Image

At approximately the age of 20, Shakur acquired an AK-47 assault rifle and began to express different views about violence, tying it to authentic black experience and rap music, "I'ma pack a gat cos that's what niggas do" (Spirer 2002). While at a firing range, Shakur explained on camera, "We [black people] could never take the stance, which was our true stance, to be straight soldiers, straight warriors … until hip hop came" (Spirer 2002).

When Shakur was 21-years-old, the film *Juice*—in which he plays an unhinged homicidal thug named Bishop—was released. It was at roughly this time that people around Shakur began to notice a change in his personality, as if Shakur had taken on Bishop's persona (Russell 2000). During this same transformative period, Shakur had the words "Thug Life" with a bullet replacing the letter "I" tattooed across his abdomen. Subsequent tattoos read "Outlaw," "Trust Nobody," "Heartless," and "Notorious" amongst others (Scott 2014, Kindle Locations 1346–1357). Some of the images accompanying these words included a "bloody skull and crossbones" (Scott 2014, Kindle Locations 1346–1350), an AK-47 (Scott 2014, Kindle Locations 1354–1357), and a rifle (Scott 2014, Kindle Locations 1346–1361).

In a 1996 interview with *Vibe*, Shakur proclaimed "There's nobody in the business strong enough to scare me" (Scott 2014, Kindle Locations 1684–1685) and later befriended ex-boxer and fellow convicted sex offender, Mike Tyson. After watching Tyson defeat Bruce Seldon on the night of Shakur's murder, Shakur identified himself with Tyson, suggesting that the professionally violent Tyson and Shakur's identity as a gangsta rapper represented sanctioned representations of violence, notwithstanding their shared experiences as incarcerated black men.

Age 20–25: Substantially Violent Period
SUMMER OF 1992 (unsubstantially violent act): *Charged with battery for slapping a woman who asked for his autograph.*

AUGUST 22, 1992 (unsubstantially violent act resulting in accident): *Pulled weapon on a third party and a male child is accidentally shot and killed.*

APRIL 5, 1993 (unsubstantially violent act): *Charged with felonious assault accused of attempting to hit rapper Chauncey Wynn with a baseball bat. Pleaded guilty.*

OCTOBER 1993 (unsubstantially violent act, victim precipitated): *Charged with shooting two intoxicated off-duty police officers in Atlanta after one of the police officers pointed a gun at him.*

NOVEMBER 1993 (substantially violent act): *Charged with sexually assaulting woman in hotel room. Convicted of first-degree sexual abuse.*

EARLY 1994 (unsubstantially violent act): *Found guilty of assault and battery on Menace II Society co-director Allen Hughes*

FEBRUARY–OCTOBER 1995: Incarcerated in Clinton Prison.

SEPTEMBER 7 1996 (unsubstantially violent act): *Assault on Orlando Anderson captured by casino cameras.* (Scott 2014)

The impetus for a hip hop artist such as Shakur to conceptualize and promote himself as an aggressive criminal and act violently is at least partially explained by the Communication Theory of Identity (Jung & Hecht 2004). Jung & Hecht propose that our identities consist of a *personal identity*, "an individual's self-concepts or self-images" existing "at the individual level of analysis as a characteristic of individuals" (266), and an *enacted identity*, an "individual's performed or expressed identity" (266). The basis for this division is the *front stage* and *back stage* selves of Goffman's dramaturgical theory. Though both aspects of identity may be influenced by the attitudes of the *phantom* and *fandom* communities, the *enacted identity* that the gangsta rapper performs is particularly affected.

Jung & Hecht (2004) posit that gaps between an individual's *personal* and *enacted* identities occur when his attempts to convey his identity (*enacted identity*) to others are either unsuccessful or perceived to be unsuccessful, resulting in communication dissatisfaction. Another possibility that Jung & Hecht do not adequately explore is that an individual's *enacted identity* may be purposefully deceptive. Intending to grossly misrepresent his *personal identity* to others, the individual may become fearful that a lack of success in this venture may lead to him being exposed as a phony. In hip hop music, the need to convince others that both the *personal* and *enacted* identities are consistent with one another, and thus authentic, is crucial for a successful career. Another possibility, then, is that if one's *enacted identity* is that of "thug" or "gangsta", he may seek to change his *personal identity* to match it, narrowing or closing the gap between these two aspects of his identity and resulting in communication satisfaction. What better way for an individual with an *enacted identity* of a dangerous criminal to live up to this than committing violence and/or threatening violent acts? This could account for Athens' (1997) findings that one's capacity for violence is related to self-image.

Violence inflicted as communication to negotiate or affirm the perpetrator's identity, as in the case of Tupac Shakur, is thus *expressive/transformative* in nature (Mellor in press). As the victim of a hip hop feud tends to be specific, and is typically targeted in a blitz style act-focused attack (eg. "Drive-by shootings"), such crimes often fall into the Type 1 category of *expressive/transformative* violence. The attack on the specific person (*symbolic victim*) is the message itself (*victim as soapbox*), rather than the message residing in any symbolism implicit in the manner of violence (*victim as canvas*—eg. when organized criminals sever the tongue or place a rat in the mouth of a suspected informant). This paradigm, the *expressive/transformative* theory of violence, is one where literary criminology, criminal violence, and performance art overlap, and is expressed schematically in Figure 1 below:

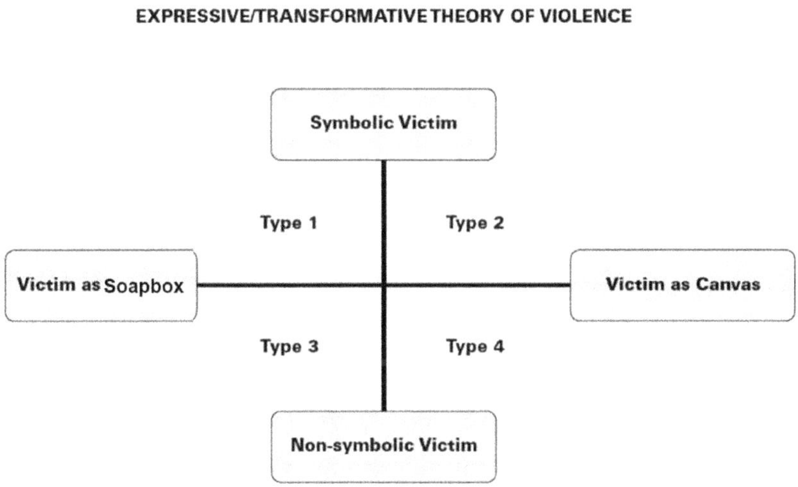

Figure 1. A Typology of Expressive/Transformative Violence.

Braggadocio, Battle Rap, and Communication Dysfunction

Gangsta rap, when combined with the hip hop conventions of "braggadocio" and "battle rapping," births a distinct form of violence based upon the need to create and/or maintain *face* and call into question the *face* of another rapper. The qualities of this *face* are largely determined by the attitudes of the *phantom* and *fandom* communities. Due to their roles as entertainers and/or celebrity status, hip hop artists spend an inordinate amount of time as *actors* in Goffman's *front stage* social position (1959), defined as "that part of the individual's performance which regularly functions in a general and fixed fashion to define the situation for those who observe the performance" (22). By "performance," Goffman means that there is a certain conduct that is expected of a hip hop artist by his *audience*—a role to which he generally conforms (Goffman 1959). In this case, Goffman's *audience* encompasses members of Athens' *phantom community* and our proposed *fandom community*.

As previously mentioned regarding a rapper's *fandom community*, hip hop audiences demand of their artists the *accrediting attributes* of street smarts, ghetto authenticity, loyalty to one's faction, lack of cooperation with police, unwavering confidence, heterosexuality, aggressive masculinity, and a willingness to embrace confrontation. Thus, like society at large, it is the broader hip hop community that "establishes the means of categorizing persons and the complement of attributes felt to be ordinary and natural for members of each of these categories" (Goffman 1963, 2). If, at any time, one or more of the *accrediting attributes* is visibly absent, or if the *audience*'s suspicion is raised as to whether the hip hop artist possesses the attribute, then he may be "reduced" in the minds of hip hop fans and peers "from a whole and usual" rapper "to a tainted, discounted one" (Goffman 1963, 3). This will likely mean the death of his career.

The mechanism of such *front stage* communications as "battle rapping" or the exchanging of carefully crafted disses (disrespectful comments) on recordings (Goffman 1959) is essentially that of an *actor* expressing *significant symbols* (Mead 1934/1967) in the form of rhyming words that either highlight a stigma that has already *discredited* another *actor* or reveals the stigma of a *discreditable actor* (Goffman 1963). The artist, through *performing* his role of rapper, defines his identity and that of any other *actors* in the situation to his audience. Goffman (1963) refers to those attributes which cause others to turn away from us as "stigma," demarcating stigma where a person is *discredited* from stigma where a person is *discreditable.* A person is automatically *discredited* if their stigma is visually observable such as skin colour or a physical deformity. Conversely, a person is *discreditable* if there is information about them that, if revealed, would lead to their stigmatization. Following from these two types, Goffman additionally proposes three different manifestations of stigma. In "Hit 'Em Up" Shakur draws attention to Notorious B.I.G.'s obesity and Prodigy from Mobb Deep's sickle-cell disease: both *abominations of the body* (Shakur et al. 1996). On "Ether", Nas reveals information about Jay-Z which raises questions about his sexuality, honour, and attitudes towards women; all of which are *blemishes of individual character* (Jones & Turner 2002). Ja Rule criticizes Eminem in "Loose Change" for being a white rapper who is unable to know black pain. Here, Ja Rule is highlighting Eminem's racial stigma of being Caucasian in the predominantly Black hip hop culture. This latter case is a fascinating example of Goffman's (1963) assertion that stigma can be situational, considering that in most American occupations, being white would be advantageous and African-American heritage would be stigmatized. Hip hop is thus the definitive exception to many rules.

Dissing, then, is a process of trying to discredit the authenticity of a rival hip hop artist's identity by referencing his stigmas in a *front stage* social region. This is done by referring to those visible attributes of a rival artist that have already *discredited* him to some members of the *audience*, or by truthfully exposing or slyly fabricating *discreditable* attributes that the rival artist may or may not possess. An unanswered diss may be seen as revealing a blemish on the individual's character—discrediting him by showing that he lacks willingness to embrace confrontation.

Hip hop allows a number of options for a dissed artist to save or enhance his credibility and career. These include openly addressing the stigma and even sympathizing with the reasons for its existence. Eminem has taken his approach concerning his race in the song "White America". In the case of Rick Ross—who was exposed as a former Corrections Officer—he at first denied that he had ever occupied this stigmatized (in hip hop culture) role. On another occasion he tried to incorporate this role into his gangsta mythology, loosely implying that he had taken the job at the prison to infiltrate it on the part of his "team" (305Resident August 15, 2012). Of theoretical interest, here Ross admitted that he was indeed a duplicitous *performer*, however, where the initial accusation was that the *back stage* Rick Ross was a former corrections officer *front*ing like a gangsta, Ross's face-saving strategy was to socially re-package the situation, proposing that he was a gangsta performing *front stage* in the prison as a corrections officer. Finally, Ross claimed that he had taken the role of a corrections officer to put food on the table—just part of the "hustle" of getting by in life (Hezakya Hendrix March 7, 2014). This last explanation is illustrative of Goffman's (1959) observation that when a social performance has gone very badly, occasionally, the *actor* will take off his mask and appeal to our shared sense that we are all *actors* in a variety of situations, and that this differs from our *back stage* conduct.

There are times when the rapper can perform a "defensive practice" to manage the stigma. Through his lyrics and fashion sense, the Notorious B.I.G. bore his obesity (Goffman 1963), as a trademark of his rapper identity. But by far the most common way of managing diss-related stigma in hip hop is for the rapper to communicate a diss response which reveals or highlights one or more stigmatizing attributes of his opponent, and minimizes, or sometimes ignores, the rapper's own stigmas. Clever rhymes, humorous wordplay, and the sheer intensity of the rapper's performance enhance the audience's sense that the communication is credible hip hop, and skill in this artistic medium can be an an *accrediting attribute.*

Disses can belong to one of several types identified here:

1. **Direct/individual**—directed at a specific individual who is named in the lyrics, eg. "I know you missing Nas [a rival rapper] all the fame/ But along with celebrity comes about 70 shots to your frame/Nigga, you are lame"—Jay-Z (Shawn Carter), "The Takeover" (Carter et al. 2001).

2. **Direct/communal**—directed at a specific community or group who are named in the lyrics, sometimes along with specific individuals, eg. "This Gay-Z [rapper Jay-Z] and Cock-a-Fella Records [Jay-Z's record company] wanted beef/Started cocking up my weapon, slowly loading up this ammo/to explode it on a camel/and his soldiers"—Nas (Nasir Jones), "Ether" (Jones & Turner 2002).
3. **Indirect/individual**—directed at an individual who is not named but whose identity can be inferred by the content of the diss, eg. [in reference to rapper MC Shan] "Party people in the place to be, KRS-One attack/You got dropped off MCA cause the rhymes you wrote was wack/So you think that hip-hop had its start out in Queensbridge?/If you pop that junk up in the Bronx you might not live"—Boogie Down Productions, "South Bronx" (KRS-One & La Rock 1987).
4. **Indirect Personal Elevation**—directed at all or many rappers in general, usually more as an act of braggadocio rather than specifically "dissing" anyone, eg. "[Spoken] There are too many overnight MCs … [Rapped] You couldn't wet shit up in a motherfuckin' water fight"—Naughty By Nature, "Yoke the Joker" (Criss, Brown & Gist 1991).

Unlike dissing, braggadocio originated in the 1980s from the artistic collaboration between the DJ (disc jockey) and MC (master of ceremonies). According to Ice-T, "[The] DJ said 'here's a microphone, somebody tell everybody how great I am … Now this MC has the microphone, so what he would do is say 'you know, by the way, y'know the DJ's this, but I'm kinda nice and I'm kinda fly'…" (Spirer 2003). As DJ/MC collaborations would compete against others to see who was the most popular at a given event, naturally they would try to outdo each other by responding to the previous MC's braggadocio. In this way, braggadocio can elicit a response as an Indirect Personal Elevation diss.

The combination of dramaturgical theory with Athens' (1994, 1997) qualitative research regarding identity and violence provides a remarkable window into this potential lethality. Following his qualitative study of 47 male and 11 female inmates incarcerated for substantially violent acts[1] at four separate institutions,[2] Athens, whose approach shares its symbolic interactionist underpinnings with dramaturgical theory, concluded that violent actors always first (1) *interpret* the situations in which they commit violence, then (2) form a *judgment* as to how they should react by taking the attitude of their *phantom community*. In the case of hip hop artists, they may also take the attitude of their *fandom community*, either exclusively or in conjunction with that of the *phantom community*.

During the interpretive phase, Athens' (1997) research shows that an *actor* interprets communications by his victim(s) in one of four ways:

1. *Defensive*—The perpetrator or his loved ones are either being physically attacked or the perpetrator perceives that they are going to be attacked, so he either attacks pre-emptively or in retaliation;
2. *Frustrative*—The perpetrator either interprets that the victim is going to resist complying with what he wants them to do, or alternatively, that the victim is going to force him to do something that the perpetrator doesn't want to do;
3. *Malefic*—The perpetrator interprets that the victim is insulting him, concludes that the victim is evil or malicious, and decides that the appropriate response is to attack the victim;
4. *Frustrative-Malefic*—The perpetrator either interprets that the victim is going to resist complying with what he wants them to do, or alternatively, that the victim is going to force the perpetrator to do something that he doesn't want to do. The victim is perceived by the perpetrator as evil or malicious, and the perpetrator concludes that he will commit an act of violence upon the victim in response (Athens 1997).

The types of interpretation available to an individual depend upon his self-image: *non-violent*, *incipiently violent*, and *violent*. A *marginally violent* person has a *non-violent* self-image and *phantom community*, and will only commit defensive acts of physical violence. In addition to defensive violent acts, the *violent* person will also respond with violence to *frustrative-malefic* interpretations, and has an *incipiently violent* self-image and a *mitigated violent phantom community*. Finally, the *ultraviolent* person will commit all four of Athens' types of violence egged on by his *unmitigated violent phantom community* and in accordance with his *violent self-image*.

Once the communication has been *interpreted*, the actor takes the attitude of his *phantom community*, and in the case of the hip hop artist, his *fandom community*, to form a *judgment* as to how he should react. Oftentimes, if a *defensive*, *frustrative*, *malefic*, or *frustrative-malefic* interpretation has been formed, a person will *judge* that he is being encouraged to respond with vitriol or violence by members of his *phantom community*, and in the case of the rapper, his *fandom* community. This does not mean that he necessarily will; Instead, he may form a "restraining judgment" (Athens, 1997, 45). Lil' Cease talks about how this pressure was exerted on the Notorious B.I.G. following 2Pac's epic Direct/Communal diss "Hit 'Em Up" of him and his associates on the east coast:

> "They [the fans on the street on the east coast] wanted that [an aggressive response]. Even some members of the [Junior] M.A.F.I.A. wanted to respond … Niggaz was already in the lab the day after they heard it. And B.I.G. was like 'yo, if you put that record out, or any bars out [I won't be happy]. I'm not fucking with you'." (This is 50 June 6, 2012)

Athens studied only physically violent responses to actions interpreted as *defensive*, *frustrative*, *malefic*, or *frustrative-malefic*, but in hip hop, the appropriate reaction is generally thought to be to respond with a better, and often viciously insulting, diss track. To quote KRS-One (Lawrence Parker):

> "[Y]ou verbally attack your opponent, and your opponent verbally attacks you until somebody breaks down and either wants to fight, cries … or a judge deems the battle won by either opponent … It was Zulu Nation that first brought up the idea of we [African-Americans] don't have to shoot at each other or beat on each other or this, we can actually use this tradition of 'the dozens' to actually have verbal warfare through art." (Ice-T 2004)

Unfortunately, though many rap feuds are initiated on purpose and subsequently "squashed", the ambiguous nature of the Indirect/Individual diss means that hip hop artists often wrongly interpret that they are the target of the diss. The deadly feud between 2Pac and The Notorious B.I.G. occurred when 2Pac (wrongly, according to The Notorious B.I.G. and his colleagues), formed a *defensive* interpretation of the lyrics of B.I.G.'s "Who Shot Ya?", believing that they where directed at him and in reference to 2Pac's being shot five times in 1994.

Such interpretations can also occur during an Indirect Personal Elevation diss. However, more commonly in this type of diss, a hip hop artist will take offence at the implication that he or other rappers that he respects have been placed on a lower level than the artist making the Indirect Personal Elevation diss. An example of this occurred at New York City's Harlem World when MC Busy Bee, performing before a live crowd, proclaimed that he should be given the trophy already because "I'm knocking out all bums" (Spirer 2003). Rapper Kool Moe Dee who was in attendance took offence because Busy Bee "didn't acknowledge that he couldn't beat me in a battle" (Spirer 2003), and signed up for the rap battle, winning decisively with his intricate lyrics.

A second problem occurs when a hip hop artist forms a *defensive*, *frustrative*, *frustrative-malefic*, or *malefic* interpretation of another rapper's lyrics, when in actuality, there was no malicious intent. One such incident occurred when KRS-One of Boogie Down Productions supposedly misinterpreted the lyrics from Queensbridge's The Juice Crew as being a Direct/Communal diss aimed at his neighbourhood, the South Bronx, and responded with the song "South Bronx", an Indirect/Individual diss track directed at The Juice Crew's MC Shan. This ignited a legendary feud between Boogie Down Productions and The Juice Crew. But according to MC Shan:

> "KRS claimed that I said that hip hop started in Queensbridge, which I didn't. In the beginning of the song you hear Marley Marl say 'yo, they wanna tell you a story about where *they* [The Juice Crew, not hip hop] come from.' That's the key word: where *they* come from." (Spirer 2003)

Further complicating matters is the possibility that an artist may intentionally diss another artist directly or indirectly, then pretend that this was a misunderstanding in order to avoid a feud, while simultaneously avoiding being discredited. Ultimately, however, so long as the conflict in hip hop remains verbal in nature, there are no serious ramifications of a feud. At worst, it will mean the destruction of the losing party's career. As record executives and music journalists learned long ago, a public battle between hip hop artists or factions often leads to increased record and magazine sales (Spirer 2003).

Finally, feuding can be competitively entertaining in a way that other genres of music can't. West coast G-Funk rapper Snoop Dogg (Calvin Broadus) explained that "[Hip hop's] like a sport to me because it's like you're driving me to outdo you" (Ice-T 2012). But, as any hockey fan will attest, sports can quickly escalate from healthy competition to physical violence. Having grown as an art form from the Mertonian enclaves that gave rise to gangsta rap and the salience of an authentic criminal image, hip hop-related violence is often armed and taken to extremes. As the Notorious B.I.G. learned, a simple lyrical misinterpretation can result in being shot four times.

Conclusion

Following the murder of The Notorious B.I.G. in 1997, several artists made attempts to settle "beefs" in a non-violent self-effacing manner, often under the arbitration of Louis Farrakhan and the Nation of Islam (Spirer, 2003). Yet, less than a year later, in response to LL Cool J's "4, 3, 2, 1" Canibus released the epic diss track "Second Round K.O." mocking those who would engage in this peace process, and warning LL that he would, "Make your wife get on the horn/call Minister Farrakhan/So he could persuade me to squash it/I say naw he started it/He forgot what a hardcore artist is/A hardcore artist is a dangerous man, such as myself" (Williams, Wonder & Jean 1998).

"Second Round K.O." is widely considered one of the best diss tracks ever recorded. Though in most social situations a public overture to avoid violence is considered commendable, the confrontation and potential for misinterpretation woven into rap as an art form, combined with the incorporation of gangsta morality by the artists' *phantom* and *fandom communities*, which Athens has demonstrated can prefigure acts of violence, has created a working consensus that, in hip hop culture, extending an olive branch is actually a discrediting act (Goffman 1963). Thus, some level of violent identity and self-conceptualization, whether authentic or not, must always be maintained and projected as *face* (or *enacted self*) by the hip hop artist—an identity that the artists may embrace or feel the need to live up to. As the saying goes, truth is the first casualty of war—even if it is (merely) a war of words.

Notes

1. Athens defines an act as "substantially violent" if "[t]he victim was either (1) substantially physically injured, that is, nonaccidentally injured either fatally or to a degree that usually calls for a physician's attention such as results from a shooting, stabbing, clubbing, or relentless beating; or (2) substantially sexually violated, as in the case of coitus, sodomy, fellatio, or cunnilingus, under either the threat of the infliction of substantial physical injury or the actual infliction of substantial or less severe physical injury" (Athens, 1997, p. 31).
2. These institutions included a woman's maximum security prison, two men's maximum security prisons, and a large county jail in a "far western state" along with a "men's maximum security prison in a midwestern state" (Athens, 1997, p. 101).

References

Athens, L. The Self as a Soliloquy. *The Sociological Quarterly*. 35 (1994): 521–532.

Athens, L. *Violent Criminal Acts and Actors Revisited*. Urbana, Chicago & Springfield: University of Illinois Press, 1997.

Baxter, L. Rap Music Began on Jamaica in the 1960s. *New York Times*. June 15, 1988. Accessed September, 2, 2015. http://www.nytimes.com/1988/06/15/opinion/l-rap-music-began-on-jamaica-in-the-1960-s-659388.html.

Blumer, H. (1969). *Symbolic Interactionism: Perspective and Method*. New Jersey: Prentice Hall.

Cooper, A, & Smith, EL. *Homicide Trends in the United States, 1980–2008*. USA: US Department of Justice, 2011.

Goffman, E. *The Presentation of Self in Everyday Life*. New York: Anchor Books, 1959.

Goffman, E. *Stigma: Notes on the Management of Spoiled Identity*. New York: Touchstone, 1963.

Johnson, S. "Rap music originated in medieval Scottish pubs, claims American professor". *The Telegraph.* December 28, 2008. Accessed September, 2, 2015. http://www.telegraph.co.uk/culture/music/3998862/Rap-music-originated-in-medieval-Scottish-pubs-claims-American-professor.html

Jung, E, & Hecht, M. Elaborating the Communication Theory of Identity: Identity Gaps and Communication Outcomes. *Communication Quarterly.* Vol 52 Issue 3 (2004), 265–283.

Kreps, D. Report: Rick Ross Worked as a Florida Corrections Officer. *Rolling Stone.* July 22, 2008. Accessed September 2, 2015. http://www.rollingstone.com.

Mead, GH. *Mind, Self, & Society from the Standpoint of a Social Behaviorist.* Charles W. Morris (Ed.). Chicago: University of Chicago Press, 1934/1967.

Mellor, L. (2015) Mincing Words: Refining the Language of Mutilation. *Understanding Necrophilia: A Global and Multidisciplinary Approach.* Lee Mellor, Anil Aggrawal & Eric W. Hickey (Eds.) San Diego: Cognella.

Mellor, L. (in press). The Expressive-Transformative Offender: Communication and Negotiation of Identities Through the Process of Violence. Dissertation manuscript in preparation.

Merton, R. Social Structure and Anomie. *American Sociological Review*, 3 (1938), 672–682.

Scott, C. *The Killing of Tupac Shakur.* Las Vegas, NV: Huntington Press, 2014. Kindle Edition.

Venkatesh, V, Wallin, J, Walschots, N, Netherton, J, & Podeshon, J. "Giving Head to the Dead": Penetrating, Defiling and Polluting the Ethos of Death in Necrophilic Death Metal. Understanding Necrophilia: A Global Multidisciplinary Approach. Lee Mellor, Anil Aggrawal & Eric W. Hickey (Ed.) San Diego: Cognella, 2015.

Wald, E. The Dozen's: A History of Rap's Mama. Oxford: Oxford University Press, 2012.

Washington, TN. "Rapping with the Gods: Hip Hop as a Force of Divinity and Continuity from the Continent to the Cosmos," *Journal of Pan African Studies.* 6, no. 9 (2014): 72–100.

Documentary Films

Beef. Directed by Pete Spirer. 2003. United States: QD3 Entertainment. 2003. DVD.

Beef II. Directed by Pete Spirer. 2004. United States: QD3 Entertainment. 2004. DVD

Something From Nothing: The Art of Rap. Directed by Ice-T. 2012. United States: Art of Rap Films Ltd. 2012. DVD.

Thug Angel: The Life of an Outlaw. Directed by Pete Spirer. 2002. United States: QD3 Entertainment, 2002. DVD.

Tupac Shakur: Thug Immortal. Directed by Toby Russell. 2000. United States: Xenon Pictures. 2000. DVD.

Musical Recordings

Carter, S, West, K, Parker, L, Burdon, E, Lomax, A, Chandler, B, Lemay, R, Morrison, J, Densmore, J, Krieger, R, & Manzarek, R. The Takeover. Recorded by Jay-Z. On *The Blueprint* [CD]. New York City: Rockafella, 2001.

Coronel, F. The 4th Branch. Recorded by Immortal Technique. On *Revolutionary Vol. 2* [CD]. New York City, USA: Viper Records, 2003.

Criss, A, Brown, V, & Gist, K. Yoke the Joker. Recorded by Naughty By Nature. On *Naughty By Nature* [LP]. New York City: Tommy Boy Records, 1991.

Fletcher, E, Glover, M, Robinson, S, & Chase, J. The Message. Recorded by Grandmaster Flash and the Furious Five. On *The Message* [Vinyl]. Englewood, New Jersey USA: Sugar Hill Records, 1982.

Jones, N, & Turner, R. Ether. Recorded by Nas. On *Stillmatic.* [CD] New York City: Sony, 2001.

KRS-One, & La Rock, S. South Bronx. Recorded by Boogie Down Productions. On *Criminal Minded.* [LP] New York City: B-Boy Records, 1987.

Marrow, T, & Glenn, C. 6 'N the Morning. Recorded by Ice-T. On *Rhyme Pays* [Vinyl]. Los Angeles, California USA: Sire/Warner Brothers, 1987.

Henderson, A, & Marrow, T. New Jack Hustler (Ninos' Theme). Recorded by Ice-T. On *O.G. Original Gangster* [CD]. Los Angeles, California USA: Sire/Warner Brothers, 1991.

Mathers, M, Hale, N, & Resto, L. Till I Collapse. Recorded by Eminem. On *The Eminem Show* [CD]. USA: Aftermath, Goliath, Interscope, Shady, 2002.

Shakur, T, Fula, Y, Washington, B, & Greenidge, M. Hit 'Em Up. Recorded by 2Pac. On *Hit 'Em Up* [CD Single]. California, USA: Death Row, Interscope, 1996.

Smith, J, Smith, C, Noble, R, Williams, G, & Simmons, E. 4, 3, 2, 1. Recorded by LL Cool J. On *Phenomenon* [CD]. USA: Def Jam, 1997.

Williams, Wonder, J, & Jean, W. Second Round K.O. Recorded by Canibus. On *Second Round K.O.* [Vinyl Single]. USA: Universal Records, 1998.

YouTube Videos

"1988 Tupac Interview at 17 Years Old." YouTube video. Posted by "UHATIn uni." April 24, 2012. https://www.youtube.com/watch?v=1EUAALItX4Q

"Lil' Cease Breaks Down When Tupac Was Shot & Past Beef He & Biggie Had With Him." YouTube Video, 7:15. Posted by "This is 50." June 6, 2012. https://www.youtube.com/watch?v=sxgYMdwas34

"MTV News presents Tupac Shakur: In His Own Words (13.09.1997) (HQ)." YouTube video, 22:29. Posted by "Tupar Amaru Shakur Unofficial Channel," September 16, 2012. https://www.youtube.com/watch?v=DTQU1gsTcVY

"Officer Ricky Telling a Different Story On Being a C.O. (2009)" YouTube video, 5:37. Posted by "305Resident." August 15, 2012. https://www.youtube.com/watch?v=Jdw3rx8RUKg

"Rick Ross SPEAKS OUT On his Past as a Corrections Officer: 'I'd do it again!!'" YouTube Video, 3:00. Posted by "Hezakya Hendrix." March 7, 2014. https://www.youtube.com/watch?v=4914BXj7Ex8

"Tupac Claiming Oakland." YouTube video, 7:15. Posted by "Xirix Seven." July 9, 2014. https://www.youtube.com/watch?v=sxgYMdwas34

"Tupac Shakur with Tabitha Soren Interview (26.10.1995)." YouTube video, 13:26. Posted by "Tupac Amaru Shakur Unofficial Channel," April 29, 2012. https://www.youtube.com/watch?v=NfHJGj4-oJs

3. *Metonymy & Mass Murder: Diagnosing "Splitting" Through Automatic Text Analysis*

YAIR NEUMAN, YOCHAI COHEN & JAMES KNOLL

Introduction: Objectives of the Study & Background

Psychiatrists are well aware that diagnosis is an art no less than a science. While this metaphor is usually taken for granted as pointing to the intuitive and complex nature of psychiatric diagnosis, one can push it further to suggest that the same as the artist, whether a painter or a pianist, is both empowered and constrained by the tools s(he) uses so is the psychiatrist. Therefore, it is important to enrich the toolkit of the psychiatrist in order to provide him with additional tools for diagnosis. Indeed, the complexity of symptoms facing the psychiatrist (Berrios & Markova, 2006) has led into intensive attempts to create a shared language for mental disorders as epitomized by the DSM, but at the price of sharp criticism launched from the core of the field's experts (e.g. Cuthbert & Insel, 2013; Frances & Widiger, 2011; Hyman, 2010; Nesse & Stein, 2012). Regardless of the criticism it is a fact that psychiatric "language" has been enriched while no similar advancement has been made in providing tools for validly diagnosing the *individual patient*. We emphasize the "individual" level of analysis as psychological inventories governing the assessment of personality (e.g. DSQ, Andews, Singh & Bond, 1993), have been designed and tested on the group level of analysis and therefore cannot be trivially used for drawing conclusions in individual cases (Molenaar, 2004, 2009, 2013) which is the psychiatrist ultimate source of interest.

The aim of this paper is to enrich the psychiatrist's diagnostic tool kit by introducing a methodology for automatically identifying the existence of the splitting defense mechanism in a patient's written communications. Defense mechanisms have been an important concept for clinical psychiatrists and the ability to accurately identify a defense mechanism in the patient's dynamics may be highly important for a diagnosis. Therefore, our aim is more modest and focal than pursuing diagnostic validity. Nevertheless, we believe that providing a tool for the micro-diagnosis of a defense mechanism may provide the psychiatrist with a practical tool for better understanding her patient. As splitting is an important primary defense mechanism associated with various disorders, most notably Borderline personality, the identification of splitting through automatic text analysis may enrich the psychiatrist tool kit. In addition it may be particularly helpful in the context of forensic psychiatry where texts are sometimes analyzed postmortem, as the only significant information available for the diagnosis (Knoll, 2010a, 2010b).

Here we illustrate the proposed methodology by analyzing *three case studies* of texts written by mass-murderers to include Seung Hui Cho, perpetrator of the Virginia Tech Massacre. In line with our informal diagnosis and hypotheses, the computerized analysis provides strong indications for the existence of splitting in Cho's "manifesto". We conclude by pointing to the importance of developing new technologies supporting the more traditional forms of diagnosis.

Splitting as a Defense Mechanism

The idea of "defense mechanisms" has been one of the most important and fruitful concepts for the development of modern psychological diagnosis (McWilliams, 1994). In this context, primary or primitive defenses are those that involve the boundary between the self and the world (McWilliams, 1994). Splitting epitomizes this primitive form of defense mechanisms as it involves the segregation or compartmentalization of experience into "all-good and all-bad categories" with no room for ambiguity (ibid. p. 99). A lack of ambiguity will be one of the dimensions we use for the identification of splitting in a text.

Splitting is one of the main archaic defense mechanisms (Grotstein, 1981) used for anxiety reduction and for the maintenance of positive self-esteem. However, it is used at the price of distortion of reality and chaotic shifts in feelings of self-worth and self-representations (Akhtar & Byrne, 1983; Myers and Zeigler-Hill, 2008).

It is argued that splitting is a defense mechanism associated with several personality disorders such as the Borderline Personality Disorder (Kernberg, 1967; Peer & Cooper, 1986; Zanarini et al. 2009). However, it was found (Zanarini et al. 2009) that although splitting was associated with BPD, it was not included among the three most significant defense mechanisms associated with the disorder (i.e. Acting out, emotional hypochondriasis and undoing).

Splitting can be identified through a direct interaction with the patient or through psychological assessment tools such as the Splitting Index (Gould, Prentice & Aisnlie, 1996). Both of these methods suffer from difficulties, whether in identifying splitting under the cognitive load of a direct, real-time interaction with the patient or in gaining access to the existence of this defense mechanism through the mediation of the subject's self-report.

A more straightforward way to identify the existence and intensity of splitting is through a structured analysis of the patient's text, whether spoken during a therapeutic session or written in the form of a diary, "manifesto", or suicide letter.

The benefits of analyzing the patient's text, is in gaining a direct access to his *first person perspective*, or what is known as the "phenomenology" of the subject. That is, instead of observing the complexity of the subject's behavior with its verbal and non-verbal aspects *in vivo*, we may analyze the text, assuming that it is the patient's first person perspective, as evident in his written/spoken text, which is the psychiatrists primary source of information.

Moreover, a structured, and as we propose an automatic analysis of the text, may reduce the cognitive load of the psychiatrist and provide him with more time and energy for interpreting the relevant dimensions that have been extracted from the text in a theoretically and empirically grounded manner.

In sum, we propose a methodology that aims to identify the existence and the intensity of the splitting defense mechanism through the automatic analysis of the patient's text. This methodology is detailed below.

Materials and Method

The idea of introducing novel technologies into psychiatric practice has been raised in the past, specifically with regard to the promise of Artificial Intelligence and natural language processing (e.g. Garfield, Rapp & Evans, 1992; Hand, 1985; Morelli, 1989; Servan-Schreiber, 1986). However, this promise has not yet fulfilled and novel technologies are entering at a slow paste to psychiatric diagnosis, such as in the case of measuring pupil size for diagnosing autism (Martineau et al. 2011), using neuroimaging for borderline diagnosis (Sato et al. 2012) or using text processing for the diagnosis of depression (Neuman et al. 2012). We are not familiar, though with a natural language processing approach for the identification of defense mechanisms in general and splitting in particular.

The proposed methodology and hypotheses are straightforward. We assume that the splitting of the world into "good" and "bad" objects is evident in the text through the "positivity" and "negativity" of words associated with the first person pronoun "I" representing the first person perspective, and the "positivity" and "negativity" of words associated with the pronoun "You" as indicating the other/s to which the patient points.

More specifically, we hypothesize that the splitting is evident whenever there is a significant gap between the positive and negative "valence" of words associated with the first person pronoun used by the patient, as well as between the positive valence of words associated with the "I" and the negative valence of words associated with "You".

In other words, a patient using the splitting mechanism should express a split of the self into "good" and "bad" categories as evident from the emotional valence of words associated with his use of the linguistic marker indicating his first person perspective (i.e the "I").

The same splitting should be evident with regard to the difference between the positive value the patient attributes to himself, which is contrasted with the negative values he attributes to the other/s (i.e You).

The use of pronouns for a psychological analysis isn't new as the use of personal pronouns (e.g., "I," "him," and "they") has been shown both in the clinical and empirical research to be indicative of perspective-taking (e.g. Meissner, 1996; Pennebaker, Mehl & Niederhoffer, 2003; Ricard, Girouard, & Decarie, 1999).

In addition, to the above hypotheses, we followed the theory and hypothesized that if "no room for ambiguity" is a characteristic of splitting then the ambiguity or uncertainty level of words in a text, suspected to express this mechanism, should be higher than the ambiguity level of a text in which the splitting is hypothesized to exist to a lesser extent.

To test the proposed methodology, we analyzed three texts: The texts were the manifesto written by Seung Hui Cho who murdered 23 students at the Virginia Tech Massacre, the manifesto of Christopher Dorner, a former police officer who murdered four people in a series of shooting attacks and the writings of "Kip" Kinkel the perpetrator of the Thurston High School shooting who murdered four people.

Our decision to analyze these case studies was based on a close expert analysis of texts written by civilian mass-murderers and the hypothesis that Cho's manifesto expresses a high-level of splitting in contrast with Dorner's manifesto that expresses a relatively lower level of splitting and the text of Kinkel that expresses a level of splitting which is in-between the previous texts.

Based on our expert analysis of the texts, we hypothesized that stronger indications of the splitting mechanism would be found in Cho's manifesto than in Kinkel and Dorner's texts respectively.

As there is no gold standard for determining the level of splitting in a text, comparing the level of splitting in three texts of mass-murderers may provide us with the appropriate framework for testing our methodology and our clinical and informal impressions from in-depth manual analysis of these cases.

Data Analysis and Results

To test the methodology and the hypothesis, we first identify the positivity and negativity of words associated with the "I" and "You" in the text. We considered the possibility of identifying these words through the automatic grammatical analysis of the sentences and the identification of syntactic relations between our pronouns and their associated words. However, using a linguistic parser (e.g. Stanford Parser), it was found that the grammatical structurness of some of the texts, specifically Cho's manifesto, is not appropriate for this kind of analysis. Therefore, we chose a simpler and heuristic procedure and analyzed each text by identifying the words co-located up to four places to the right of the pronouns "I" and "You". The choice to identify the words collocated four places to the right of the pronouns, was inspired by the default of the most comprehensive corpus of American English (i.e. COCA). This heuristic aims to identify the words associated with the pronouns in a highly economical manner, although we were aware of the fact that this heuristic may be quite noisy.

A Part-of-Speech Tagger (Roth & Zelenko, 1998) was used to identify only words belonging to one of the following categories: Nouns, Verbs, Adjectives and Adverbs. To test the positivity and negativity of words, we used the most updated norms of words' valence (i.e., pleasantness) in English (Warriner, Kuperman & Brysbaert, 2013), ranked the 13,915 words in the norm's database according to their valence and selected the top 50 words and the bottom 50 words. The most pleasant words included: vacation, happiness and fun, and the most unpleasant words included: pedophile, rapist and AIDS.

Next, we've used the idea of vectorial semantics according to which the meaning of words can be represented as a vector in a high-dimensional semantic space (Neuman & Cohen, 2014). By using the Latent Semantic Analysis engine (http://lsa.colorado.edu), we measured the semantic similarity between the vectors of words that were found to be associated with the I/You and the vectors of the positive/negative words.

The resulting similarity score is an indication of the words' "positivity" and "negativity". The difference between (a) the positivity and negativity of the I-WORDS and (b) between positivity of the I-WORDS and negativity of the You-WORDS, for the three cases appears in the next table:

Table 1. Differences in Positivity and Negativity.

Case	Difference within I	Difference between I-Positive and You-Negative
Cho	0.15	0.29
Dorner	0.00	0.02
Kinkel	0.10	0.22

As can be seen, the results confirm our hypotheses. A bigger difference was found within Cho's "I" than within Kinkel and Dorner. This difference was used to indicate the gap between the positive and negative self perception of the subject. As our analysis involves three case studies, there is no sense in using statistical significance tests and we consider the results' rank only.

The biggest difference between the positivity of the I-WORDS and the negativity of the You-WORDS was found for Cho followed by Kinkel and Dorner as hypothesized. If we consider the gap between positive self-perception and negative perception of the other, then this result indicates that splitting is evident in a higher degree in Cho's manifesto.

No Room for Ambiguity

As we have previously mentioned, "no room for ambiguity" is a characteristic of the splitting mechanism that divides the world into "black" and "white" without leaving a place to shades of gray. In linguistics the term "speculative language" is used to describe different mechanisms, such as "hedging", for dealing with vagueness, uncertainty and fuzziness. Words such "probably", "approximately", and expressions such as "a sort of" are all semantic and discursive markers of uncertainty. For measuring the ambiguity in each of our texts, we draw on the most updated research in computational linguistics for measuring uncertainty (Sauri & Pustejovsky, 2012; Szarvas, Vincze, Farkas, Móra, & Gurevych, 2012; Vincze, 2013) and used a dictionary of uncertainty cues that appears in these studies.

The uncertainty dictionary appears in Appendix 1. For determining the level of ambiguity in each text, we measured the proportion of uncertainty cues in each text. It was found that the proportion of uncertainty cues was

0.033 for Cho, 0.025 for Dorner and 0.040 for Kinkel. These results, at least in term of their rank, further confirm our hypothesis as the ambiguity level was the lowest for Cho's manifesto. Another way of measuring the uncertainty in the text is to measure the similarity of the uncertainty dictionary vector and the vectors of words collocated with I and You. Table 2 presents the results of this measurement.

Table 2. Similarity of the I-WORDS and YOU-WORDS with the Uncertainty Vector.

Case	I-WORDS	You-WORDS
Cho	0.10	0.06
Dorner	0.20	0.10
Kinkel	0.16	0.10

As we can see, the lowest level of similarity with the uncertainty vector was found for Cho both for the I-WORDS and YOU-WORDS. This result converges with our previous findings and provides another indication that the splitting defense mechanism was much more intense in Cho's text than in the two other texts.

Discussion

Our proposed methodology emerged from several years of a close and in-depth analysis of clinical texts, and the attempt to develop novel computerized supported tools for clinical and mainly forensic diagnosis. These tools cannot be described as Artificial Intelligence, at least not in the classical sense of this term. They should be better described as "Augmented Intelligence" or the attempt to provide human beings with tools that may leverage their "intelligence" or more accurately their clinical practice. Therefore, the methodology described in this paper has no pretension of substituting the expertise of the practitioner, whether the psychiatrist or the clinical psychologist, but to leverage the psychiatrist's capability and enrich her tool kit. The methodology presented here is a straightforward implementation of the theory as splitting is measured through the extent in which polarity exists with regard to the self and the other. As there is no "significant" level of splitting in a text, a measurement such as the one we've presented in this paper is meaningful only as compared with other measurements, produced through hypotheses as we have done, or through other frames of reference. The difficulty of finding an appropriate frame of reference for comparison is something that should be carefully taken into consideration.

In sum, in this paper we introduce a novel computerized methodology for measuring splitting in a text. The methodology is theoretically grounded and supported by conventional tools used in natural language processing. Nevertheless, it is a methodology which is in the first steps of development and therefore should be considered with caution and rather than a complete product, an invitation for further research and inquiry.

Appendix 1. Uncertainty Dictionary

Uncertain unclear vague ambiguous unsure tentative doubtful hesitant undecided likely indefinite indeterminate undefined indecisive inexact possible probable plausible apparent imprecise fuzzy blurred elusive skeptical dubious unconvinced irresolvable unconfident exploratory speculative unconfirmed questionable shaky untrustworthy ambivalent inaccurate approximate rough May suggest indicate appear might or consider believe expect think putative whether investigate examine study determine if would will until could some many other several most various others certain number critics often usually generally very almost common much popular famous well-known notable notably important best traditionally controversial.

References

Andrews G, Singh M, Bond M. The defense style questionnaire. The Journal of Nervous and Mental Disease 1993; *181*: 246–256.

Berrios G E, Marková IS (2006). Symptoms—historical perspective and effect on diagnosis. In M. Blumenfield and J. J. Strain (eds), *Psychosomatic Medicine* (Philadelphia: Lippincott Williams & Wilkins), 27–38.

Cuthbert BN, Insel TR. Toward the future of psychiatric diagnosis: the seven pillars of RDoC. *BMC Medicine 2013*; *11*: 126.

Dutton, DG, White KR, Fogarty D. Paranoid thinking in mass shooters. *Aggression and Violent Behavior* 2013; *18*: 548–553.

Frances AJ, Widiger T. Psychiatric diagnosis: lessons from the DSM-IV past and cautions for the DSM-5 future. *Annual Review of Clinical Psychology 2012*; *8*: 109–130.

Garfield DA, Rapp C, Evens M. Natural language processing in psychiatry: artificial intelligence technology and psychopathology. *The Journal of Nervous and Mental Disease* 1992; *180*: 227–237.

Grotstein, J. S. *Splitting and projective identification*. New York: J. Aronson, 1981.

Gould, J. R., Prentice, N. M., & Aisnlie, R. C. (1996). The Splitting Index: Construction of a scale measuring the defense mechanism of splitting. *Journal of Personality Assessment*, *66*(2), 414–430.

Hand, D. J. (1985). Artificial Intelligence and Psychiatry. Cambridge: Cambridge UP.

Hyman SE. The diagnosis of mental disorders: the problem of reification. *Annual Review of Clinical Psychology 2010*; *6*: 155–179.

Kernberg O. Borderline personality organization. *Journal of the American Psychoanalytic Association* 1967; *15*: 641–685.

Knoll JL. The "pseudocommando" mass murderer: Part I, the psychology of revenge and obliteration. *Journal of the American Academy of Psychiatry and the Law Online* 2010a; *38*: 87–94.

Knoll JL. The "Pseudocommando" Mass Murderer: Part II, The Language of Revenge. *Journal of the American Academy of Psychiatry and the Law Online* 2010b; *38*: 263–272.

Martineau J, Hernandez N, Hiebel L, Roché L, Metzger A, Bonnet-Brilhault F. Can pupil size and pupil responses during visual scanning contribute to the diagnosis of autism spectrum disorder in children?. *Journal of Psychiatric Research* 2011; *45*: 1077–1082.

McWilliams, N. Psychoanalytic diagnosis. N.Y.: The Guilford Press. 1994.

Meissner WW. The self-as-object in psychoanalysis. *Psychoanalysis & Contemporary Thought* 1996; 19: 425–459.

Molenaar P C. A manifesto on psychology as idiographic science: Bringing the person back into scientific psychology, this time forever. *Measurement* 2004; *2*: 201–218.

Molenaar P C, Campbell CG. (The new person-specific paradigm in psychology. *Current Directions in Psychological Science* 2009; *18*: 112–117.

Molenaar PC. On the necessity to use person-specific data analysis approaches in psychology. *European Journal of Developmental Psychology* 2013; 10: 29–39.

Morelli, R. (1989, November). Artificial intelligence in psychiatry: issues and questions. In *Engineering in Medicine and Biology Society, 1989. Images of the Twenty-First Century., Proceedings of the Annual International Conference of the IEEE Engineering in* (pp. 1812–1813)

Myers EM, Zeigler-Hill V. No shades of gray: Splitting and self-esteem instability. *Personality and Individual Differences* 2008; *45*: 139–145.

Nesse RM, Stein DJ. Towards a genuinely medical model for psychiatric nosology. *BMC Medicine* 2012; *10*: 5.

Neuman Y. & Cohen Y. A vectorial semantics approach to personality assessment. *Scientific Reports* 2014; 4: 4761.

Neuman Y, Cohen Y, Assaf D, Kedma G. Proactive screening for depression through metaphorical and automatic text analysis. *Artificial Intelligence in Medicine* 2012; 56: 19–25.

Pennebaker JW, Mehl, MR, Niederhoffer KG. Psychological aspects of natural language use: Our words, our selves. Annu Rev Psychol 2003; 43: 547–577.

Perry JC, Cooper SH. A preliminary report on defenses and conflicts associated with borderline personality disorder. *Journal of the American Psychoanalytic Association* 1986; *34*: 863–893.

Ricard, M.; Girouard, P. C.; Decarie, T. G. Personal pronouns and perspective taking in toddlers. J Child Lang 1999; 697: 681–697.

Roth D, Zelenko D. Part of speech tagging using a network of linear separators. In *Proceedings of the 36th Annual Meeting of the Association for Computational Linguistics and 17th International Conference on Computational Linguistics—Volume 2* (pp. 1136–1142). Association for Computational Linguistics. 1998.

Sass L, Pienkos E. Beyond words: linguistic experience in melancholia, mania, and schizophrenia. *Phenomenology and the Cognitive Sciences* 2013; 1–21.

Sato JR, de Araujo Filho GM, de Araujo TB, Bressan RA, de Oliveira PP, Jackowski AP. Can neuroimaging be used as a support to diagnosis of borderline personality disorder? An approach based on computational neuroanatomy and machine learning. *Journal of Psychiatric Research* 2012; *46*: 1126–1132.

Servan-Schreiber D. Artificial intelligence and psychiatry. *The Journal of Nervous and Mental Disease* 1986; *174*: 191–202.

Shari R, Pustejovsky J. Are you sure that this happened? Assessing the factuality degree of events in text. *Computational Linguistics* 2012; *38*: 261–299.

Szarvas G, Vincze V, Farkas R, Móra G, Gurevych I. Cross-genre and cross-domain detection of semantic uncertainty. *Computational Linguistics* 2012; *38*: 335–367.

Vincze, V. Weasels, Hedges and Peacocks: Discourse-level Uncertainty in Wikipedia Articles. International Joint Conference on Natural Language Processing, pages 383–391, Nagoya, Japan, 14–18 October 2013.

Warriner AB, Kuperman V, Brysbaert, M. Norms of valence, arousal, and dominance for 13,915 English lemmas. *Behavior Research Methods* 2013; 1–17.

Zanarini MC, Weingeroff JL, Frankenburg FR. Defense mechanisms associated with borderline personality disorder. *Journal of Personality Disorders* 2009; *23*: 113.

Part II

Film & Media Studies

4. *Psychopaths in Film: Are Portrayals Realistic and Does It Matter?*

JOAN SWART

Introduction

Despite the fact that what the clinical or forensic literature might classify as "realistic" depictions of psychopaths remain underrepresented in popular film, such depictions continue to influence wider public perception of the association between mental illness in general, and psychopathy in particular, and the ensuing criminal behaviors. These misconceptions, which often focus on violent and homicidal acts, bizarre mannerisms and appearance, sexual depravity, above average intelligence, and a calm, calculating demeanor, perpetuate myths of psychopathy that hinder the diagnosis and treatment of those who qualify according to professionally accepted criteria. The realistic depiction of a psychopathic character is made more problematic by the fact that psychopathy is not a homogeneous personality construct. Various researchers, including Karpman (1941), Hare (2003), and Hervé (2003) have proposed differentiated constructs, but their validity remains largely untested. Among these subtypes, in film we have seen a graduated change in popular depictions that range from socially misfit, violent, and chaotic mass murderers in horror and slasher films to more sophisticated and calculating iterations among more dramatic or ostensibly "serious" motion pictures. However, although very few psychopaths are violent and become murderers, it is here that the focus and fascination remains very much attached to such misconceptions.

Certain psychopathic traits are also well suited to successful careers, and despite the fact that harm and mayhem is also created by psychopaths in these circles, the corporate psychopath continues to attract relatively little attention with the exception of a few films such as *Wall Street* (1987) and *The Wolf of*

Wall Street (2013). Here, television seems to lead the way. The trends of the depiction of psychopaths in film and the reasons and implications are further explored, including in two other largely ignored groups: women and youth.

Therefore, it is the aim of this discussion to emphasize the importance—and to some extent a tacit responsibility—of film to advance the general knowledge about psychopathy. It might be argued that there is a heightened duty among filmmakers in their attempt to appropriate the related nomenclature to balance commercial interests with credible information. By bringing together the scientific status and understanding of psychopathy with the cultural views that are guided by film, the principal interest here is to analyze trends and the effective and realistic, and not so effective and realistic, portrayals of psychopathic characters in these media channels. Following a discussion of the development of the conceptualization of psychopathy, including its current definitional status and nosological classifications that include those proposed by Cleckley (1941), Hare (2003), and Millon (1998), examples of the depictions of psychopathic characters found in some better-known film are offered. More specifically, these examples disaggregate the filmic psychopath into discrete classifications that include adult male, adult female, the young, and the corporate psychopath. By focusing on psychopathy in such a selection of fictional characters, the effect that film and television has on the public perspectives of psychopathy is highlighted.

Development of the Psychopath Concept: From Cleckley to Hare

Psychopathy was initially associated with general mental illness and psychotic conditions, but after its definition settled, mainly due to the important conceptualizing of Hervey Cleckley (1941), the impact and magnitude of such characters became better understood. In this same era came a focus on capitalism and individual enterprise in the Western world that some have since argued came to celebrate and even lionize psychopathic traits in its culture and institutions (Olson, 2012; Boddy, Miles, Sanyal, & Hartog, 2015). In fact, capitalism at its most ruthless rewards psychopathic behavior as a rule with a requisite glibness, cunning, manipulation and lack of empathy. As such, capitalism, with its inherent remorselessness, is the material manifestation of psychopathy.

Capitalist culture also celebrates a predatory spirit and fearless attitudes in life, which are probably part of the widespread fascination that psychopathy holds for consumers of fiction. Maybe we recognize in it a part of our darker self, a part that we go to great lengths to hide from others; or, maybe we wish we had some of the same qualities to protect ourselves against abuse and exploitation by others like that. Whatever the case may be, it is in the best interest of societies to understand psychopathy correctly, including the tremendous impact that psychopaths have in terms of social harm and financial cost, in order to be prepared and able to act appropriately. Psychopathy is not a medical problem; rather, it is a societal problem. According to an estimate by American neuroscientist Kent Kiehl and Judge Morris Hoffman (2011), the cost of psychopathy in the U.S. alone amounts to $460 billion per year based on the direct and indirect cost of the criminal justice system, which does not even account for costs of the treatment of victims and their emotional suffering and financial losses. This is barely lower than the estimated combined annual cost of substance abuse and obesity ($529 billion), and roughly 10 times the cost of depression.

Although the concept of psychopathy emerged mostly in the nineteenth-century based on the works of French psychiatrist Phillipe Pinel and American psychiatrists Benjamin Rush and JC Pritchard as a synonym for aggressive and irresponsible behavior, it was still a generalized attempt to explain 'moral insanity'. In the late nineteenth-century J. L. Koch introduced the term "psychopathic inferiority," but with Garofalo and Lombroso in the late 19th century, continued to equate a lack of intelligence to the characteristics of irrational behavior, lack of insight, moral non-sensitivity and the lack of shame in adulthood that they observed (Buzina, 2012). The first mention of psychopathy in terms of the current construct, instead of in the general sense of mental illness, was in 1904 when German psychiatrist Emil Kraepelin addressed moral insanity by referring to specific psychopathic subtypes involving antisocial, criminal or dissocial behavior (Millon, Simonsen, & Birket-Smith, 1998). After the First World War, Kraepelin and others developed categorization schemes under the heading "psychopathic personality," only some subtypes of which were thought to have particular links to antisocial behavior. In 1917, the Statistical Manual for the Use of Institutions for the Insane, a forerunner to the American Psychiatric Association's guiding text, the Diagnostic and Statistical Manual of Mental Disorders (DSM), included a category of psychoses with constitutional psychopathic inferiority. A clear distinction was therefore beginning to take form between psychopathy (as a behavioral and personality disorder) and psychosis (as the impairment of thoughts and emotions that results in a break with external reality).

Beginning in the late 1920s American psychologist George E. Partridge influentially narrowed the definition of psychopathy to antisocial personality, and from 1930 onward suggested that a more apt name for it would be sociopathy. The concepts slowly crystallized, but it was American psychiatrist Hervey Cleckley's (1941) seminal work *The Mask of Sanity* that produced the basis for the modern conceptualization of psychopathy. The first version of the DSM in 1952 included sociopathic personality disturbance, and identified four subtypes: antisocial, dyssocial, sexual, and addiction. As it was very broad compared to later definitions, only antisocial personality disorder was included in subsequent versions of the DSM, while sociopathy was relegated. Until today, psychopathy has never been included in any formally accepted mental health classification as a distinct disorder. Instead, it is recognized, at varying levels, in the criminal justice systems of many countries and jurisdictions, primarily as a measure of risk of violence.

Cleckley's treatise was first published in 1941, yet the basic elements of psychopathy outlined therein remain relevant today. Cleckley's clinical profile listed 16 behavioral characteristics of a psychopath, which Gowlett (2014) has subdivided into three categories:

A. Positive Adjustment

1. Superficial charm and good intelligence
2. Absence of delusions and other signs of irrational thinking
3. Absence of nervousness or psychoneurotic manifestations
4. Suicide threats rarely carried out

B. Behavioral Deviance

5. Inadequately motivated antisocial behavior
6. Poor judgment and failure to learn by experience
7. Unreliability
8. Fantastic and uninviting behavior with drink and sometimes without
9. Sex life impersonal, trivial, and poorly integrated
10. Failure to follow any life plan

C. Emotional-Interpersonal Deficits

11. Untruthfulness and insincerity
12. Lack of remorse and shame
13. General poverty in major affective reactions
14. Pathologic egocentricity and incapacity for love
15. Specific loss of insight
16. Unresponsiveness in general interpersonal relations

According to Cleckley, the main characteristic of a psychopathic person is that he is able to outwardly mimic a normally functioning person with precision, masking or disguising his impaired internal personality structure to achieve his self-centered goals in a repeated and purposeful way that is often destructive to himself and others. Nearly 75 years later, Cleckley's work continues to act as a cornerstone to modern research and clinical practice, which included the embracement of the psychopathy label, the Psychopathy Checklist—a measurement tool of psychopathy developed by Robert D. Hare—and continued refinement of the scientific understanding of the construct. As is evidenced in this paper, Hare's classification of psychopathy in particular has also been embraced by popular culture where, through representations that vary greatly in terms of accuracy, it is used to simultaneously entertain and frighten audiences.

The Psychopathy Checklist (PCL) is a psychological assessment tool that was developed to measure psychopathy in male offenders and forensic inmates. It is a 20-item inventory of perceived personality traits and recorded behaviors that is completed by means of a semi-structured interview and supplemental information such as public records. The items were largely based on Cleckley's characteristics of psychopathy, but with Hare's amended version widely considered to be the gold standard among practitioners. With a maximum score of 2, each item is scored as either a 0 (does not apply at all), 1 (applies somewhat), or 2 (applies fully). The scores are later added and in the United States a total score of 30 or above (max=40) indicates a serious, or clinical, psychopath. The most current version known as the Psychopathy Checklist-Revised (PCL-R) officially divides the 20 items into two factors. These are sometimes further divided to form a four-facet structure.

Factor 1 Traits: Interpersonal/Affective Expression

Facet 1: Interpersonal

1. Glibness/superficial charm
2. Grandiose sense of self-worth expressed as pompous arrogance
3. Pathological/compulsive lying
4. Cunning and manipulative

Facet 2: Affective

5. Lack of remorse or guilt
6. Shallow affect/lack of emotional depth
7. Callousness or lack of empathy
8. Failure to accept self-responsibility

Factor 2 Traits: Social Deviance

Facet 3: Lifestyle

9. Need for stimulation and proneness to boredom
10. Parasitic lifestyle (living off others)
11. Lack of realistic, long-term goals
12. Impulsivity
13. Irresponsibility

Facet 4: Antisocial

14. Poor behavioral controls (unpredictability; never learning from mistakes)
15. Early behavioral problems
16. Juvenile delinquency
17. Revocation of conditional release
18. Criminal versatility

Additional Factors

19. Promiscuous sexual behavior
20. Many short-term marital relationships

Despite its widespread acceptance and use to identify psychopathy, there have also been several criticisms of Hare's scoring model. Of note, Skeem and Cooke (2010) argue that the checklist does not represent or equate with the definition or theoretical construct of psychopathy by leaving out key factors, and that it places excessive emphasis on criminality. This may lead, they argue, to diagnostic problems and inappropriate applications such as securing convictions or harsher punishments in court. Also, some contend that its use in real world settings and non-forensic populations is questionable. However, regardless of these concerns, the PCL-R remains the best validated instrument to measure psychopathy at this time.

Psychopath Subtypes: A Brief History

There continues to be growing scientific support for the heterogeneity of psychopathy, but there remains little agreement on the basis of differentiation. Although the primary-secondary distinction is still the most widely used, many other researchers have opted for more nuanced multi-faceted classifications. Despite the fact that there are many more in various stages of empirical investigation, I have opted for three types of classifications: the two-factor model, a multi-facet (three- to five-factors) model, and a personality-based classification.

Cleckley (1941) first hinted at the distinction between two major types of psychopathy; namely, a prototypical, or primary psychopath whose dysfunctional characteristics are not due to social disadvantage, low intelligence, neurotic anxiety, or other psychopathology—different from the secondary type. Therefore, the inappropriate behavior of a primary psychopath is presumed to be due to some intrinsic deficit that prevents self-regulation and normal adjustment. It does not appear to be influenced by environmental and societal experiences that can be linked indirectly to "inadequate intelligence, psychotic thinking, excessive neurotic anxiety, unusual sex drive, or other attributes that increase a person's vulnerability to chronic misbehavior" (Newman, MacCoon, Vaughn, & Sadeh, 2005, p. 319). These associations underlie the secondary type of psychopath, a person who appear to be more fluid and less encumbered by inherited psychopathic traits.

Since Karpman's (1941) original development of the concepts of primary and secondary psychopathy, several classification systems have expanded on it to further nuance differences. Hervé (2003) has used these distinctions as basis to follow on from a proposed three-factor model that distinguished between interpersonal, affective, and lifestyle types. Four main clusters emerged from Hervé's study of 202 Canadian federal prison inmates with PCL-R score of 27 and above. He termed these groups as follows:

1. *Classic/idiopathic/prototypical subtype*: Typified by high overall PCL-R scores, as well as high scores on the interpersonal, affective, and lifestyle factors. They are most related to the primary type.
2. *Manipulative subtype*: Distinguished by high scores on the interpersonal and affective factors, but lower scores on the lifestyle factor. These are the 'talkers' who use cons and ruses to defraud and deceive their victims.
3. *Macho subtype*: Has the second highest overall PCL-R score while scoring high on the affective and lifestyle factors, but low on the interpersonal factor. As such, the group lacked the charm and social skills to con and manipulate others, relying on force and intimidation instead to achieve their objectives
4. *Pseudopsychopath subtype*: These are akin to sociopaths, and have the lowest overall PCL-R scores, low scores on the interpersonal and lifestyle scales, but high in affective characteristics. (Morana, Arboleda-Flórez, & Câmara, 2005)

Personality psychologist Theodore Millon (1998) recognized that psychopathic behaviors are also rooted in appreciably different personality patterns that could not always be associated with only one personality disorder. Different pathways to psychopathy therefore exist that may stem from fundamentally dissimilar styles of life to end in varying forms of social deviance. As a result, Millon and Davis (1998) described 10 variants of psychopathy to account for a great majority of behavioral patterns and expressions of psychopathy. By placing a focus on the discriminant characteristics beyond the common core of a marked self-centeredness and disdain for the needs of others, the differential classification was devised to add more distinction to various clinical and personality backgrounds. A short description of each of the 10 subtypes of psychopathy follows.

1. *The unprincipled psychopath* is highly narcissistic, and gets satisfaction from exacting vengeance through humiliation. They exploit and abuse other people, and generally enjoy the anguish they create.
2. *The disingenuous psychopath* enjoys popularity and usually has a convincing social façade that is used to charm others in the short-term. However, long-term relationships eventually suffer due to their unreliability, their intense resentment, and their tendency to plot against others. They view life as a zero-sum game, and always strive to be on the winning side of the inevitable win-lose outcome.
3. *The risk-taking psychopath* lives for the rush that they get when they take risk and put their lives or the lives of others in danger. They thrive on a lifestyle of dangerous and treacherous activities, and are convinced that they are invincible.
4. *The covetous psychopath* displays envy and revenge as core characteristics. They are exhibitionistic and self-indulgent as they relentlessly pursue aggrandizement, believing that they have been deprived of their rightful share of love, support, and material rewards. In the process they often have little concern for the people that they deceive and exploit.
5. The *spineless psychopath* views himself as defenseless and weak and will therefore strike out first in a counterphobic manner to avoid or preempt the aggression of other people. They tend to project a false bravado and are desperate for others to see them as invincible and not to be provoked.
6. *The explosive psychopath* is defined immediate and frequent access to deep feelings of rage that are directed against those who are innocent or vulnerable. Their main difference from the other types lies in their tendency to erupt instantaneously in a sadistic and savage manner. These tantrums are unpredictable and often erupt when they feel thwarted or threatened, as a reaction to cope with frustration or fear.
7. *The abrasive psychopath* is oppositional and surly by nature, who resembles a rebellious teenager. They are unable to build deep relationships due to their enduring and defining personality traits that are contentious and quarrelsome. They often use insults in an indirect, but intentionally antagonistic, manner, causing and magnifying incessant discord with others. They feel entitled to do and say anything that they please, relishing their contemptuous stance. They exhibit

no remorse for their cruel insults, even when leveled at their most intimate associates.

8. *The malignant psychopath* is driven by paranoid beliefs and follows power hierarchies. Compared with other types of psychopaths, they are often less effective, and their efforts to inflict harm on others tend to backfire. They have often endured terrible abuse in the past and see the world as a dangerous and treacherous place, thus resorting to fantasy rather than to action, and they invent scenarios that place people around them in dark and menacing roles.
9. *The tyrannical psychopath* is stimulated by the vulnerability of others, which supports his cunning and calculating demeanor. They find satisfaction in subordinating and subjugating their victims, while delighting in their fear, humiliation, and intimidation. An important distinctive feature is that they target those who they predict will submit, while avoiding conflict with those more likely to fight back. They relive and relish the memories of their conquests and their victims' suffering, even to the point of amusement. The tyrannical psychopath is one of the most violent, cruel, and treacherous types, and use crude and vulgar methods to force victims to cower and submit.
10. *The malevolent psychopath* is also cold-blooded and ruthless, and perhaps the most prototypical of the psychopathic types with a blend of paranoid and sadistic features. They are intolerant and deeply suspicious of tender emotions, which they generally view as a tool to manipulate and hurt them. They seek and enjoy power, which they demonstrate in the deliberate mistreatment of others.

Quickly becoming evident from the brief summaries of Millon's 10 subtypes of psychopathy, adequate distinction between the groups are not always clear-cut, which may add to the conceptual confusion among creators of these fictional characters and the audience.

Filmic Depictions of the Criminal Psychopath: Message and Meaning

Initially, and to a certain extent still today, fictional portrayals of psychopaths in the visual media are mostly limited to criminal types. Many earlier depictions in the horror/slasher genre featured antagonists with psychopathic traits as misfits with some obvious impairment resulting in social rejection that caused their deep resentment towards society or specific groups. They are depicted as feeling wronged—an approximation of the covetous psychopath—which fuels the human monster narrative, in some sense justifying their clear motivation for hunting their victims—the malevolent psychopath. It is in their hatred for their advantaged peers, which sometimes involves sexual compulsion that fuels their obsession with revenge. They are opportunistic, but organized. Characters such as Jason Voorhees in the *Friday the 13th* franchise (1980–2009) and Michael Meyers in the *Halloween* series of films (1978–2009) are two better-known examples of this characterization of psychopathy that diverge significantly from the accepted profile. Other social misfits with a sexual motivation to kill include Norman Bates of *Psycho* (1960) fame and his younger version in the contemporary A&E television series *Bates Motel* (2013–2015).

These grotesque and caricature-type psychopaths eventually decreased in their prevalence in commercial films into the late 1980s as several high profile (and real life) psychopaths in the 1960s and 1970s lead to the public becoming more knowledgeable about the clinical description of psychopaths and their behaviors and methods. The Zodiac Killer, John Wayne Gacy, Ted Bundy, the Hillside Stranglers (Angelo Buono and Kenneth Bianchi), and the Son of Sam (David Berkowitz) represent some of the most publicized psychopaths and serial killers from this epoch—their heinous crimes simultaneously fascinated and informed the public, leading, in circuitous fashion, to an enhanced public understanding of the clinical and forensic underpinnings of psychopathy and the associated nomenclature. In a sense, these real life cases also became the backdrop for broader misconceptions in popular culture reified through disinformation conveyed via Hollywood. This included, most notably, the belief that all psychopaths are intelligent and serial killers (Ted Bundy's reported IQ was 136 and that of John Wayne Gacy and David Berkowitz, both 118).

The spectacle-driven allure of horror and slasher films continued unabated, however, based in large part on the sensational marketability of the villains in these films—characters molded on real-life sexual murderers and thus, by extension, similarly depicted (or erroneously classified in film) as psychopaths. Towards the dawn of the 1990s, the increase in publicity and information flow about criminal investigations, including criminal profiling, also lead to more realistic depictions of psychopaths in film. This arguably lead to the "birth" and popularity of the "elite" psychopath, or a psychopath "exhibiting exaggerated levels of intelligence, sophisticated manners, and cunning" (Leistedt and Linkowski, 2014, p. 171), which often surpassed or contradicted the typical traits of a psychopath. As such, as the times and information flow changed, fictional psychopathic characters in popular media continued to perpetuate common myths rather than dispelling or addressing those. The most notable of these depictions in film from the 1990s, one that would later spawn countless imitators and engender a great deal of misunderstanding about the nature of psychopathy, is of course Hannibal Lecter in the films based on Thomas Harris's acclaimed crime novels.

Hannibal Lecter as Exemplar of Psychopathy in Film

The character Hannibal Lecter, who in the wake of Harris's novels has been solicitously featured in three movies, three seasons on television, and countless publications and discussions, is widely regarded in popular culture as the ultimate prototypical psychopath—the exemplar of the clinical and forensic nomenclature to which all filmic psychopaths should aspire. He is perhaps the most arrogant, cunning, manipulative, callous, and cruel character to ever grace fiction and has become a cultural icon and model for later portrayals of seriously disturbed offenders (Gullhaugen & Nottestad, 2011). Yet, his variety of characteristics includes many that are in fact, upon closer inspection, *contrary* to the accepted symptoms of psychopathy. He had an adverse childhood, but cannot truly be thought of as antisocial. He demonstrates some affection and grief that appears genuine (as far as fiction goes), and fulfills 8 out of 10 items of the criteria from the PCL-R Factor 1 (the interpersonal and affective domain), but only 4 out of 10 from Factor 2 (the lifestyle and antisocial domain). According to Gullhaugen and Nottestad (2011), this provides Lecter with PCL-R score of 24 (max = 40), which is below the generally applied cutoff in America (≥30) or Europe (≥25) for severe—or clinical—psychopathy. Similar conclusions seem to apply to Dexter Morgan, eponymous serial killer in Jeff Lindsay's series of novels and the subsequent, and arguably better-known, Showtime series. Fulfilling seven criteria from Factor 1 and only one from Factor 2, he scored even lower at 16. Both scores are still moderate to high with the average score of the general public around five. While Dexter Morgan is a television creation rather than one based in film—the more common habitat of the fictive criminal psychopath—it is curious to note that he and Lecter share mutual literary origins and that Dexter Morgan, as a television analog of Lecter in many respects, shares a number of traits that contradict the accepted literature with respect to diagnosing psychopaths.

As explained, the depiction of psychopathic characters in film—both antagonists and tortured protagonists that court public interest, such as Hannibal Lecter—evolved in part due to the expectations of audiences that were based on the information that they had available. It helped shaped their fascination, which also changed with time. From the majority of violent and antisocial misfits or earlier horror, slasher, and other serial killer narratives, psychopathic characters eventually became more nuanced in their construction, their being aligned more closely with the clinical understanding of their traits and behaviors. As a result, psychopaths with a wider and more realistic array of affective and interpersonal deficits (primary type), as well as those who primarily utilized manipulation instead of overt violence, became more prominent in popular culture (see Figure 1). As such, the focus shifted away from the idiosyncratic misfits of the previous genres to the "elite" iconography seen in the case of Hannibal Lecter, beginning with the 1991 film *The Silence of the Lambs.*

While Lecter was previously depicted in the 1986 film *Manhunter* directed by Michael Mann of *Miami Vice* fame, the character was then portrayed by British actor Brian Cox and the surname spelled as "Lecktor" in original billing. The film, while since becoming a cult favorite, is often considered non-canonical in the Lecter series, the preferred reading of Lecter beginning in 1991 with the character being re-cast with Anthony Hopkins and *Manhunter* later being re-made, true to the title of the original Harris novel, as *Red Dragon* in 2002. It would therefore seem as though it is not just Hannibal Lecter that has become the referent for filmic depictions of psychopaths, but specifically Hopkins's interpretation of the character. It is a distinction that may help chart future research with respect to what Danesi (2014) and Arntfield (2016) refer to second order forensic semiotics, or the feedback loop between actual crime, media depictions of that crime, and the ensuing—and erroneous—nexus drawn between actual events and so-called "true crime" which is actually interpretative and performative.

Based on analyses of the data provided by Leistedt and Linkowski (2014) of 125 films screened between 1915 and 2010, it appears that the 1990s were the decade where the psychopath had the most presence (a central psychopathic character appeared in a total of 51 movies). Just focusing on the 30 years between 1981 and 2010, secondary psychopaths featured slightly more often (55%) than primary psychopaths. During the same period, based on Hervé's classification, the classical/idiopathic/prototypical subtype made up the most prominent group (30%), followed by macho (25%) and pseudo psychopaths (25%). The presence of classical psychopaths reached a high in the 2010s (42%), while the macho type was least used (16%). The manipulative type was the most featured in the 1980s (37%). This implies that the primary, prototypical psychopath has enjoyed greater attention in film recently.

Hannibal Lecter was, and still is, an important influence on the idea of a psychopath in popular culture: intelligent, successful, sophisticated, manipulative, cunning, callous, almost with no perceptible emotions, self-centered, and acting without hesitation using extreme violence when required. With his

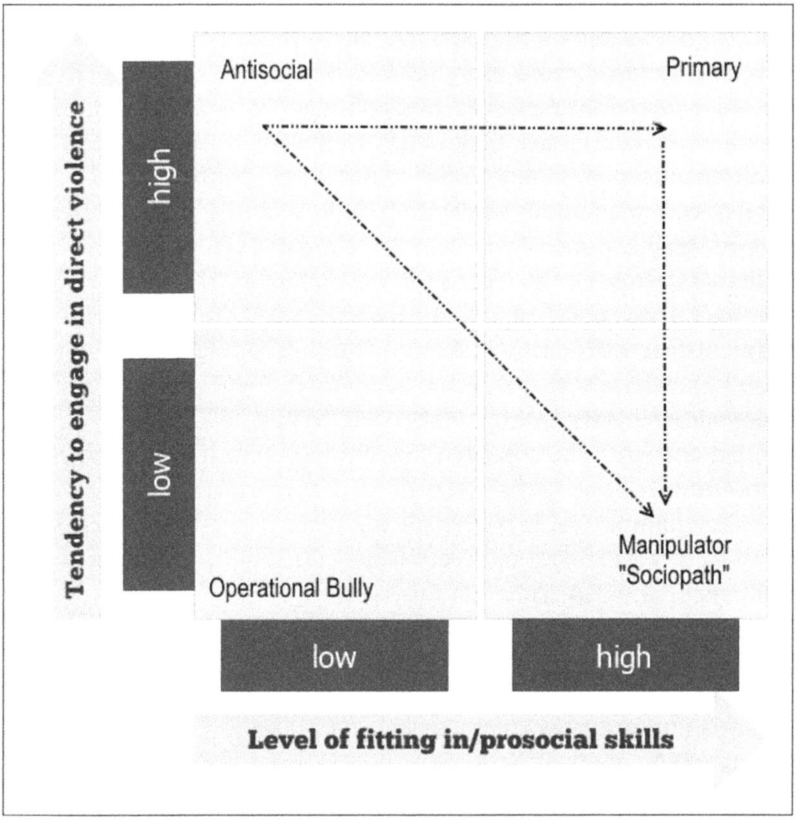

Figure 1. Four-Quadrant Model of Psychopathy.

calm, calculating, stylish, and always-in-control demeanor Lecter became the venerable psychopath for some time. But, the problem is that, in the context of the literature, the character traits are simply too extreme, even flawless to a point, thereby caricaturizing psychopathy to a point where it became an unrealistic portrayal that created and sustained many of the misconceptions for the sake of sensationalism.

But, popular culture also has a point beyond simple entertainment: reflecting real life to ponder important societal questions. These include questions that cannot be asked and explored in unrealistic portrayals. Since the early 2000s, psychopathic characters in fiction became more vulnerable, struggling with the changes that they knew are required, with their weaknesses, adverse pasts, and their relationship issues. The chaos and damage left in their wake became more apparent and relatable. As a result, a more realistic depiction of psychopaths emerged in film and the characterizations of psychopathy became more accurate. These included symptoms of lack of empathy and remorse, cold-bloodedness, impulsivity, and capacity for violence. Earlier depictions especially, tended to ignore two important symptoms of psychopathy, namely lack of goals and focus, and impulsivity. Many psychopathic characters in film, especially ones at the height of the Lecter era in the 1990s, were meticulous in devising and executing plans motivated by a longer-term goal and focus. In reality, psychopaths are far less organized and premeditated. Films like *No Country for Old Men* (2007), based on the 2005 Cormac McCarthy novel of the same name, with the realistic prototypical idiopathic/primary psychopath, Anton Chirgurh, is a leading example. He is incapable of love, lacks shame, remorse, empathy, and psychological insight, is unable to learn from past experiences, and has a cold-blooded, ruthless, and determined attitude. The absence of psychological insight is an important, if heretofore unmentioned, characteristic of a psychopath that creates unique problems for filmmakers. It is perhaps the main reason why psychopaths are unwilling to seek treatment or accept help—a detail that is seldom accounted for in the diegesis of on-screen narratives.

Corporate Psychopaths in Film

Compared to criminal populations, there are little information and understanding available about corporate psychopathy and its implications, although it is estimated that one in twenty-five high level business people can be considered a psychopath (Babiak, Neumann, & Hare, 2010). With their ruthless and callous predatory behavior that is sometimes exposed as criminal, businesses and entire industries are impacted by psychopaths, likely more than anyone would freely acknowledge. After all, it is often said that capitalism awards psychopathic behavior, including the exploitation of the vulnerable—a detail famously first depicted with great candor in the 2003 documentary film, *The Corporation.* It is then understandable that corporations are not interested to avail themselves of research in psychopathy.

Whatever the reason, there has also been relatively little attention paid to corporate psychopaths in film. Among Leistedt and Linkowski's (2014) list of motion pictures, there is only one corporate psychopath among the many crime, action, apocalyptic, war, and horror characters: Gordon Gekko in the 1987 film *Wall Street.* With his credo being that "Greed is good. Greed is right, greed works [...] Greed captures the essence of the evolutionary spirit," Gekko personifies both affective and interpersonal traits of psychopathy (e.g. grandiose sense of self-worth, cunning/manipulative, lack of remorse/guilt, callous/lack of empathy). As most psychopaths do, he justifies his exploitive actions with complete disregard, even disdain, of others for his own benefit. He has a complete sense of entitlement, and an overriding devotion to personal profit at the expense of morality.

Two subsequent Hollywood films also portrayed psychopathic characters: the 2010 sequel, *Wall Street: Money Never Sleeps* and the 2013 biographical black comedy *The Wolf of Wall Street,* directed by Martin Scorsese. Both movies were criticized for glorifying psychopathic behavior, but became part of a Wall Street pop culture that vilifies its ruthless exploits, but adores its riches. An open letter written by a victim of Jordan Belfort, the stockbroker portrayed in *The Wolf of Wall Street*, claims that the depiction is a "reckless attempt at continuing to pretend that these sorts of schemes are entertaining, even as the country is reeling from yet another round of Wall Street scandals" (McDowell, 2013, para. 5) and that the cultural message that aligning with a criminal who left victims destitute and degraded women is acceptable, is both irresponsible and despicable.

There is also a film, at the time of this writing, presently in development based on the story of Bernie Madoff, the American corporate criminal and former stockbroker convicted of fraud of an estimated 65 billion dollars. The Madoff case made headlines worldwide in 2008–2009, and he is widely considered to be the consummate corporate psychopath, which will no doubt form an important character part in the film. Madoff, claiming to have been simply misunderstood, continues to rationalize and minimize his behavior. He took risks without regard for investing clients, distributes guilt, consistently lied to his family, became obsessed with wealth, was a master manipulator according to family and friends, and obsessively upheld a façade of success and genius. These features are all symptomatic of a corporate psychopath.

The Female Psychopath in Film

Although the male psychopath continues to dominate in film, perhaps in part as psychopathy is associated much more with males than females in the related real world literature, there have been a few notable representations of female psychopaths in contemporary cinema. While about 1% of Western general populations are thought to meet the criteria for psychopathy, the ratio between men versus women has been documented as high as 20:1 (DeLisi & Vaughn, 2016). It is thought that some of the difference between men and women may not be in the existence of deceitful, manipulative, and exploitive personality traits but in the expression of them, particularly as aligned with and diagnosed as another mental illness (Sprague, Javdani, Sadeh, Newman,

& Verona, 2012). Also, female psychopaths are outnumbered 3:1 by their male peers in violent prison populations (Wynn, Hoiseth, & Pettersen, 2012).

According to Logan (2011), "on the whole, women are not physically harmful to the same degree or with the same frequency as men and they rarely attack strangers, and this is thought to be the case with psychopathic women too" (p. 119). However they can still be equally damaging and devastating to others, if not on a physical level, then definitely at an emotional and relationship level. Fictional portrayals in particular highlight their deep-seated insecurity and need for the admiration of others that underlies their hostile, manipulative, and coercive behavior. In a sense, it is a protective mechanism to safeguard a perilous fragile ego. Not surprising then, female psychopathic characters in film tend to exhibit features of manipulative and pseudopsychopathic (sociopathic) subtypes rather than those that are more physically oriented.

According to the data set of Leistedt and Linkowski (2014), there are only 21 female psychopathic characters in film history up to 2010, with almost half being portrayed in movies produced in the 1990s. Almost three-of-four are secondary psychopaths, with the most the pseudo (47%) and manipulative (40%) subtypes. As expected, there were no female macho psychopathic characters and only two classical psychopaths in this period (Sadie in *The Last House on the Left*, 1972; and Mona Demarkov in *Romeo is Bleeding*, 1993). Although the harmful potential of women has been overlooked for a long time in fictional portrayals, the more 'equal' depiction of women behaving badly is arguably a reflection of a willingness to acknowledge the devious intentions and behavior of some women to achieve a goal or express themselves. Atwood (2009) explained the possibilities of "evil" female characters in fiction as follows:

> [...] female bad characters can also act as keys to doors we need to open, and as mirrors in which we can see more than just a pretty face. They can be explorations of moral freedom—because everyone's choices are limited, and women's choices have been more limited than men's, but that doesn't mean women can't make choices. Such characters can pose the question of responsibility, because if you want power you have to accept responsibility, and actions produce consequences. I'm not suggesting an agenda here, just some possibilities; nor am I prescribing, just wondering. If there's a closed-off road, the curious speculate about why it's closed off, and where it might lead if followed; and evil women have been, for a while recently, a somewhat closed-off road, at least for fiction-writers. (p. 20.8)

So, "evil" women have, in many respects, taken a rightful place in film. Sometimes, but not often, there is a more direct relation to reality. Although the 2003 film *Monster* was not included in the Leistedt and Linkowski (2014) analysis, it is mentionable here for a couple of reasons. The crime drama was based on the life of U.S. female serial killer, Aileen Wuornos. The film also got overwhelming praise from critics and won several awards, including an Academy Award for Best Actress by Charlize Theron. It grossed a respectable $60 million and ranks number 13 in the true crime genre, according to the Box Office Mojo website statistics. Wuornos, who was executed in 2002 for the murder of seven men in Florida between 1989 and 1990, is recognized as one of a handful of female serial killers worldwide outside the medical field and who targeted strangers. She was diagnosed with Borderline Personality Disorder (Krop, 1992), but her PCL-R score of 32 also evidenced a psychopathic personality (Myers, Gooch, & Meloy, 2005).

The second cinematic portrayal of a female psychopath that received significant critical attention was the character of Amy Dunne in the 2014 film *Gone Girl*, based on the 2014 Gillian Flynn novel of the same name. Dunne's devious, revengeful, and manipulative schemes, dishonesty and lack of remorse is indicative of a textbook example of a primary psychopath, or in terms of Hervé's classification, a classical subtype that does not hesitate to use violence when required, even seeming to revel in the opportunity. But, unlike many typical real-life psychopaths, she is not that impulsive—observing, collecting information, and meticulously planning her revenge for over a year before acting. However, her anger when things don't go her way brings an intensity and urgency that threatens to derail her carefully made plans. Her lack of perspective of her behavior in the context of acceptable norms is another aspect of psychopathy. She continually creates her own narrative where she has to be in the center of attention. All things considered, the character of Amy Dunne reflected mainstream willingness to consider a female psychopathic character, albeit one that is over the top and shocked most audiences. Where the 1990s brought viewers frightening psychopathic characters such as Alex Forrest in *Fatal Attraction*, Annie Wilkes in *Misery*, Catherine Tramell in *Basic Instinct*, and Tracy Safian in *Malice*, which were written by men, more recent depictions, including *Gone Girl* were created by female authors, which is still a rare occurrence, especially in popularity. However, it perhaps brings with it a less sexualized character version with psychopathic traits more integrated and pervasive in a primary sense.

Children and Adolescent Psychopaths

There has been a great deal of controversy about the labeling of youth as psychopaths, both from a developmental and ethical viewpoint. The label of being assessed as a psychopath carries with it the burden of stigmatization and possible inaccuracy. A child and adolescent's brain and personality is still developing, and therefore there is an increased chance of a wrong diagnosis or changed condition later in life. Remember that 'psychopath' is not a true diagnostic type, but is mostly used in criminal offender populations. Using it outside these settings is often thought to cause proneness to over-diagnosis of traits that could lead to psychopathic tendencies if they persist. Such a premature label may actually have the opposite effect by traumatizing and marginalizing the child and family, exacerbating symptoms, and decreasing the willingness to commit to an assessment and treatment. The most widely used test instrument to measure psychopathy in children is the Psychopathy Checklist-Youth Version (PCL-YV), which has not been well-validated outside of youth offender settings. It consists, like the PCL-R, of a list of 20 items that are rated on a scale of 0 to 2.

Despite the associated controversies in academic and clinical circles, however, the film industry has been fascinated by the concept of young psychopaths for some time now. Earlier depictions focused on "evil" children as demonically possessed cold-blooded killers, such Damien in the *The Omen* (1976–1985) and *The Children of the Corn* (1984–2011) franchises. Many newer films and television present children and adolescents with traits that are closer to those exhibited by prototypical psychopaths, though there are thought to be a number of conceptual problems with the way children and teenagers are featured as psychopaths in fiction. These often perpetuate myths and misconceptions held by the lay public about the condition, which may hinder early identification.

In the first place, the children are usually depicted as having superior intelligence and being from affluent homes with both, loving parents present. In real life, this seems to be the exception rather than the norm. Empirical studies have shown that there are no intelligence differences between psychopaths and non-psychopaths (Johansson & Kerr, 2005). Higher psychopathy scores on the PCL-YV are associated with physical abuse and non-parental living arrangements during childhood (Campbell, Porter, & Santor, 2004).

The second issue is a conceptual one. Although the diagnostic distinction of sociopathy was eliminated with the publication of the DSM-II in 1968, there is a reluctance in the popular media to abolish the classification. Therefore, as a pop psychology term it has become confounded with the psychiatric diagnosis of antisocial personality disorder (APD) and the legal concept of psychopathy. Only APD is officially recognized in the DSM-5, the current mental health classification system in use in the U.S. Today, psychopathy is, in professional terms, mostly defined by the Psychopathy Checklist-Revised

(PCL-R), which contains a significant criminal/antisocial construct, and used to evaluate risk of future violence and recidivism in adult offender populations. With few exceptions, fictional characters of child and adolescent in film and television are referred to as sociopaths, technically a redundant and nonscientific term, and therefore conceptually confusing.

The third issue is that the youth version of the instrument (PCL-YV) that was previously mentioned and most widely used to identify youth psychopaths is controversial in terms of its predictive ability. There is no established threshold score for the PCL-YV, which causes concerns of inconsistency, and a potential increase of false positives if the cutoff is lowered in non-offender populations. Although research by Lynam, Caspi, Moffitt, Loeber, and Stouthamer-Loeber (2007) found that psychopathy from early adolescence in a middle school sample (13-year-old) into young adulthood (24-year-old) was moderately stable, predictive power was poor. In simpler terms, this means that a low percentage of boys who were identified as psychopathic at age 13 were psychopathic at age 24. The dangers of false positives should be clear here. Not only is treatment and institutionalization expensive, the effect of a pejorative label is unknown, as are effectiveness of treatment for a young psychopath, and distinction of those young psychopaths whose antisocial behavior will remit over time.

The fourth issue that pertains to child and adolescent psychopathy in the popular media is the need to highlight legal implications of such a diagnosis. It has varying impact and meaning between jurisdictions and there is a lack of knowledge and opportunity to cover the implications. In many instances, especially barring acts of serious violence, a child cannot be committed for treatment involuntarily (without the consent of parents and legal guardians), and in more serious cases heard in juvenile court, proper care will not be available after conviction. Proper education of the condition and availability of options is important to ensure early identification and intervention. The entertainment media can play a responsible role here, but is perpetuating misinformation, perhaps for the sake of sensationalism, that can make positive efforts more challenging.

A more recent example of the portrayal of an adolescent psychopath in mainstream film is *We Need to Talk about Kevin* (2011). In most other films the effect of psychopathy on the individual, their family, and community is obfuscated in the vilification of unambiguous characters. The cause-and-effect of dysfunctional interpersonal relationships on psychopathic behavior is rarely illustrated. No person can be thought of as exclusively bad. This is a misconception that is most often perpetuated in entertainment media where ambiguity is not easily absorbed. Society does not want to be blamed or associated with her 'monsters'. Instead, they provide a fascination from afar. Such a shortsighted view is limiting, but in Kevin's case the evolution pf psychopathy in a person is a refreshing (albeit somber) take. Having basic childhood needs fulfilled helps protect a person against genetic imperfections, enabling a young person to learn functional ways to cope with it. However, although the film offered this not-often-seen interpersonal perspective of psychopathy, it remains a fairly shallow view offering many of the same conclusions that the media often does about the 'pure evil', unconditional nature, and untreatability of psychopathy that perpetuate the usual misconceptions.

Conclusion: Psychopaths on Television ... a New Standard?

Psychopathy is not straightforward and unitary condition. Film provides a vicarious experience that we can parallel to an extent to our own lives and those around us, helping us to understand and navigate our own and others' complex personalities more effectively. Hopefully such an improved insight helps us to appreciate the profound impact that we can have on our children. Collectively, children's health and wellbeing is a reflection of the status of entire societies and nations. Through fictional characters, people can absorb their experiences and interactions, shaping discourses about responsibility, accountability, empathy, and moral values. Such characters can blunt our senses or bring new hope. Universal boogeymen and archetypes may hold a fascination and appeal to many, but they can also increase aggression and violent behavior in some consumers by desensitizing them and normalizing bad behavior.

Therefore, there is a compelling argument for the realistic depiction of psychopaths in film, or at least a thoughtful consideration by producers of how to portray (and market) characters with psychopathy to audiences. This will help people beyond professional fields to gain insight into the interpersonal dynamics, inner complexities, and behavioral inconsistencies of those with psychopathy that they may encounter in real life. After all, there is a great need to learn about dealing with psychopaths in order to protect oneself against their threats, manipulation, and exploits.

As television continues to espouse an increasingly post-broadcast model and continuously competes with conventional motion pictures in terms of production values, serialized storytelling, and its ability to attract high profile talent, depictions of psychopaths in television can be expected to follow a similar evolutionary design when looking back at its various iterations in film, although a survey of texts produced post-2000 suggests that television may in fact be charting a new—and more accurate—course.

Table 1. List of Main Psychopathic Characters in Contemporary TV Series.

No.	Character Duration	Television Series	Psychopathic Main Character
1	2001–2003	24	Nina Myers
2	2011–2013	American Horror Story	Bloody Face
3	2011	American Horror Story	Tate Langdon
4	2013–2015	Bates Motel	Norman Bates
5	2008–2013	Breaking Bad	Walter White
6	2001–2003	Coronation Street	Richard Hillman
7	2006–2007	CSI	The Miniature Killer
8	2008–2010	CSI	Nate Haskell
9	2011–2013	CSI Miami	Esteban Carlos Navarro
10	2009	Dexter	Arthur Mitchell
11	2006–2013	Dexter	Dexter Morgan
12	2011–2014	Game of Thrones	Joffrey Baratheon
13	2013–2015	Game of Thrones	Ramsay Bolton
14	2013–2015	Hannibal	Hannibal Lecter
15	2013–2015	House of Cards	Frank Underwood
16	2012–2014	House of Lies	Monica Talbot
17	2010–2013	Luther	Alice Morgan
18	2007–2015	Mad Men	Don Draper
19	2014	Murder in the First	Eric Blunt
20	2005–2009	Prison Break	T-Bag
21	2011–2015	Revenge	Emily Thorne
22	2005–2006	Rome	Gaius Octavian
23	2015	Secrets and Lies	Abby Crawford
24	2013	The Fall	Jamie Dornan
25	2013–2015	The Following	Joe Carroll
26	1990–2015	The Simpsons	Sideshow Bob
27	2001–2002	The Sopranos	Ralph Cifaretto
28	2010–2012	The Walking Dead	Shane Walsh
29	2012–2014	The Walking Dead	The Governor
30	2014	True Detective	Errol Childress

As a series that generally lacks a storyline and characters with emotional stability or healthy relationships, the HBO production *Game of Thrones* (2011–2015) in particular offers a veritable buffet of psychopathic types. Although Joffrey Baratheon was only 18-years-old when he was murdered, he displayed characteristics consistent with Millon's spineless psychopath type. He was a sadistic and cruel young man who commanded others to fight his battles for him, thereby hiding his own fears of being weak and defenseless with a false bravado. Another character in the same show, Ramsay Bolton, can be seen as a malevolent psychopath according to Millon's classification. He delighted in the torture and domination of others, and he used his victims' emotions against them, often by offering a glimmer of hope before ruthlessly crushing it. He derived personal pleasure and satisfaction from the torture and murder of others. But, as a medieval fantasy, *Game of Thrones* is far from modern real life and its everyday challenges. A nuanced view of many different types of psychopathic characters has entertainment merit, but the caricaturized depictions offer minimal real insight. Other series are better positioned to reflect real-life situations—a characterization that remains lacking in a balanced understanding of psychopathy.

Silicon Valley prodigy, Eric Blunt, main protagonist in the first season of *Murder in the First* (2014), is a prototypical manipulative psychopath in Hervé's nosology. He was a pathological liar, manipulated others to get what he wants, but also for amusement, used and coerced others to perform his crimes, but also did not hesitate, and took pleasure, to murder someone up-close-and-personal. He was extremely impulsive and aggrandized himself, which eventually led to his fall. In fact, Eric Blunt may be a good fictional example of the so-called dark triad personality—a particularly malevolent and destructive blend of psychopathic, narcissistic, and Machiavellian traits. Akin to some psychopathic symptoms, narcissism is characterized by grandiosity, pride, egotism, and a lack of empathy, while Machiavellianism is characterized by manipulation and exploitation of others, a cynical disregard for morality, and a focus on self-interest and deception (Jakobwitz & Egan, 2006).

Television has also taken much of the initiative in the increasing depictions of child and adolescent psychopaths, also called a 'budding psychopath'. The growing popularity of criminalistic shows such as CSI and Criminal Minds had an important contribution to this trend. In addition to these single-episode depictions, youth with psychopathic traits have also played main characters in television series. The list of television characters in Table 1 features teenager Norman Bates in *Bates Motel* (2013), Joffrey Baratheon who was 16-years-old in the first season of *Game of Thrones* (2011), and 12-year-old Abby Crawford in *Secrets and Lies* (2015). Nevertheless, despite the growing fascination with young psychopaths in the popular media, the merits of such a concept and labeling remains highly questionable.

Psychopathy has become a topic of increasing interest to armchair viewers in the last decades, not just because 'evil' makes for compellingly entertaining material, but viewers can feel complacent that they are different and uninvolved. This is perhaps symptomatic of a collective need to confirm that 'evil' is only a problem of the 'other'; that the labels and stereotypes do not apply to oneself. In a sense the complexity of the human experience is simplified by erecting boundaries between "good" and "evil."

Unfortunately, the media continues to perpetuate this effect; thus, one should always ask: *Cuo bono*? Meaning, literally, "who benefits?," it is a Latin coinage that questions the producer's motivation for a specific portrayal—in this case the psychopathic character. In news and fiction alike, it is often beneficial to promote a dichotomous "us-and-them" mentality in order to evoke positive feelings of one's own group. The medium of film, however, has to much more to offer in terms of realism, including its acting as a catalyst for insight and positive change instead of further alienation and labeling that is encouraging negative values and sustaining misconceptions about "evil" and the nature of psychopathy and other mental disorders. Television is even better situated to make a positive contribution in the perception about psychopathy as it offers increased scope for character nuances and development in serial storytelling, access to broader audiences, and more opportunities to experiment and make adaptive changes. However, both film and television continue to fall short in an accurate portrayal of psychopathy. There consequently endures a need for the professional mental health, film, and television industries to collectively collaborate to counter inaccurate stereotypical portrayals of psychopathy that sustain misconceptions and stigma, discourage help-seeking, and, ultimately, impede rehabilitation initiatives.

References

Arntfield, Michael. *The Forensic Gothic: Criminal Investigative Procedure in Victorian Horror & Mystery*. New York: Palgrave-Macmillan. 2016.

Atwood, Margaret. "Spotty-handed Villainesses: Problems of Female Bad Behavior in the Creation of Literature." In *Curious pursuits: Occasional writing*. London: Hachette Digital. 2009.

Buzina, Nadica. "Psychopathy: Historical Controversies and New Diagnostic Approach." *Psychiatria Danubina* 24 (2012): 134–142.

Babiak, Paul, Neumann, Craig S., and Hare, Robert D. "Corporate Psychopathy: Talking the Walk." *Behavioral Science & the Law* 28 (2010): 174–193.

Boddy, Clive, Miles, Derek, Sanyal, Chandana, and Hartog, Mary. "Extreme Managers, Extreme Workplaces: Capitalism, Organizations and Corporate Psychopaths." *Organization* 22 (2015): 530–551.

Caldwell, Michael, Skeem, Jennifer, Salekin, Randy, and Van Rybroek, Gregory. "Treatment Response of Adolescent Offenders with Psychopathy Features: A 2-Year Follow-up." *Criminal Justice and Behavior* 33 (2006): 571–596.

Campbell, Mary Ann, Porter, Stephen, and Santor, Darcy. Psychopathic Traits in Adolescent Offenders: An Evaluation of Criminal History, Clinical, and Psychosocial Correlates. *Behavioral Sciences and the Law* 22 (2004): 23–47.

Cerny, Cathleen, Friedman, Susan H., and Smith, Delaney. "Television's "Crazy Lady" Trope: Female Psychopathic Traits, Teaching, and Influence of Popular Culture." *Academic Psychiatry* 38 (2014): 233–241.

Cleckley, Hervey M. "*The Mask of Sanity: An Attempt to Clarify Some Issues About the So-called Psychopathic Personality.*" Maryland Heights, MO: C. V. Mosby Co., 1941.

Coid, Jeremy. W., Yang, Min, Ulrich, Simone, Roberts, Amanda, Moran, Paul, Bebbington, Paul, Brugha, Traolach, Jenkins, Rachel, Farrell, Michael, Lewis, Glyn, Singleton, Nicola, and Hare, Robert D. "Psychopathy Among Prisoners in England and Wales." *International Journal of Law and Psychiatry* 32 (2009): 134–141.

Danesi, Marcel. "*Signs of Crime: Introducing Forensic Semiotics.*" Berlin: DeGruyter, 2013.

DeLisi, Matt, and Vaughn, Michael G. "Correlates *of Crime*". *In The Handbook of Criminological Theory*, edited by Alex R. Piquero, 18–36. Malden, MA: John Wiley & Sons, 2016.

Diagnostic and Statistical Manual of Mental Disorders: DSM-5. Washington: American Psychiatric Association, 2013.

Dutton, Kevin. "*The Wisdom of Psychopaths: What Saints, Spies, and Serial Killers can Teach Us about Success.*" New York: Scientific American/Farrar, Straus and Giroux, 2012.

Fazel, Seena, and Danesh, John. "Serious Mental Disorder in 23,000 Prisoners: A Systematic Review of 62 Surveys." *The Lancet* 359 (2002): 545–550, 2002.

Gowlett, Christopher T. "Does Secondary Psychopathy Exist? Exploring Conceptualizations of Psychopathy and Evidence for the Existence of a Secondary Variant of Psychopathy." *Internet Journal of Criminology*, 2014. Accessed August 29, 2015. http://goo.gl/k5HA5W.

Gregory, Sarah, Ffytche, Dominic, Simmons, Andrew, Kumari, Veena, Howard, Matthew, Hodgins, Sheilagh, and Blackwood, Nigel. "The Antisocial Brain: Psychopathy Matters (A Structural MRI Investigation of Antisocial Male Violent Offenders)." *Archives of General Psychiatry* 69 (2012): 962–972.

Gullhaugen, Aina S., and Nottestad, Jim A. "Looking for the Hannibal Behind the Cannibal: Current Status of Case Research." *International Journal of Offender Therapy and Comparative Criminology* 55 (2011): 350–369.

Hare, Robert D. "*Manual for the Revised Psychopathy Checklist* (2nd ed.)." Toronto: Multi-Health Systems, 2003.

Hervé, Hugues F. M. "*The Masks of Sanity and Psychopathy: A Cluster Analytical Investigation of Subtypes of Criminal Psychopathy*" PhD diss., The University of British Columbia, 2003.

Jakobwitz, Sharon, and Egan, Vincent. "The Dark Triad and Normal Personality Traits." *Personality and Individual Differences* 40 (2006): 331–339.

Johansson, Peter, and Kerr, Margaret. "Psychopathy and Intelligence: A Second Look. *Journal of Personality Disorders* 19 (2005): 357–369.

Karpman, Benjamin. "On the Need of Separating Psychopathy Into Two Distinct Clinical Types: The Symptomatic and the Idiopathic." *Journal of Criminology and Psychopathology* 3 (1941): 112–137.

Kiehl, Kent A., and Hoffman, Morris B. "The Criminal Psychopath: History, Neuroscience, Treatment, and Economics." *Jurimetrics* 51 (2011): 355–397.

Koenigs, Michael. "The Role of the Prefrontal Cortex in Psychopathy." *Reviews in the Neurosciences* 23 (2012): 253–262.

Krop, Harry. "*Psychological Evaluation of Aileen Wuornos.*" Gainesville, FL: Community Behavioral Services, 1992. Accessed on August 29, 2015. http://goo.gl/P7tp6i.

Leistedt, Samuel J., and Linkowski, Paul. "Psychopathy and the Cinema: Fact or Fiction?" *Journal of Forensic Sciences* 59 (2014): 167–174.

Logan, Caroline. "La Femme Fatale: The Female Psychopath in Fiction and Clinical Practice." *Mental Health Review Journal* 16 (2011): 118–127.

Lynam, Donald R., Caspi, Avshalom, Moffitt, Terrie E., Loeber, Rolf, and Southamer-Loeber, Magda. "Longitudinal Evidence that Psychopathy Scores in Early Adolescence Predict Adult Psychopathy." *Journal of Abnormal Psychology* 116 (2007): 155–165.

Mathieu, Cynthia, Hare, Robert D., Jones, Danial N., Babiak, Paul, and Neumann, Craig S. "Factor Structure of the B-Scan 360: A Measure of Corporate Psychopathy." *Psychological Assessment* 25 (2012): 288–293.

McDowell, Christina. "An Open Letter to the Makers of *The Wolf of Wall Street*, and the Wolf Himself." *LA Weekly*, December 26, 2013. Accessed September 2, 2015. http://goo.gl/zgJ9rh.

Millon, Theodore, and Davis, Roger D. "Ten Subtypes of Psychopathy." In *Psychopathy: Antisocial, Criminal, and Violent behavior*, edited by Theodore Millon, Erik Simonsen, Morten Birket-Smith, and Roger D. Davis, 161–170. New York: Guilford, 1998.

Millon, Theodore, Simonsen, Erik, and Birket-Smith, Morten. "Historical Concepts of Psychopathy in the United States and Europe." In *Psychopathy: Antisocial, Criminal, and Violent Behavior*, edited by Theodore Millon, Erik Simonsen, Morten Birket-Smith, and Roger D. Davis, 3–31. New York: Guilford, 1998.

Morana, Hilda C. P., Arboleda-Flórez, Julio, and Câmara, Fernando P. "Identifying the Cutoff Score for the PCL-R Scale (Psychopathy Checklist-Revised) in a Brazilian Forensic Population." *Forensic Science International* 147 (2005): 1–8.

Morton, Robert J. "*Serial murder: Multi-disciplinary Perspectives for Investigators.*" Quantico, VA: Federal Bureau of Investigation, 2008.

Myers, Wade C., Gooch, Erik, and Meloy, John R. "The Role of Psychopathy and Sexuality in a Female Serial Killer." *Journal of Forensic Sciences* 50 (2005): 1–6.

Newman, Joseph P., MacCoon, Donal G., Vaughn, Leah J., and Sadeh, Naomi. "Validating a Distinction Between Primary and Secondary Psychopathy with Measures of Gray's BIS and BAS Constructs." *Journal of Abnormal Psychology* 114 (2005): 319–232.

Olson, Gary. "Corporations: Empathy-Devoid Psychopaths." In *Empathy Imperiled: Capitalism, Culture, and the Brain*, 53–60. New York, Springer, 2013.

Salekin, Randall T., Worley, Courtney, and Grimes, Ross D. "Treatment of Psychopathy: A Review and Brief Introduction to the Mental Model Approach for Psychopathy." *Behavioral Sciences & the Law* 28 (2010): 235–266.

Skeem, Jennifer L., and Cooke, David J. "Is Criminal Behavior a Central Component of Psychopathy? Conceptual Directions for Resolving the Debate." *Psychological Assessments* 22 (2010): 433–445.

Skeem, Jennifer L, Johansson, Peter, Andershed, Henrik, Kerr, Margaret, and Louden, Jennifer E. "Two Subtypes of Psychopathic Violent Offenders that Parallel Primary and Secondary Variants." *Journal of Abnormal Psychology* 116 (2007): 395–409.

Sprague, Jenessa, Javdani, Shabnam, Sadeh, Naomi, Newman, Joseph P., and Verona, Edelyn. "Borderline Personality Disorder as a Female Phenotypic Expression of Psychopathy?" *Personality Disorders: Theory, Research, and Treatment* 3 (2012): 127–139.

Vitacco, Michael J., Neumann, Craig S., and Wodushek, Thomas. "Differential Relationships Between the Dimensions of Psychopathy and Intelligence: Replication with Adult Jail Inmates." *Criminal Justice and Behavior* 35 (2008): 48–55.

Wynn, Rolf, Hoiseth, Marita H., and Pettersen, Gunn. "Psychopathy in Women: Theoretical and Clinical Perspectives." *International Journal of Women's Health* 4 (2012): 257–263.

Yu, Rongqin, Geddes, John R., and Fazel, Seena. "Personality Disorders, Violence, and Antisocial Behaviour: A Systematic Review and Meta-Regression Analysis." *Journal of Personality Disorders* 26 (2012): 775–792.

5. *The Hammer and the Hummingbird: Spectating Crime Inside the Documentary Film*

Trevor Grant

Introduction

The few who have experienced violent crime first hand know the reality—the smell, the fear, the shock and the surreal suspension of time and space. For those who have not, it is difficult, if not impossible, to fully imagine the grotesque realism inherent in a life ending human-to-human confrontation. The true crime genre in literature, popular criminology, cinema and television spins out thousands of non-fiction stories to place the spectator as observer inside a moment they cannot imagine, but do want to experience. While criminality comes loaded with natural born dramatic curves, arcs, conflict and tension—a natural hunting ground for the narrative ambitions of storytellers—it is the conceit of the real that audiences crave. The more believable the claim of authenticity the closer to the scene of the crime the spectator is positioned and the more intimate the imagining.

Absent the camera from the immediate scene of a violent crime, the story then is dependent upon the narrative imagination of the author to re-construct truth from the archival remnants and then present the fictionalization as believable fact. A non-fiction approach to any story, in any genre, including true crime, 'always fictionalizes, emphasizes, exaggerates, interprets, constructs, and creates "truth," and any relationship to the facts is mediated and compromised' (Murley 2008: 13). There is no doubt that at some level the spectator understands authenticity is compromised in the re-imagining. However, the form in which the crime story is constructed directly influences the perception of the degree of truth within a narrative. Within the world of film, it is the documentary form that is best positioned in the psyche of the spectator to deliver authenticity. The documentary form is constructed not on fantasy as we find in cinema, but ostensibly on facts that present audiences with, 'accounts in which the viewed is to be taken as effectively indistinguishable from the real' (Corner and Richardson 1986: 141). Within the narrative world of the documentary there are several approaches to constructing meaning. In general this chapter investigates two primary modes of documentary making, the persuasive expository type and the ambiguous performative approach, in relation to truth claims and the spectator. It is however of benefit to first consider true crime stories through the implied promises made to the spectator in cinema in relation to ones made through the differing types of the documentary form.

Crime centered cinema often signals to the audience that the narrative is "based on a true story." In contrast, the documentary form comes with the unstated, but implicit promise that what is about to unfold is indeed true. In Hollywood produced movies the trumpeting of "based on a true story" is a means to market and is, as film writer Tasha Robinson says, 'the attempt to have it both ways: to demand the respectability of "This really happened!" while not operating under any obligation to what really happened' (Robinson 2013). While many crime-based films weave in some small bits of reality, others indicate they are based on truth when the truth is they are fully fictionalized. *The Texas Chainsaw Massacre* and *Fargo* state they are based on true stories, however neither film has any grounding in a crime story that occurred in the real world. As Thomas Leitch argues, in cinema it would seem there is no threshold between authenticity and blatant fabrication, whereby 'If *Fargo* creates its own textual source by creating an original story and then framing it as if it were true, it would seem that anything can be made to assume textual authority even if its not a source, not a text, not true and non existent' (2007: 302). However, when we enter the world of cinema it is fair to say that the spectator enters with their eyes wide open and accepts the substantive dramatic license a film will take. Not so in the documentary experience given the wide acceptance of the form as non-fiction which 'elevates it above narrative fiction in the hierarchy of truth in cinematic representation' (Harindranath 2009: 107). The documentary film, heretofore not being critically unpacked by either scholars or practitioners within the framework of crime alone, necessitates that the spectator enters the narrative largely accepting the implicit promise that what is about to unfold on screen is not just loosely based on the truth, but it *is* the truth. Paradoxically, expository documentary types that stress their objectivity are often less honest than performative documentaries, which Bill Nichols argues do not "hide their signifieds [...] these films stress their own tone and expressive qualities while also retaining a referential claim to the historical' (1994: 98–99). The performative is an approach that declares its subjectivity, rather than the expository type and its tenuous claims of objectivity.

This chapter's discourse will examine performative documentary narratives in contrast to expository constructions in "true crime" documentaries—analyzing how each mode intersects with the world of the spectator in challenging, altering or re-enforcing existing perceptions of violent crime. It will be argued that the expository obscures the narrative mechanics behind the manufacturing of reality, while the performative openly celebrates its creative treatment of reality. Central to this discussion is the type, form and arrangement of narrative voices.

Narrative Voices Inside Ambiguous Space

The term "voices" in this chapter should be understood as encompassing a vast system of narrative devices. In part, the choice of characters, questions asked, interview clips selected, authorial perspectives, voice over narration, text, the camera (camera type, lens, movement, composition), *mise-en-scène*, musical tracks, inclusion of both diegetic and non-diegetic sounds, colorization, the screening space (watching a documentary on television carries different meaning than screening in a theatre space), etc. are layered into the narrative. Further, the multiplicity of voices is then arranged within a scene, the scenes within the structure and the structure placed chronologically or fractured inside the overarching narrative. The consideration in the conception, the application during filming and the arrangement in editing of these narrative voices has a distinctive contribution in the construction and creation of meanings (the true and the not so true) in a documentary's narrative. Many or all of these technical elements of film production as they are employed to construct the diegesis of crime stories have been examined in the context of feature films and through multiple lenses by theorists ranging from Gilles Deleuze to Edward Branigan. It is the objective of this chapter however to disaggregate the performative crime documentary as its own discrete area of scholarship—one demarcated by the unrivalled multiplicity of voice as, oddly enough, evidence of verisimilitude.

Given the distinction of the performative crime documentary from other modes of story-telling, including those ostensibly modeled on actual events, the narratology approach to the subject matter in documentary film making might be seen as engaging Mikhail Bakhtin's postulates concerning the similar role of the novel. Such postulates are both germane and exportable to the crime documentarian's experience in that they serve as a means of defining, in part, narrative voices through the lens of the novel: 'The novel orchestrates all its themes, the totality of the world of objects and ideas depicted and expressed in it, by means of … differing individual voices' (2004: 263). The voices enunciated might be lyrical, epic, dramatic or hybrid in nature and either arranged in the classical expository method of a "causal chain" constructed from 'exposition, complication, resolution' (Wollen) or the disjointed narrative techniques prevalent within performatory documentaries. In considering Bakhtin's theories in relation to narrative techniques, David Bordwell (1985: 17) writes that the 'novel, according to Bakhtin, is not a spectacle organized around Jamesian straight lines; it is a polyphony, even a cacophony, of different registers of speech and written language: a montage of voices,' Through what might partially be described as a Deleuzian crystal—speech types, space and time being reflected (and refracted) inside the narrative and projected to the receiver—the spectator's reception of the narrative becomes in and of itself an additional voice. It is in the arrangement of voices that, in part, serve to engage the spectator as an active participant or reduces the spectator to the role of passive recipient.

Organizing Voices: Influencing the Spectator as Witness

Some eight decades ago, John Grierson, the first head of the National Film Board (NFB) of Canada, defined the emerging documentary form as the creative treatment of actuality. Within this rather loose (and often debated) framework—documentaries approach the task of representing reality through six differing narrative constructions. While the performative and expository types will be explored in depth in this chapter, it is beneficial to have at least a surface understanding of the principals of the other four as each type does carry some influence within the discussion. While each type has multiple levels of complexity and meaning, in simple terms:

> *Poetic* organizes images of the lived world through patterns and associations and arrange the "narrative" through impressionistic interpretations.
>
> *Observational* observes lived life with minimal intervention by the documentarian.
>
> *Participatory* features the documentarian within the film and in obvious rather than subtle ways. The inter-action between the author and subject is a key defining element in this type. Many viewers will come to the experience to watch a favored (or disfavored) documentarian, rather than solely for the story.
>
> *Reflexive* types draw attention to their own constructed representations as a means to confront the audience, to demand the spectator challenge the authenticity of the narrative.

Seldom, however, do any of the six documentary types stand-alone. As documentary theorist Bill Nichols (2001: 17) points out, "the characteristics of a given mode function as a dominant in a given film [...] but they do not dictate or determine every aspect of its organization." The performative type, which engages the director to the story as author in constructing subjective truths, weaves in nuances from most other documentary modes. Many of the critically acclaimed crime documentaries, including, most notably, *The Thin Blue Line*, *The Jinx* and *Into the Abyss*,[1] are documentaries that are, in part, 'characterized by a mix of participatory, performative and reflexive techniques which have helped documentarians express their idiosyncratic worldviews' (Ricciardelli 2015: 28). The straight ahead expository type, premised on persuasion through arguing rhetorical content, is the least likely to incorporate other types. All other documentary types carry signifiers, either writ large or small that signal a subjective authorial voice as one of many that combine to *represent* truth. However, acknowledging subjectivity exposes the expository type's manufacturing process and makes meaningless the assembly line arguments. The methods the expository documentary utilizes to conceal the conceit are varied, many and consistent no matter the story being told.

The story-telling mechanics within the expository documentary type suppress the spectator's voice through a diegetic approach—utilizing a disembodied, omniscient and authoritative sounding narrator who, "guides the viewer's interpretation of the images on the screen [...] The audience is passive more than active: we are invited to listen more than to interpret and evaluate' (Melnyk 2014: 22). The viewer is restricted to the world of the narrative thereby assuming the role of a passive witness to the crime. The power of the expository type to persuade is partially dependent on concealing subjectivity behind a veil of objectivity. As Bill Nichols (1999) writes: "An expository documentary may also try to mask or diminish its own shaping and modifying activity so that it seemed self evident that the world is indeed cast in the image the film proposes" (113). The concealment of modifying activity is a standard construction in propaganda films, which, in turn, are a fabricating story factory inside the expository type. Grierson, who oversaw the manufacturing of the NFB's propaganda films during the Second World War, is considered by some theorists and film historians to have had substantive influence on the mechanics of the expository style. In *Theorizing Documentary*, Michael Renov (1993: 29) writes that 'persuasion is the dominant trope for nonfiction films in the tradition of John Grierson [...] for this son of a Calvinist minister, the screen was a pulpit, the film a hammer.' The expository type of documentary still wields a hammer, one loud enough and insistent enough to eliminate the voice of the spectator, while the performative construction serves to mirror society and provide space for voices beyond that of the narrator.

In contrast to the expository type, the voices within a performative documentary often conflict which serves to challenge and provoke the spectator to bring their own lived histories to the documentary in order to sort seemingly ambiguous meanings. The classic form of narration that is integral in the expository form is largely absent in the performative, consequently there is, 'no single, authoritative voice, no unified interpretation, but rather many voices that give us information from a variety of sometimes conflicting perspectives' (Renov 1993: 22) The spectator becomes a filmic decoder of symbols and sub-text who is then challenged to do some sleuthing of self in order to make meaning and, as a consequence, are pressured to reconsider their preconceived notions, stereotypes and perceptions of criminality. Engaging the audience is thus also dependent upon the levels of ambiguity in the documentary. The expository documentary reflects one world; indeed the arguments depend on confining the spectator to the singular world within the narrative. The performative too builds a world the audience can recognize through mimetic construction, but to a different end. Mimetic construction recreates a known world that grounds the spectator within the real as a means to imply truth within the narrative: "expository devices make it recognizable as documentary—its credibility is dependent on its successful mimesis' (Harindranath 2009: 107). The mirroring of the known world, of a crime scene as we might imagine it, of a villain, of a victim as we think we know them is then infused with ambiguity emanating from the heteroglossia of voices. The world the spectator has built, the assumptions they have made and the stereotypes they draw within that world are called into question. As the spectator sorts through ambiguous imagery and sound, broken chronologies, unexpectedly sympathetic villains and multidimensional victims their known world is suddenly not so well known. Absent an authoritative narrator to guide the spectator, the director/author of the performative documentary instead offers spaces for thinking, for reflection and for accessing memory, resulting in an individualized spectator experience. The performative does first offer a mimetic construction, one that is then probed and challenged by voices other than our own. The documentary transforms from a thing to observe to a thing in which to participate: 'Mimetic elements of the documentary discourse interweave argument and story, reason and emotion and contain [...] the film-maker's creativity. Such a conception of the documentary incorporates both the 'truth claims' as well as the ineluctable fictive elements in non-fiction' (Harindranath 2009: 121–122). The critical differentiation here, as interpreted within a documentary discourse centered on expository and performative documentaries, is that of the director's influence on the narrative.

To this end, Bakhtin (2004: 314) also brings to the surface another integral aspect in this discussion of the performative type, that of a system of voices that emanate from the author: 'We acutely sense two levels at each moment in the story; one, the level of the narrator, a belief system filled with objects, meanings and emotional expressions, and the other, the level of the author, who speaks (albeit in a refracted way) by the means of this story and through this story.' Rather than masking subjectivity, the multiple levels emanating from an authorial voice both announce and celebrate subjectivity in pursuit of their truth.

Voices in the Abyss: Echoes of Authenticity

Criminality, and more directly any earnest attempt to document its occurrence beyond murder as entertainment and violence as spectacle is fertile ground for the narrative ambitions of a documentarian intent on immersing the spectator inside the human condition. Crime documentaries like *Into the Abyss*, *The Thin Blue Line* and *The Jinx* hew strongly toward a director driven creative treatment of reality. *The Jinx* is a six part documentary mini-series and breaks new ground on a few fronts and is contentious on a few others. Of most interest in this documentary discourse is the final scene in which the spectator bears witness to director Andrew Jarecki's sudden and profound realization that he, as observer (rather than solely as author), has fallen prey to the main character's web of persuasion. A few muttered words by the main character in the dénouement of this six-hour narrative reveal the duping of the documentarian. Here we have a moment in which several voices collide (those of the character, author, spectator and the reversal of arguments made and pre-conceptions held) conflict, transform and re-emerge as a new "truth," one revealed seconds before the closing credits. In this way, the narrative voices speak long past the end of the documentary as the spectator continues to debate what they have experienced and attempt to re-assemble Jarecki's altered perspective against their own.

Within a substantive body of work Werner Herzog utilizes documentary text to explore the human condition through universal themes, utilizing narrative intransitivity, first person narrative, and an ambiguous aesthetic constructed within a hybrid of performative, participatory and reflexive documentary modes. Herzog's *Into the Abyss* serves as an example of a documentary that is dominantly performative, but carries elements of the participatory and the reflexive, adding even more voices to the mix.

The narrative spine that holds together Herzog's *Into the Abyss* is structured around three brutal murders, the impending execution of one of the killers and lifetime incarceration for the other. Within what might be considered standard crime fare (horrific murders at the hands of ones painted purely evil and non-redeemable) we are instead subtly challenged by director Herzog to consider the seemingly obvious beyond simplistic and persuasive binaries like good/evil, saint/sinner and villain/victim. *Into the Abyss* begins with on screen text that states simply "A Film by Werner Herzog," immediately after which the spectator is then positioned inside a conversation between two social actors in the documentary. The participants include Herzog (off camera) as director/author and the death house minister (on camera) who will attend the execution. We first hear Herzog as he poses a question concerning the pending execution:

> **Herzog**: "Reverend you are on duty today, can you just think about the man whom you are going to encounter in less than an hour from now?"

The minister side steps personal reflection concerning the killer as an individual human and ends his response with:

> **Minister**: "We have a loving, caring, forgiving, merciful God."

The answer is one we would expect and as such, places the spectator into a passive position. However, Herzog guides the minister away from his agenda by politely asking a question many would like asked:

> **Herzog**: "Why does God allow capital punishment?"
> **Minister**: "I don't know the answer"

The minister goes on to share an anecdote about almost accidently killing two squirrels. He is laughing a bit when he says this, but then we experience him connecting the dots between saving the squirrels and the unstoppable execution of the murderer (which the minister will bear witness to in less then one hour). In this moment, Herzog allows the spectator to simply observe the minister. There is no narrator telling the spectator what to think, simply the image of the minister becoming human rather than singularly as a man of God. In considering more deeply Herzog's question about God and capital punishment, the man digs down and finds something closer to his personal truth:

> **Minster**: "Life is precious whether it is a squirrel or a human being … make a little noise and squirrels will take off, but I cannot do that for someone on the gurney, I cannot stop the process for them. But I wish I could."

In this deceptively simple opening sequence, a number of complex and contradictory voices are introduced which begin to immerse the spectator inside and outside the world of the documentary—the *mise-en-scène* suggests a specific and highly subjective point of view. The minister is framed with the state cemetery in soft focus in the background; the headstones are simple, identical crosses.[2] Buried here are the executed whose bodies were not claimed. They are buried anonymously; no names on the headstones only numbers. The narrative voice of the minister is on one level simply his reflections on state sanctioned executions through a deeply imbedded religious filter. At a deeper level, manifesting itself physically as well as tonally, the minister adds a conflicting voice—that of an internal, relatable and emotional conflict as he struggles to offer Herzog answers that hold real truth for the minister. Yet another layer of voice is transmitted through the composition of the minister—the camera lens remaining largely static effectively confining the minister as he reaches deep into self while searching for answers to unanswerable and even inscrutable questions. The spaces for thinking allow the audience to reflect on what has just been shown and said, to filter the content through their own perceptions concerning capital punishment and to begin bringing their own voice to the narrative through the necessity of decoding signs and sub-texts.

Hidden Voices: The Levers of Deception

At the other end of the documentary spectrum from the performative type is the expository documentary. Crime narratives are arguably among the lowest hanging fruit for this largely manufactured, and often episodic, documentary type. As previously discussed, the expository mode, at least in the context of crime documentaries, tend to lack the verisimilitude of the performative mode—in spite of the nomenclature suggesting the inverse. For the purpose of this paper, crime based docudramas, quasi documentaries, and propaganda productions qualify as expository documentaries, though not all of these formats will be directly discussed. Excluded from this discussion are long-form stories that are grounded in journalistic practices within social, cultural, political and economic spheres, including investigative current affairs programming. While expository in construction, the motivations of these formats (accountability, information dissemination, etc.) carry radically different and more complex purposes (public concern, public discourse, etc.) than formulaic persuasion. For example, current affairs programming is predicated on the investigation and revelation of pertinent facts within an issue of societal concern and presented in a fair and balanced discourse.[3] All sides of an issue are examined and given voice. In a criminal trial the assessment of the evidence is left to the jury, similarly in current affairs programming the evidence is presented to the spectator as though a jurist and they have final judgment. In contrast, the expository documentary works within one side of an issue, although they often conceal bias by presenting ostensibly differing sides of a story, however they all flow from the same standpoint. This is an evidentiary slight of hand at work and unseen in the expository type. Consequently, the spectator's *verdict* is based only on prima facie evidence that cannot be challenged within the confines of the expository documentaries "tell" construction.

Expository story constructions are centered on a diegetic approach that tells rather than shows. The seemingly authoritative—rather than authorial—narrator tells the audience what to think. The authoritative narrator functions as the all-knowing voice that speaks directly to the spectator, while the authorial voice within the performative type serves as the threshold through which all imagery, sound, content is passed before reception by the spectator and further is "framed by several embedded textual and intentional layers' (Hatavara 2016: 290) that insist the viewer travel beyond the immediate world of the narrative.

In the expository type, the story unfolds within the world of that disembodied narration and the number of complex narrative voices are reduced—if not removed entirely. Rather than the pursuit of *a* truth through an exploration of universal themes that underlie the performative type, the bread and butter of the expository type is cold bloodied murder, vulnerable victims and the monstrous villains. Murder as entertainment, murder as spectacle and murder re-enactments that serve as persuasive arguments that what the viewer is "witnessing" is the true (and unimaginable) grotesque realism inherent in a life ending human-to-human confrontation. The individuals chosen by the producers to appear on camera to pontificate and condemn, be they characters or experts, are restricted in their responses through question lines, editing and/or their complicity in becoming a social actor within a specific docudrama role. Regardless of their connection to the crime, they all speak from a similar standpoint. As Chapman (2009: 105) describes, 'interviewees can appear like puppets or stereotypes recruited for the line of the film, while in more complex documentaries the filmmaker will establish a voice for the textual system that rises above the voices of individual contributors, that is greater than the sum of its parts.' The volume of the voices that remain in service of the argument are in turn exaggerated through typically quick-cut interview clips, dramatic musical cues (the timpani drum having proven to be a recurring favorite within this genre based on a cursory inventory) and what might be described as a "say it-see it" system of dramatic recreations complete with images of lurid stylized violence. As a consequence of removing textual layers—something akin to putting a peel back on an onion—and hammering out any remaining ambiguity, the narrative is sliced down into simplistic and easily accessible bits and pieces. This mode also follows a causal chain of events (often fully unfolded in the opening sequence) that tacitly leads the viewer to become something of a voyeur who experiences the thrill of the kill—as seen through the killer's point of view. Only trace evidence of the complex human story is uncovered and, in general, the killer, the police investigators, the victim and the families are one-dimensional and interchangeable from one episode to the next and from one program to another.

In this mode of the expository crime documentary, more accurately described as docudrama than *cinema verité*, production tends to adhere to a strict formula. Through this formula, one that remains largely unchanged when shifting between film and television as the storytelling medium, we can take the opening scene from any one of hundreds of titles and witness how the spectator is made passive and voices are designed to persuade rather than provoke or challenge the spectator. For the purposes of comparison between the subjective performative construction and the modifying activity of the "objective" expository approach, the 2013 docu-drama series, *Deadly Women: Malicious Hearts*[4] serves as something of an exemplar.

Malicious Hearts is an episode framed around the 2009 murder of Jeanette Maples by her mother Angela McAnulty. The narrative evinces a clear and cogent beginning, middle and end to the narrative based on a causal construction and linear timeline played out in the diegesis. Between a mix of omniscient narrator, interview clips from experts, soaring Gregorian chants to ensure the audience understands the gravity of the situation and literal recreations of the crime, the audience is told directly and unequivocally that the villains in this episodic series are all one dimensional: "These women have ice in their veins and malicious hearts." There are no visual representations of the murderer or the victim or, in this case, the stepfather (who is characterized singularly as "the perfect husband for Angela because he wasn't very smart"). With the exception of on camera experts, no real human appears on screen.

Actors portray the roles of the principal characters. Whippings, beatings and the murder are re-enacted. McAnulty's daughter Jeanette is reduced to a one-dimensional thing—a victim (a constant within the expository form). Jeanette cowers in corners, is lessened by camera angles and is at all times doomed and helpless. Not so much an approach that blames the victim, but re-defines them as a good one—that is to say docu drama ready: 'smallness or weakness in anything or anyone that makes it helpless and unable to fight back is a prime quality of a good victim' (Klapp 1964: 80)

In speaking beyond the specific docudrama under discussion here—the reduction of the human being to the singular voice of a victim, sanitizing the grotesque realism of violence and using evidentiary editing techniques that "prove" the argument has, I would suggest, consequences for the viewer and for society at large as these are the precise methods used in propaganda films (as discussed earlier). Some, like *The Eternal Jew*, had unfathomable, but predictable consequences.[5]

Back into the Abyss: The Documentarian Inside the Threshold

Also notably absent in the expository mode is the system of voices that emanate from the author and this has perhaps the most profound and direct impact on the spectator and their perception of objectivity. As Nichols (1991: 128–129) famously posited:

> "The primary point is to identify a level of authorial presence or voice that is felt and experienced by the viewer as different from the mere replication or reproduction of the world. What we experience is less the world reproduced than represented. Perspective can embody both objective and subjective moments; it can defer to those individuals recruited from the world to speak in the film but not for the film; it can be a voice wholly embedded within stylistic choices of selection and arrangement."

In *Into the Abyss* there is a pivotal early scene in which we are exposed to a polyphony of differing voices that positions our expectations and then as the narrative unfolds the expectations are fractured and re-arranged into multiple meanings as they intersect and build upon the known world of the spectator. It is a powerful scene that is all the more evocative and truthful when we understand the multiplicity of voices at work including the director's standpoint and the documentary making process. In this scene, one that might be described as anti-evidentiary editing, the camera is inside the death house and begins a slow, relatively long handheld shot that travels through the holding area where the condemned are brought shortly before their execution. The handheld, *verité* approach suggests a number of motivations that prompt an equally varied number of queries. Does Herzog want to position the spectator in the shoes of the minister who will soon hold the killers leg as the needle is inserted? Does the camera perspective represent the spectator's footsteps as they are taken to bear witness? These are but two of several possible meanings, and establishing a single unambiguous meaning behind this aesthetic treatment is problematic, if not impossible. Within this continuous travelling shot, Herzog also reveals metaphors with multiple meanings and a distinct role within the larger narrative. Bibles on a table, then a telephone, then the death house holding cell and finally the camera stops at the doorway to the execution room—pausing in the threshold between life and death. Herzog then edits to a prisoner entering a cubicle with Plexiglas separating Herzog from the smirking inmate. At this point we are well into the documentary yet we do not know who this person is, nor what he did, nor to whom. The condemned inmate reaches for the phone to communicate with Herzog, who tells the prisoner that he first needs a microphone. This is a highly reflexive moment that clearly indicates the presence of Herzog and the process of film-making thereby adding several more layers of voices. It is at this point that the spectator is given context as to the crime and the perpetrator, Michael Perry, through on screen text utilizing non-inflammatory, non-judgmental language. Herzog then constructs and reveals his subjective threshold—through which all voices must now pass:

> **Herzog**: "I have a feeling that in a way, destiny has dealt you a very bad deck of cards. It does not exonerate you and when I talk to you it does not necessary mean that I have to like you, but I respect you and you are a human being and I do not think human beings should be executed, as simply as that."

In identifying and sharing his personal worldview on capital punishment Herzog declares his subjectivity. However, there are yet more voices at work. Through Herzog's universal themes the spectator will likely come to realize that *Into the Abyss* is not really about capital punishment or a specific murder, but of fathers and sons and generational cycles of violence. In this we are likely to more deeply question our own truths as we internally debate Herzog's standpoint in relation to our own.

Conclusion: The Hammer and the Hummingbird

The closing of an expository documentary is formulated to provide a neat, tidy and unambiguous end to the matter, loose ends are tied up and there is a period at the end of the argument—much as a criminal lawyer would do in a summation to the jury. *Deadly Women Malicious Hearts* is no exception. We learn the murderer, Angela McNulty, was sentenced to death and then, in the form of a concluding clip from an expert, the hammer drops, "I'd like to think there is a special place in hell for Angela, but I don't think Satan wants her there." The curtain falls. The story ends. The spectator disengages. Full stop.

In contrast, Herzog takes his leave from *Into the Abyss* through an open ending. While the documentary ends, life for the characters goes on. One of the many sub stories inside the overarching narrative is framed around a man who was the captain of the death house guard where Perry will be executed. He had laid hands on hundreds of the soon to be dead. Ultimately he could not come to terms with his role and walked away leaving a a pension behind. Herzog leaves us with the last words in the documentary coming in the form of a flutter rather than a hammer. In considering his decision to walk away from the death house, the former captain says, "Once you start feeling good about your life you start to watch what the birds do and the ducks do. Like the hummingbirds—why are there so many of them?" With this ambiguous "end" the spectator is required to draw their own conclusions calling upon the signs and symbols left behind by the documentarian, their individual lived histories and deeply ingrained preconceptions of criminality.

In sorting through the multiple levels of meanings the spectator becomes active within a performative documentary rather than a passive receiver of information and persuasive arguments. *Into the Abyss* is unlikely to change whatever perspective on state sponsored executions a spectator brings to the documentary, however it will make you internalize and debate the ones you already have.

As a scholarly teacher of the medium and as a director who has worked both sides of the street (performative and expository documentaries), I have wielded hammers and looked for hummingbirds. In my experience it is beyond any form of narrative to authentically articulate the grotesque realism inherent in violence. Given that there is an implicit promise, and I would argue an acceptance by the spectator, that the documentary form is a purveyor of truth then it seems an author who declares subjectivity and explores crime through their authorial perspective and universal themes is closer to the "truth" than a narrative masking subjectivity behind a veil of objectivity. Documentarian Errol Morris, quoted in *New Documentary: A Critical Introduction*, shares his perspective on truth: 'There is no reason why documentaries can't be as personal as fiction filmmaking and bear the imprint of those who made them. Truth isn't guaranteed by style or expression. It isn't guaranteed by anything' (Bruzzi 2000: 127). Perhaps, then, the only true thing about true crime stories is that the audience has an insatiable need to experience them.

Notes

1. The Thin Blue Line, directed by E. Morris (1995); The Jinx, directed by A. Jarecki (2015); Into the Abyss, directed by W. Herzog (2012).

2. Throughout the documentary Herzog returns again and again to visual manifestations of the cross as a metaphorical halo of influence. In Herzog's hands, the camera serves as pen in writing the metaphors that Herzog wishes to present to the spectator in order to challenge or reaffirm beliefs and to express his own.
3. The CBC's *The Fifth Estate* and PBS's *Frontline* are excellent examples of fair and balanced current affairs programming. As in all genres based on true stories, there are exceptions as some current affair programs are constructed around the theatrics of the journalist, for entertainment and spectacle at the expense of truth.
4. *Deadly Women: Malicious Hearts*, directed by Jane Manning (2013).
5. *The Eternal Jew*, directed by F. Hippler (1940) is a Nazi propaganda film that claims the title "documentary" in the opening credits. This devastating expository/propaganda approach to the "Jewish question" was instrumental in persuading the German citizenry to give the Nazi Reich tacit approval to begin transporting Polish Jews to concentration camps.

References

Bakhtin, Mikhail. *The Dialogic Imagination: Four Essays.* 1981. Reprint. Austin: University of Texas Press. 2004.

Bordwell, David. *Narration in the Fiction Film.* Madison, Wisconsin: University of Wisconsin Press. 1985.

Bruzzi, Stella. *New Documentary: A Critical Introduction*, Londres, Routledge. 2000.

Chapman, Jane, and Kate Allison. *Issues in Contemporary Documentary.* Cambridge: Polity Press. 2009.

Corner, John. "Documentary Studies: Dimensions of Transition and Continuity." In *Rethinking Documentary: New Perspectives and Practices*, edited by Wilma De. Jong and Thomas Austin. Berkshire: Open University Press. 2008.

Hatavara, M., Hyvärinen, M., Mäkelä, M., Mäyrä, F., & Hatavara, M. *Narrative Theory, Literature, and New Media: Narrative Minds and Virtual Worlds.* New York, NY: Routledge. 2016.

Harindranath, Ramaswami. *Audience-citizens: The Media, Public Knowledge and Interpretive Practice.* New Dehli: SAGE Publications India. 2009.

Herzog, Werner. *Into the Abyss: Tales of Death. Tales of Life.* United States. IFC Films. 2012.

Hippler, Fritz. *The Eternal Jew.* Germany: International Historic Films. 1940.

Klapp, Orrin Edgar. "Dramatic Encounters." *Symbolic Leaders: Public Dramas and Public Men.* Chicago: Aldine Pub. 1964.

Manning, Jane. *Deadly Women: Malicious Hearts.* Beyond International. 2013.

Melnyk, George. *Film and the City: The Urban Imaginary in Canadian Cinema.* Edmonton, Alberta: Athabasca University Press. 2014.

Morris, Erroll. *The Thin Blue Line.* United States. Public Television Playhouse. 1988

Murley, Jean. *The Rise of True Crime: Twentieth Century Murder and American Popular Culture.* Westport, Conn.: Praeger Publishers. 2008.

Nichols, Bill. "Documentary: A Fiction (Un)like Any Other." In *Representing Reality: Issues and Concepts in Documentary*, Bloomington, IN: Indiana University Press. 1981.

Nichols, Bill. *Introduction to Documentary*. Second ed. Bloomington, IN: Indiana University Press. 2001.

Nichols, Bill. "Performing Documentary." In *Blurred Boundaries: Questions of Meaning in Contemporary Culture*, Bloomington, IN: Indiana University Press. 1994.

Renov, Michael. *Theorizing Documentary*. New York, NY: Routledge. 1993.

Ricciardelli, Lucia. *American Documentary Filmmaking in the Digital Age: Depictions of War in Burns, Moore, and Morris*. New York, NY: Routledge. 2015.

Robinson, Tasha. "The Problem with "based on a True Story" *The Dissolve*. Accessed August 18, 2015. https://thedissolve.com/features/the-conversation/156-the-problem-with-based-on-a-true-story/. 2013.

Wollen, Peter. "Godard and Counter Cinema: *Vent d'Est*," *Afterimage* 4. 1972.

Part III

Religious & Cultural Studies

6. *Looking Inside the Coffin: An Overview of Contemporary Human Vampirism and Its Relevance for Forensics Professionals*

DJ WILLIAMS & JOHN EDGAR BROWNING

Introduction

This chapter provides an overview of human vampirism and its relevance to criminology and forensics. To begin, however, we will first introduce how supernatural vampire legends and myths reflect human attributes and sensibilities, helping to give rise to the vampire's widespread popularity, and afterwards discuss the blurring of legend and reality as illustrated through such historical figures as Vlad Tepes and Erzebet Bathory. We will then discuss Caroline Picart and Cecil Greek's work on "Gothic criminology" and introduce diverse forms and interpretations of contemporary vampirism, including human or real vampirism vs. clinical vampirism and Renfield Syndrome. We hope to demonstrate how understanding diverse forms of vampire self-identification can be valuable for forensics professionals, particularly in showing its complex inter-workings and relative benignity. Rare modern cases of violent criminal vampirism, particularly involving brutal killings, also will be noted. In short, we will highlight what forensics professionals need to know in distinguishing between criminal/dangerous and acceptable forms of contemporary human vampirism.

The Vampire(s) of Legend and Myth

Brief Historical Overview

The vampire of folklore hitched a ride to America aboard colonial ships brimming with old-world legend and rumor. However, Paul Barber's (1998) seminal treatment of the European "revenant" or vampire of folklore helps to show that the figure these passengers had in mind little resembles its undead counterpart on screen. The vampire that haunted Central and Eastern Europeans 300 years ago was essentially the ghost of a recently deceased relative or neighbor who at night would feed upon villagers to satiate its hunger for blood or "energy." After several attacks, frightened villagers usually assembled at the grave of the suspected vampire, in many cases, the first deceased villager, and proceeded to exhume the body after it had lain for weeks in the earth. Unfortunately, little was understood at the time about natural decomposition (e.g. the bloating of the body, blood-tainted liquid around the orifices, opened eyes, mouth agape, etc.), so naturally they assumed that what lied before them in the open grave was irrefutable evidence that the deceased had indeed been issuing forth from its final resting place and attacking the living. Villagers would then proceed to kill the corpse a "second time," often using a stake, decapitation, fire, or any number of means.

Meanwhile, across the Atlantic, the vampire began to appear in American newspapers as early as the 1700s, though not always in the folkloric sense. Instead, it often appeared as a pejorative to describe various corporations and professions, especially bankers and politicians. Even manufacturers began to employ the figure of the vampire to describe certain illnesses and sell new medicinal treatments. Science, too, invoked the vampire to characterize and name new species of squid and bat, a development newspapers at the time were eager publicize on account of John Polidori's enormously popular *The Vampyre; A Tale* (1819). Polidori's novella was an instant success throughout Europe, but its real impact was in helping to metamorphose the corpse-like revenant or vampire of the peasantry that had for centuries dominated folklore into the suave, blue-blooded vampire or "Fatal Man" (Pirie, 2009).

Meanwhile, New England and surrounding areas suffered from their own vampire scourge, employing, just like their European cousins, similar apotropaics (means of warding off or defending against evil) to defend themselves against the "dangerous dead," to use Barber's apt term. From Vermont, New Hampshire, Connecticut, Massachusetts, New Jersey, Rhode Island, and Maine, to New York, Illinois, Pennsylvania, and Ontario, eighteenth and nineteenth century newspapers documented stories of locals exhuming the graves of their relatives and neighbors in order to perform certain rites.

According to Michael E. Bell's (2010) seminal work on the topic, these events lasted right up until the turn of the century. Indeed, the nineteenth century marked a curious, yet exciting time for the vampire: science, folklore, grave disinterment, literature, all converged to produce a period that would transform the vampire forever.

Human Attributes—Anthropomorphic Vampires or Vampiric Humans, or Both?

Humans have long been fascinated with vampires. Vampire-like myths have existed for thousands of years across a range of cultures and locations (Melton, 1999), and vampires in movies and contemporary popular culture continue to attract large audiences (Fischoff et al., 2002/2003). So what is it that accounts for such a longstanding fascination with vampires? An obvious answer, yet one that surprisingly is sometimes overlooked, is that vampires seem to occupy a curious space between life and death. Unlike other species, human beings know that death is inevitable, and from sometime in early childhood we realize that each of us will die. Such knowledge of the inevitability of death impacts all sorts of human beliefs and practices in profound ways.

In his classic *Denial of Death*, Becker (1973) explained how character development is formed around the process of denying mortality and that such denial is necessary in order to function. More recently, sociologist James Aho (2011), exploring a similar vein, discussed in *Sociological Trespasses: Interrogating Sin and Flesh*, how a variety of diverse social issues and practices involving the corporeal body, including racism, collective violence, body obsession, sickness, and environmental concerns, are products of the transference of aspects of ourselves onto objects that are independent of ourselves. He explains how this transference occurs in response to a hope that such objects and social causes "out there" enable us somehow to escape or deny the existential crisis of knowing that personal death is coming.

As Becker and Aho have documented, the unconscious denial of death and attempts at navigating personal existential crises seem to be widespread and common. They have argued that "normal" social and cultural practices with a popular rationale still function to distract us from the reality of our own death. Vampires, of course, directly play with those fears while perhaps feeding a small sense of hope that somehow we may escape death's finality. The increased sexualization of vampires in popular culture adds another dimension of power to unrecognized hopes of transcending death.

Besides fucking (quite literally) with the ultimate binary of life and death,[1] mythical vampire figures also blur other common binaries. Despite common socially constructed binaries in everyday life that are present everywhere we turn—such as self/other, us/them, child/adult, private/public, personal/professional—our lived realities are far more complex and ambiguous. Vampires remind us of this. Vampires are intelligent, strong, assertive, powerful, and seductive, yet at the same time they are abhorrent and frightening. They possess a wide range of attributes that are both desirable and repulsive. This curious mix of attributes provides a powerful allure to vampires because vampires are reflections of ourselves as humans. Human beings are capable of amazing things, yet at the same time we all have limitations and imperfections. Importantly then, vampires bridge, or hint at, core binary fallacies that deal with interpretations of ourselves and our lived experiences.

Historical Figures like Vlad Tepes and Erzebet Bathory and the Blurring of Legend and Reality

While mythical vampire figures have long reflected human characteristics, an accelerated blurring of legend and reality occurred based on factual reports of two specific rulers in Europe, Vlad Tepes and Erzebet Bathory. Vlad Tepes, the son of Vlad Dracul, ruled in Romania during the 1400s and seemed to take great delight in finding creative ways to torture and impale, and then publicly display, his enemies. Not only is he well-known for his viciousness, but also for the tens of thousands of people he killed during his brief reign. Erzebet Bathory, sometimes referred to as the “Blood Countess” or the “Female Dracula,” was born in the next century (1560) and held power at Castle Sarvar in Hungary. She was particularly sadistic and enjoyed devising creative ways to torture and kill, such as stripping victims during the winter, taking them outside in freezing temperatures, and pouring water on them until they froze to death. However, it was her practice of capturing peasant girls, killing them, and then bathing in their blood that led to her being labelled a human vampire. Historical nuances of Vlad Tepes loosely helped in shaping Bram Stoker’s creation of the classic *Dracula*, as well as more recent versions of the contemporary vampire.

The Vampire’s Popularity and Cultural Dissemination

Following *Dracula*’s publication in England by Bram Stoker in 1897, then in America in 1899, the vampire found a prosperous home both in short fiction and in Vaudeville variety acts. However, today’s iconic vampiric figure did not emerge internationally until the release of Tod Browning’s *Dracula* (Universal, 1931), starring Béla Lugosi. In the early part of the twentieth century, film became the fastest growing entertainment medium in the world, especially among the lower classes. As a result, Lugosi’s endearing portrayal firmly enshrined into popular entertainment not only Stoker's indelible Count but the figure of the vampire as well. Filmic portrayals of the vampire continue to prosper throughout the 1930s and, if to a lesser extent, in the 1940s, until by the 1950s England's Hammer Film Productions effectively revitalizes Dracula and the vampire. In 1958, Christopher Lee emerged as the new Dracula, and over the next fifteen years vampire and *Dracula* films explode onto the market once more, not only in English-speaking nations but also in international markets influenced by American and English cinema. After the mid-1970s, however, vampire and *Dracula* films slowed down once more without regaining substantial strength again in America or abroad until just prior to and with the release of *Bram Stoker's Dracula* (Columbia 1992), starring Gary Oldman. Since the early-1990s, vampires generally and Dracula particularly have prospered across multiple genres outside film, including television and documentaries, as well pornography, animated features, comic books, and video games (Browning & Picart, 2010).

The vampire is inextricably tied to culture; the vampire is a shape-shifter, refusing encapsulation, reduction, or restriction. And, its ability to transmute and evolve alongside national and social ills has and continues to afford it much prosperity, in not only film but literature as well. Of particular note in the vampire's lineage in the last fifty years, and of modern import, are *Dark Shadows*'s (1966–1971) and Anne Rice's *Interview with the Vampire* (1976), the latter's central character of Louis de Pointe du Lac exceeding *Dark Shadows*'s unforgettable Barnabas Collins in further creating the real possibility of a sympathetic vampire. The importance of this development is twofold. For it leads to notable twenty-first century examples of sympathetic or outright positive vampire figures, as in Charlaine Harris's *Sookie Stackhouse Novels* (2001-) (and its television spin-off with HBO's *True Blood* [2008-]) or Stephenie Meyer's *Twilight* series (2005–2008), both playing central roles in the "vampire renaissance" that arose and fell during America's recent economic recession. However, as we will explain momentarily, developing alongside Barnabas, Louis, Sookie, and Edward is a subcultural community of equal or greater genealogical significance in the development of the modern vampire.

Gothic Criminology

Theoretical Overview

Caroline Picart and Cecil Greek (2007) treat of how our "ongoing fascination with evil, as simultaneously repellant and irresistibly attractive, both in the Hollywood film, criminological case studies, popular culture and even public policy," gestures towards the emergence of what they term "Gothic criminology," an area of study that focuses particularly on themes likes "blood lust, compulsion, fear, godlike vengeance, and power and domination" (p. 11). Picart and Greek take the position that "[r]ather than assuming that film and the media tell us little about the reality of criminological phenomena, 'Gothic criminology'... recognizes the complementarity of critical academic and aesthetic accounts of deviant behavior as intersecting with public policy in complex, nonreductive ways" (p. 11). In short, "Gothic criminology," in "connect[ing] reel worlds with the look of the 'real' world, while still mythologizing the serial killer as a Gothic construction," (Picart & Greek, 2009, p. 40) effectively

> gestures towards an account that moves in between the realms of Gothic fiction and film, which entertains its horrified and fascinated readers with unreal horrors attendant upon a realistically/cogently imagined fictional world, and factual cases (e.g. of stalkers, serial murderers, terrorists, rouge cops) framed in Gothic terms, which are essential to plotting the social construction of where evil resides within modernity. (Picart & Greek, 2007, p. 11)

Caroline Picart and Vampires

Films like *Silence of the Lambs* (1990), *Immortality* (1998), and *Hannibal* (2001) in which "the figures of the vampire and the serial killer blur into each other" (Picart & Greek, 2009a, p. 48) effectively exploit "the mythic power of the vampire narrative" and in the process demonstrate the "'natural' slippage from the realms of the natural/'cinema verite' to the supernatural/mythic [which] is what enables the Gothicization of the serial killer as vampiric" (Picart & Greek, 2009a, p. 40). Picart and Greek are also apt to note, in light of all three films, how "it is striking that in both the factual accounts and the popular imaginary, it is the white male," in keeping with criminological statistics, "who simultaneously occupies the dangerous and endangered positions of being the victimized Monster ... and glamorous and superhuman predator" as the seductive vampiric genius (p. 41). Take Hannibal Lecter, for example. Picart and Greek point out that although "there are technical differentiations between cannibals and vampires," *Silence of the Lambs* and it sequel *Hannibal* "conflate these two, such that Hannibal's vampiric and hypnotic gaze (which is characteristic of vampires, not cannibals) becomes inextricable from his blood-soaked, man-eating teeth (which is ambiguously placed in between cannibalism, an atavistic 'real life' horror, and vampirism, a supernatural horror)" (p. 48). Even still, although *Silence of the Lambs* and *Hannibal* conflate vampirism with cannibalism, both films "restore to the serial killer-cannibal the vampire's aristocraticism, combined with a supernatural intelligence and the ever-present threat of his barely contained physical power," thereby "rationally" explaining, as it were, "Hannibal's ability to terrorize and feed on others' terror" (p. 48).

Browning and Dracula's Cinematic Victimology

Proceeding from the notion of "Gothic criminology," Dracula, like the serial killer, "kill[s]out of an overpowering compulsion, and in similarly periodic and patterned ways" (Picart & Greek, 2009b, p. 97). Scholars have tended to be concerned with the xenophobic implications of blood exchange in Stoker's novel. However, blood politics in the novel have always extended beyond racial hegemony, particularly in relation to the classed and sexed demographics of Dracula's victims. This thematic continues into Dracula's subsequent filmic iterations as well. Dracula's cinematic progeny reveals at a very basic level the progression (or lack thereof) of Western political ideologies about normative sexuality, race, and class since the publication of Bram Stoker's novel in 1897.

Beginning with the Universal film in 1931, the markers of race, class, and sex have prompted studios to segregate certain victims into either visualized or censored representations. The film even goes so far as to disqualify some victims from being "turned" (based on their social or economic standing) or, in some cases, even from serving as mere nourishment for Dracula (based on their sex). Dracula's victimology, which appears to denote a procreatively- and consumptively-defined pattern, demonstrates that the physical attack itself and the subsequent "turning" (*if* it occurs) are exceedingly regulated, even discriminatory, and continue to gesture Victorian sexual politics concerning procreation and "good-breeding." However, Victorian discourses about class and miscegenation that informed Dracula's victim pattern in the novel and in the early film adaptations eventually diminish with later treatments of Stoker's novel on screen. By the end of Christopher Lee's reign as Dracula in the mid-1970s, for example, we see Lee's Dracula bite (and do so on screen) both white *and* "non-white" females of noticeably lower means in Hammer's *Dracula A.D. 1972* (1972), albeit he does so without turning them and subsequently discards their bodies. Interestingly enough, he does bite and turn a male victim. However, the action occurs off-camera. By this, we may conclude that even after 40 years (or since the Universal film), Dracula's pathology still denotes a heteronormative victim pattern in keeping with the same homophobic pattern of Stoker's original novel. Proving little different from Lee's final *Dracula* pictures for Hammer, Columbia's *Bram Stoker's Dracula* (1992) shows few, if any, male-on-male biting sequences (Prince Dracula's journey to England aboard the *Demeter* being the exception, "where, ingeniously, he viciously attacks the all-male crew in wolf form, effectively desexualizing the entire experience") (Browning, 2014, p. 229). Indeed, Dracula does not actually bite, and turn, a male victim onscreen until TriStar's *Dracula 2000* (2000); moreover, moreover the victim also happens to be "non-white." However, the act is reminiscent of early cinematic visualizations of gay male kissing: quick, violent, and forced.

Dracula's seriality in film is as much criminological as it is mythic through the sexually-, racially-, and socially-encoded victim pattern he displays. However, by reassessing the censorial and representational development of Dracula's bite through his victims and their respective typologies (in relation to sexed, raced, and socially classed demographics), we are able to uncover the complex ways blood politics have manifested across cinematic history. Equally striking, the critical lens we apply to Dracula seems to work effectively on generalized vampire narratives, too. Thus, interrogating Dracula's and the vampire's victimology offers a fruitful perspective into ideologically progressive and conservative forces at work in cinematic representations. Cultural theorist and philosopher Laurence A. Rickels (1999) offers a productive comment on the matter, that with any proper examination of the vampire, "we will find that we must first be sure we know what is being sucked and what or who exactly is doing the sucking" (p. 7).

Vampirism and Culture: Beyond Hollywood

The Vampire in Mainstream Culture: Contemporary Forms and Interpretations

There is a community of people who regard vampirism as an essential part of their being. These self-described human or real vampires consume human and/or animal blood (sanguinarian), or absorb psychic energy (psi-vamp), or do both (hybrid), out of a need which they adamantly claim derives from the lack of natural energies their bodies produce. This self-described nature is, for them, a condition in which they claim to have neither a choice nor the freedom to change. And, should they refrain from feeding on blood or energy, members of this community attest to feeling weak and experiencing an overall diminished well-being. However, it is important to differentiate this community from one of its contemporaries. As John Edgar Browning (2015) explains, real vampirism is most assuredly not

> the sole adoption of Gothic dress and prosthetic fangs for aesthetic purposes, as though real vampirism were merely a practice or fad that one might adopt one day and discard the next. Such a description denotes an entirely different class of people, which the real vampire community has termed "lifestylers." To real

> vampires, Gothic or dark clothing and fangs are … merely supplementary *identificatory* markers of, or hegemonic modes of group expression for, their *inherent* condition (much in the same way that same-sex desire, for example, is categorically distinct from, and in no way dependent upon, the myriad cultural practices of the gay community).

While people may choose to adopt the particular forms associated with lifestyle vampirism for various reasons, real vampires describe their vampirism as chronic and immutable (Laycock, 2009, 2010). In other words, it is not chosen. While some forms of vampire lifestyle identification, particularly that among younger people drawn to vampire pop culture phenomena, may be attributed to a *narrative collective-assimilation hypothesis*, where experiencing a narrative leads one to become part of the collective described therein (Gabriel & Young, 2011), real vampire identification does not seem to be based on this psychological process. Thus, it resists and challenges common explanations of vampire self-identification, and may be perceived by outsiders as pathological or perhaps dangerous in some way.

Real Vampirism: Historical and Scholarly Overview

Browning's Work

Browning's entree into the field of Real Vampire Studies came by way of intensive ethnographic fieldwork in New Orleans, whose vampire community was decimated by Hurricane Katrina. The terms "vampire community," "real vampire community," or "modern vampire community," as Browning lays out, did not achieve regular use until the late 1990s, and at that time only referring to a network of online message boards and chat rooms (Browning, 2014). Regardless, a network of people who self-identified as vampire had already existed, albeit disjointedly, for at least two decades prior to the late 1990s. Although their exact numbers are unknown, in the 1970s people openly or secretively identifying as vampire were attending many of the same social gatherings (i.e. *Dark Shadows* conventions and other vampire fan organizations, bondage and S&M gatherings frequented by blood fetishists and other willing blood donors, Goth clubs etc.), and in the process they began networking for the first time and identifying blood and energy donors. Limited print runs of self-printed newsletters (or 'zines) also began appearing at this time, and like the aforementioned conventions and gatherings, they were particularly beneficial by helping to merge into one interconnected community a number of real vampire groups and individuals scattered across the United States.

Dr. Jeanne Keyes Youngson founded the Count Dracula Fan Club (now The Vampire Empire) in 1965 as an organization dedicated to Dracula and vampire fiction and film. However, by the early to mid 1970s Youngson began receiving letters from people self-identifying as vampire, so the organization's purview was extended, making her fan club the first research organization to study real vampires and leading Youngson (1997) to publish a casebook of some of her correspondence with these individuals. Another notable early researcher was Stephen Kaplan. He formed in 1972 the Vampire Research Center and supervised a "vampire hotline" that received numerous phone calls, mostly hoaxes, but some of them did appear to be from real vampires. Kaplan, like Youngson, met in person with some of his phone responders and went on to detail these encounters in what remains in the field of Real Vampire Studies a canonical (though problematic) text (Kaplan, 1984). Following Youngson and Kaplan in chronological significance, Martin V. Riccardo founds in 1977 the Vampire Studies Society and prints a quarterly newsletter entitled, *Journal of Vampirism*. Also, the Vampire Information Exchange emerged in 1978 and continued to publish the *Vampire Information Exchange Newsletter (VIEN)* through to the mid-2000s. In the 1980s and 1990s, other pertinent scholars would include folklorists, researchers and paranormalists, journalists, and criminologists, like Norine Dresser, Rosemary Ellen Guiley, Carol Page, and Katherine Ramsland. In addition to a plethora of scholarship, the 1990s also ushered in two historically significant events that would have a profound impact on the real vampire community. Anne Rice conventions began to appear at this time, providing a bounty of socializing and networking opportunities to closeted and unaffiliated real vampires. Of perhaps greater importance, however, to the present state of the real vampire community is the publication of White Wolf's *Vampire: The Masquerade*, which lays the ground rules for a vampire role-playing game and created, if inadvertently, a social space as well within which real vampires could and did begin to congregate and network. *Vampire: The Masquerade* introduced simultaneously to real vampires a lexicon of terms, conventions, and protocols that many in the community culturally adapted for its own needs and purposes, in the end helping to solidify the mainstream identity we see today.

In the last decade, the real vampire community has grown exponentially, and it owes much of this prosperity to the Internet. Before the Internet's strengthening in the 2000s, real vampires existed in isolated pockets and depended mainly upon geographically close fan conventions and low-circulation newsletters for communication. The internet in effect dissolved these geographic limitations and made almost entirely obsolete the need for print correspondence, opening up for the first time vastly more efficient e-communication through online forums and chat rooms. As a result, the late 2000s through mid 2010s have introduced a new wave of scholarship on real vampirism, including works by actual vampire community members like Michelle Belanger, Corvis Nocturnum, and Atlanta vampire community leader Merticus of the Atlanta Vampire Alliance (AVA). Important academic works of this period include those by pioneer in the field Joseph Laycock (2009, 2010, 2015) whose body of work includes book- and article-length works in ethnology and religious studies; followed by D. J. Williams's (2008, 2009, 2013; Williams & Prior, 2015) article-length studies in sociology and leisure studies; John Edgar Browning's (2010a, 2010b, 2011, 2014, 2015) article-length studies in ethnography (informed by his intensive ethnographic fieldwork conducted in 2009–2011 in the New Orleans metropolitan area, and by supplementary ethnographic work in 2011–2013 in Buffalo, New York), film and media studies, and cultural studies; and John Morehead's religious studies.

Williams's Work

Williams has professional experience as both a former forensics practitioner (forensic social work) and as an interdisciplinary researcher (leisure studies, criminology, social work). His work in the area of criminology illustrates that many forms of crime can be explained as specific forms of deviant leisure (Williams, 2005, 2006; Williams & Walker, 2006). However, many forms of deviant leisure, including consensual bondage-discipline-sadomasochism (BDSM) and real vampirism, are neither criminal nor substantially dangerous when practiced with an ethical mindset, but may be understood in many cases as healthy forms of leisure (Williams, 2013, 2015a). It is noteworthy that the researchers (noted herein) who have spent considerable time with members of the real vampire community have reported feeling generally safe and not at significant risk when conducting their research.

Real vampirism, while understood as an alternative identity, may also be, in terms of both specific feeding practices and participation in community events, a form of positive deviant leisure (Williams, 2015a). Despite that real vampirism is commonly assumed by both professional and lay members of the mainstream as reflecting psychopathology, there is no evidence to support such a view. Not surprisingly, a recent exploratory study found that real vampires were afraid to disclose their self-identified vampirism to helping professionals, despite formal ethical admonitions for clinicians to approach clients with openness and without sociocultural bias (Williams & Prior, 2015). In contrast, a leisure perspective acknowledges that freely chosen, intrinsically motivated experiences that are thus consistent with one's identity often provide important physical, psychological, and social benefits. In other words, people choose their leisure, whatever form it may take, because it is personally meaningful, enjoyable, and provides substantial positive effects. Consistent with leisure experience generally, many vampires claim to obtain important physical and psychological benefits from feeding. Williams has observed that intimate feeding experiences potentially may provide spiritual effects in some cases (Williams, 2015b), which reflects a qualitatively different leisure benefit.

Clearly, there is much demographic diversity across the vampire community and notable variations in specific vampires' behaviors and practices. While psychological science has much to contribute in understanding real vampirism, other disciplines can, and already do, add important knowledge. Thus, it is important to avoid relying on narrow interpretations of real vampirism. Due to such rich diversity and variation associated with real vampirism, it is exciting that scholars from different disciplines and theoretical orientations have begun to explore this interesting topic.

"Real" vs. Clinical Vampirism and Renfield Syndrome

Real vampirism may be perceived by outsiders as being particularly deviant precisely because it challenges popular normalizing discourses from psychiatry and medicine to Judeo-Christian religion, and forensics. While it may be tempting for many professionals to label real vampires as simply delusional or reflecting some form of psychopathology, this is a mistake. Many real vampires seem to understand themselves as being ontologically different from others, and they have come to utilize the metaphor of the vampire as a way of structuring this ontological meaning. However, vampires function rather normally in multiple aspects of their personal and professional lives. Real vampire self-identification generally does not seem to reflect significant impairment in social and occupational functioning that often underlies psychiatric disorders classified in the *Diagnostic and Statistical Manual of Mental Disorders* (American Psychiatric Association, 2013). It is generally expected from the vampire community that vampires treat their donors respectfully and that feeding is practiced with safety and mutual consent.

Sometimes the unofficial term "clinical vampirism," which draws from vampire mythology, is used to describe various problematic psychological conditions. For example, "vampire personality disorder" has been used to describe people who seem to have a longstanding pattern of draining the psychological energy of those around them (Ramsland, 2002). Sometimes professionals may refer to "Renfield Syndrome" as a form of clinical vampirism where an individual during childhood may experience excitement at the sight of blood (perhaps after a minor injury), which is later paired with sexual fantasies during puberty, and eventually acted out via autovampirism and drinking the blood of animals. However, Ramsland (2012) explained that this "disorder" was fabricated and meant to be "fang in cheek." Also included under the umbrella of clinical vampirism are forensics cases where offenders have drunk the blood of their victims, such as Wayne Boden, "the vampire rapist," who drank blood during acts of sexual violence, or John Haigh, who claims to have drunk the blood of his murder victims. Such extreme forensics are also labeled as vampiric based on the mythical vampire figure and have well-established psychiatric explanations that are typically rooted in violent offenders' lack of empathy and their strong desires to control and hold significant power over their victims.

The "Real" Vs. the "Reel"

Understanding Diverse Forms of Vampire Self-Identification

Value to Forensics Professionals

It is important for academics and professionals to understand the many diverse forms of vampire self-identification. Indeed, there is a multitude of ways that individuals may identify as vampires, including adopting a real vampire identity or participating in numerous lifestyle vampire behaviors, or perhaps through being labelled externally as having some form of clinical vampirism. However, labels hold power that can significantly impact individuals' lives. Overgeneralization and misinterpretation when applied to specific cases potentially can be severely unjust and costly. While we want to avoid creating "false negative" cases wherein a person of interest (or suspect) is assessed to not be a significant danger to society when, in fact, he or she is, at the same time "false positive" cases, wherein the individual is judged to be dangerous or criminal but in fact is not, is also a severe miscarriage of justice.

Many forensics professionals may not be aware that there are large numbers of people who self-identify as vampires. Thus, it may be easy for professionals to defer automatically to normalizing discourses that assume psychopathological explanations for such self-identification. In this sense, self-identified vampirism has much in common with BDSM, whereas such practices frequently are assumed to reflect psychological dysfunction yet accumulating scholarly literature shows otherwise (for a review, see Williams, 2013). Similarly, existing publications on vampirism geared specifically for forensics professionals (i.e., Keyworth, 2009; Perlmutter, 2003/2004, 2004) do not adequately capture the extensive diversity of various forms, motivations, and practices of self-identified vampirism and how these may play out in very different ways. With this in mind, we offer the following recommendations for better understanding vampires, in the hopes of contributing to more thorough forensics assessments, thus reducing probabilities of both false positives and false negatives:

(a) Professionals should become familiar with the many possible ways that individuals may identify as vampires. We have discussed multiple ways that people may self-identify herein and have included numerous references to the work of other vampire scholars.
(b) Recognize that, applying gothic criminology and media studies, our perceptions and interpretations of specific crimes and criminals are heavily shaped by broader cultural (and pop cultural) myths and representations. We are always embedded in social and cultural contexts. Forensics professionals should become more aware of these unconscious contextual factors that shape our interpretations of forensic science.
(c) Ask many questions about specific cases. Simply claiming to be vampire offers little information; details matter. Professionals need to know how this person identifies as a vampire and what this label subjectively means to the individual. Is the person a real vampire or lifestyle vampire? If a real vampire, how long has the person identified this way? What is her or his preferred feeding method? How does the individual gain access to donors? Is the feeding process safe and consensual? For a lifestyle vampire, how and why does the individual identify this way? Is he or she part of a specific vampire community, house, or clan? What specific practices does this vampire engage in? How structured and organized is the group? Are there specific symbols that are utilized and what are the shared group meanings of these symbols? Professionals should seek as much information as possible and try to avoid assumptions. Obviously, professionals should consider a specific individual's past history in terms of whether or not there are prior charges that involve violence. In other words, past behavior is a much better predictor of future behavior than an unconventional label.
(d) Professionals should approach the topic of vampirism critically and from a multidisciplinary perspective. As we noted earlier, one strength of contemporary academic work on human vampirism is its transdisciplinary nature. The topic of vampirism exists in criminological and psychiatric literature, but it is also present in religious studies, history, medicine, cultural studies, media and literary studies, sociology, and leisure. Multiple approaches, of course, offer a more complete understanding, which then improves the assessment process.

Rare Modern Cases of Criminal Vampirism

Cases of well-documented criminal vampirism are rare, yet these extreme cases, usually involving serial murder, receive much media attention and are thus well-known among both law enforcement personnel and the public. Such famous cases include Fritz Haarmann (Germany), John Haigh (Great Britain), Richard Chase (U.S.A.), Wayne Boden (Canada), Andrei Chikatilo (Russia), and Tsutomu Miyazaki (Japan). Sometimes distinctions are made between vampire serial killing, where victims' blood is consumed, and cannibal killers, such as Jeffrey Dahmer, wherein victims' flesh is eaten. Other reports do not necessarily distinguish between the two.

One of the most well-known criminal vampirism cases in recent years involved Rod Ferrell of Kentucky, who claimed to be a vampire and started a small clan with a few friends. The group took a road trip south and on November 25, 1996 while in Florida, Ferrell murdered Naomi Ruth Queen and Richard Wendorf, who were the parents of a friend who Ferrell earlier had assisted in running away from home. The news made worldwide news headlines in large part because Ferrell claimed to be a vampire and had started a vampire clan. Yet again, as Picart and Greek reported, this case was a blending of the "real" and the "reel," which captured, and continues to hold, public interest.

Dracula's Victimology and How It Can Inform Professional Practice

The overlap of vampiric narratology with serial murder is compelling, primarily or especially because it has and continues to hide in plain sight. Vampires "are more likely to offer," as David Punter and Glennis Byron (2004) attest, "a site of identification rather than a metaphor for what must be abjected, and with the movement from the metaphorical to the metonymical, the vampire increasingly serves to facilitate social commentary on the human world" (p. 271). Dracula's and the vampire's seriality in popular narratives offers behavioral commentary as well that may offer practical uses as a criminological tool for (re)assessing criminal patterns.

Uncovering how blood politics and vampire attacks are complexly imbricated in film or other similar popular narrative forms could open up new and meaningful ways of tracing patterned behaviors in real life, perhaps benefitting cold case files or lending to psychological studies generally. Dracula and vampire narratives demonstrate the fluidity between "real"/"reel" worlds, between fictive crimes and the human psyche. Where one ends and the other begins is a distinction that should matter less for some professionals.

Concluding Remarks

Vampires and violent criminal behavior are topics that blend together and continue to fascinate large numbers of people, yet the roots of both remain in common human experiences and processes. Herein, we have discussed the widespread development of cultural myths involving vampires as closely reflecting mere humans, the creation and continued popularity of *Dracula* and vampires in media and film studies, and Picart and Greek's "gothic criminology" in illustrating the blurring that occurs in the construction and interpretation of both vampires and particular forms of violent crimes. At the same time, there are people who self-identify in numerous possible ways as human vampires or vampire-humans. Some rare forms are legitimately dangerous; however, many others are not. When trying to understand and make sense of any particular vampire, we must approach such investigation of the vampire thoroughly, critically, while also remembering to look carefully and frequently in the mirror at ourselves.

Note

1. It should be noted that precise moments of "life" or "death" do vary, for example, "biological death" versus "clinical death."

References

Aho, James. *Sociological trespasses: Interrogating sin and flesh.* New York: Lexington, 2011.

American Psychiatric Association. *Diagnostic and statistical manual of mental disorders (5th edi.).* Washington, DC: Author, 2013.

Barber, Paul. *Vampires, burial, and death: Folklore and reality.* New Haven, CT: Yale University Press, 1988.

Becker, Ernest. *The denial of death.* New York: Free Press, 1973.

Bell, Michael. *Food for the dead: On the trail of New England's vampires.* New York: Carroll & Graf, 2010.

Browning, John Edgar. Interviews with the vampires: The real story behind New Orleans' vampire subculture. In *Deep South Magazine, Spring Issue.* (2010a).

Browning, John Edgar. Conversations with real vampires. In *Deep South Magazine, Fall Issue.* (2010b).

Browning, John Edgar. The dangerous dead: Vampire mythology in the House of Night series. In P. C. Cast (Ed.), *Nyx in the house of night.* Dallas, TX: Smart Pop, 2011.

Browning, John Edgar. Classical Hollywood horror. In Harry M. Benshoff (Ed.), *A companion to the horror film.* Malden, MA: John Wiley & Sons, 2014.

Browning, John Edgar. The real vampire community: A concise history. In Montague Summers (Author) & John Edgar Browning (Ed.), *The vampire in Europe: A critical edition.* Berkeley, CA: Apocryphile Press, 2014.

Browning, John Edgar. The real vampires of New Orleans and Buffalo: A research note towards comparative ethnography. *Palgrave Communications, 1.* doi: 10.1057/palcomms.2015.6.

Browning, John Edgar, & Picart, Caroline Joan. *Dracula in Visual Media: Film, Television, Comic Book and Electronic Game Appearances, 1921–2010.* Jefferson, NC: McFarland, 2010.

Fischoff, Stuart, Dimpoulos, Alexandra, Nguyen, Francios, & Gordon, Rachel. Favorite movie monsters and their psychological appeal. *Imagination, Cognition and Personality, 22,* 401–426. (2002/2003).

Gabriel, Shira, & Young, Ariana F. (2011). Becoming a vampire without being bitten: The narrative collective-assimilation hypothesis. *Psychological Science, 22,* 990–994.

Kaplan, Stephen. *Vampires are.* Palm Springs, CA: ETC Publications, 1984.

Keyes-Youngson, Joanne. *Private files of a vampirologist: Case histories & letters.* Chicago: Adams Press, 1997.

Keyworth, David. (2009). Crime and the contemporary vampire subculture. *Australian Police Journal, 63,* 170–173.

Laycock, Joseph. *Vampires today: The truth about modern vampires.* Santa Barbara, CA: Praeger, 2009.

Laycock, Joseph. (2010). Real vampires as an identity group: Analyzing causes and effects of an introspective survey by the vampire community. *Nova Religio, 14* (1), 4–23.

Laycock, Joseph. *Dangerous games: What the moral panic over role-playing games says about play, religion, and imagined worlds.* Oakland, CA: University of California Press, 2015.

Melton, J. Gordon. *The vampire book: The encyclopedia of the undead.* Canton, MI: Visible Ink Press, 1999.

Perlmutter, Dawn. (2003/2004). The forensics of sacrifice: A symbolic analysis of ritualistic crime. *Anthropoetics, 9*(2), 1–34.

Perlmutter, Dawn. *Investigating religious terrorism and ritualistic crimes.* Boca Raton, FL: CRC Press, 2004.

Picart, Caroline Joan, & Greek, Cecil E. *Monster in and among us: Toward a gothic criminology.* Cranbury, NJ: Associated University Presses, 2007.

Picart, Caroline Joan, & Greek, Cecil E. The compulsions of real/reel serial killers and vampires. In John Edgar Browning & Caroline Joan Picart (Eds.), *Draculas, vampires, and other undead forms: Essays on gender, race, and culture.* Lanham, MD: Scarecrow Press, 2009a.

Picart, Caroline Joan, & Greek, Cecil E. When women kill: Undead imagery in the cinematic portrait of Aileen Wuornos. In John Edgar Browning & Caroline Picart (Eds.), *Draculas, vampires, and other undead forms: Essays on gender, race, and culture.* Lanham, MD: Scarecrow Press, 2009b.

Pirie, David. *The new heritage of horror.* London, England: I. B. Tarius, 2009.

Punter, David, & Byron, Glennis. *The gothic.* Malden, MA: Wiley, 2004.

Ramsland, Katherine. *The science of vampires.* New York: Berkeley, 2002.

Ramsland, Katherine. (2012). Vampire personality disorder. *Psychology Today* (November). Retrieved from: www.psychologytoday.com/blog/shadow-boxing/201211/vampire-personality-disorder

Rickels, Laurence A. *The vampire lectures.* Minneapolis, MN: University of Minnesota Press, 1999.

Williams, DJ (2005). Functions of leisure and recreation activities within a sexual assault cycle. *Sexual Addiction and Compulsivity, 12,* 295–309.

Williams, DJ (2006). Forensic leisure science: A new frontier for leisure scholars? *Leisure Sciences, 28,* 91–95.

Williams, DJ (2008). Contemporary vampires and (blood-red) leisure: Should we be afraid of the dark? *Leisure/Loisir, 32,* 513–539.

Williams, DJ (2009). Deviant leisure: Rethinking "the good, the bad, and the ugly." *Leisure Sciences, 31,* 207–213.

Williams, DJ (2013). Social work, BDSM, and vampires: Toward empowering people with non-traditional identities. *Canadian Social Work, 15,* 10–24.

Williams, DJ (a). From purple roots to dark, sexy, and diverse: The past, present, and future of deviant leisure. In Gordon J. Walker, David Scott, & Monika Stodolska (Eds.), *Leisure matters: The present and future of leisure studies.* State College, PA: Venture, 2015.

Williams, DJ (b). Intersections of vampirism and sexuality: A narrative description of a vampire feeding. In Thomas S. Weinberg & Staci Newmahr (Eds.), *Selves, symbols, and sexualities: An interactionist anthology.* Los Angeles, Sage, 2015.

Williams, DJ, & Prior, Emily E. (2015). Do we always practice what we preach? Real vampires' fears of coming out of the coffin to social workers and helping professionals. *Critical Social Work, 16,* 79–92.

Williams, DJ, & Walker, Gordon J. (2006). Leisure, deviant leisure, and crime: Caution: Objects may be closer than they appear. *Leisure/Loisir, 30,* 193–218.

7. *A* Yiddishe *Cop: Jewish Identity, Police, and Prisoners in Contemporary Law Enforcement*[1]

Sonia Halpern

Introduction

While I was enrolled in an educational outreach initiative with the London Police Service in Ontario, Canada in 2012, consisting of lectures from several officers of varying rank and expertise, an incident compelled me to think about police work as it relates to issues of religious identity. I and the other civilian students of the program, all adults hailing from disparate educational, occupational, and cultural backgrounds were required to take an oath of secrecy as a way to ensure the confidentiality of perpetrators and victims. We were advised that we had one of two options: to recite the religion-based oath while swearing on a Bible or take the secular Oath of Affirmation. As a Jew who learned that the only available Bible was the *New Testament* (a text not part of the Jewish theological canon), I opted to take the Oath of Affirmation, despite my fundamental belief in God. As such, with neither option entirely satisfactory or equitable, I saw the potential for the exclusionary practices of police departments and correctional institutions regarding the religious beliefs and rituals of Jewish officers and Jewish prisoners, respectively.

Specifically, I pondered whether the identities and customs of Jews can be acknowledged and facilitated by these systems, especially given the relatively low numbers of Jewish police and Jewish prisoners in the historical and contemporary worlds of corrections. This article is intended to present, through the enmeshing of police studies and religious studies, an overview and to some extent an ethnography of some of the relevant Jewish issues of the police and of inmates in North America and England (corrections in Israel will not be included in this discussion, as Jews represent the majority of the country's population (74.9%), and, as such, do not face the same issues of marginality that they confront in the diaspora ("Vital Statistics: Latest Population Statistics for Israel," 2015). In so doing, this paper examines how police departments and correctional facilities face a unique challenge in how to balance the individual rights and freedoms of Jewish officers and Jewish criminals (or those of any minority group, for that matter) with the values of uniformity that are perpetuated by military-based hierarchical structures entrusted with serving the common good.

Jewish Issues of the Police

Historical Cultural Context

Although there are numerous Biblical references to Jewish police (Kitaeff 2006, 20), Jews haven't typically been associated with modern policing for several reasons. First, given that modern Jews did not have their own homeland until the 1948 establishment of Israel, Jewish cultural values have not traditionally encouraged careers which prioritize martyrdom for one's country. Second, as representatives of anti-Semitic governments in Eastern Europe where most Jews lived, the police mistreated Jews, abuse which was both anticipated and experienced by immigrants in their new countries (Passamaneck 2003, 17). Third, the police have in many cases historically deemed non-Christian values and associated customs as inherently "suspicious" (Michael Arntfield, pers. asso.), an attitude generating conformity within their organization, which Jews, as a minority group, have resisted in order to maintain their identity and rituals. Fourth, policing is a physically-oriented career for which a post-secondary education has traditionally not been necessary and for which "innovation has been seen as disruptive" (Michael Arntfield, pers. asso.), combined facts which have deterred participation by an intellectually-rooted Jewish culture. Fifth, police work has until recent years, and still today in many Western jurisdictions, been defined by lower wages and social status compared with other careers, undesirable by-products for a largely immigrant group and their offspring pursuing upward mobility (Niederhoffer 1967, 80–81). Finally, policing can be dangerous, a feature that threatens the supreme Jewish value placed on life. Notwithstanding the fact that the *Talmud*, the fundamental text of Rabbinic Judaism, implicitly sanctions the job of law enforcement by favouring work that assists individuals, pursues justice, and contributes to the well-being of society, its specific criteria for a noble occupation does not actually conform to policing's authoritative role, long hours, para-militaristic regimentation, lure of corruption, low wages, and often unseemly environment (Kitaeff 2006, 17–18; Bokser 1951, 106).

Based on all of these factors, then, it should not be unexpected that, historically, low Jewish representation characterized most North American police agencies, including the New York City Police Department (NYPD) prior to World War One (Weissman Joselit 1983, 30). Of ten thousand police officers, "only two hundred [2%], according to the reliable *American Hebrew*, were Jewish—this in a city which by 1910 numbered over one million Jews" (Weissman Joselit 1983, 30). Policing was deemed a job for the Italians and Irish, who, unlike Jews, promoted physicality as part of a masculinist ideology suited to police work, and gravitated to the post in large numbers (Kitaeff 2006, 10; Norwood 2009, 170). In fact, the ultimate compliment for a Jewish officer was to be called "Reilly," signifying that a good Jewish cop (a truncated version of the term "copper") assumed the desired and standardized "Irish traits" of policing (Niederhoffer 1967, 78).

Recognizing the small number of Jewish police officers protecting their own, New York Jewish immigrants united with the city's elite German Jews and "formed a Jewish detective agency" (Weissman Joselit 1983, 10). This organization, sponsored by the Kehillah (Hebrew for "community" or "congregation"), a self-governing body in the Jewish community, worked under the name of the Bureau of Social Morals, and, from 1912 to 1917, was deemed the "Jewish police station" whose job was to seek out criminals within their neighbourhoods and then report them to the police (Weissman Joselit 1983, 10). Jewish citizens also felt a need to prevent and respond to anti-Semitic attacks rampant during this same period, and, as a result, they established additional protective groups in major cities where Jewish immigrants flocked (Norwood 2009, 175). Norwood notes that "in Chicago, 300 Jewish peddlers in the West Side ghetto organized a Protective League in 1901" and "Jews in Boston's Roxbury ghetto in East Boston, alarmed by unprovoked assaults and lack of sympathy from police, organized similar Hebrew Citizens' Protective Leagues" (2009, 175). The formation of these groups was not just a product of the rising crime rate within and directed at the immigrant communities; it spoke to the fact that mainstream police officers lacked understanding of the Jewish plight, and that the numbers of Jewish police were insufficient to adequately address the particular needs of the growing Jewish communities.

The scarcity of Jewish police officers most assuredly contributed to their marginality. Between World War One and the Great Depression of the 1930s when the poor economy in the United States compelled Jewish men to enlist in the steady job of policing, the percentage of Jewish officers in the NYPD was a mere 1% of the standing complement (Niederhoffer 1967, 78; Kitaeff 2006, 6). The fact that, unlike other officers, most of the new Jewish recruits were college-educated also served to create a rift between the culture of "anti-intellectualism" and these recruits who, in addition to their Jewish ancestry, were socio-cultural rarities within the fraternity, a distinction that often made these Jewish officers targets of anti-Semitism (Niederhoffer 1967, 79). Their marginality in policing, in fact, inspired the 1924 establishment of the NYPD's Jewish fraternal group the Shomrim Society: a young Jewish officer was the butt of an anti-Semitic comment, prompting the formation of this organization to safeguard the interests of the Jewish police (NYPD Shomrim Society 2015). The Shomrim Society, *Shomrim* being the Hebrew word for for "watchers" or "guards," became an immediate and overt symbol of the otherness of Jewish officers in the NYPD, and their need for protection, both within and outside their Department.

Historical Cultural Treatments

Within the last four decades, popular media, such as television, has reflected this historical rarity of Jews in policing, and, when they *have* appeared, Jewish self-identification has not been a core aspect of their characters. This lack of representation, in addition to accurately reflecting the historical dearth of Jewish officers in police work, arguably also reflects a combination of the long-standing disconnect between not only Jews and policing, but also the concurrent desire of assimilationist Jewish Hollywood to downplay Jewish content more generally (Zurawick 2003, 5–6). In terms of leading roles, for example, the popular sitcom *Barney Miller* (1975–82) starred the Jewish Hal Linden as the Jewish captain of a Manhattan police station; however, "his identity as a Jew … was never discussed in the workplace or made explicit in other ways" (Gabler, Rich, and Antler 2000, 37). The question then arises: why did the sitcom's creators make him Jewish at all? According to communication and media studies professor Lance Strate, in a series whose goal was to challenge a variety of ethnic stereotypes in its major police characters, a cop who was Jewish fulfilled this objective (Ghosh 2014). Strate adds that the omission of cops who were Irish or Italian, in fact, was an exclusion with which actual officers at the time expressed some dissatisfaction (Ghosh 2014). The 1990s television movie series *Family of Cops* is similarly overt in its Jewish labeling of lead-character, Inspector Paul Fein (Charles Bronson), but the Fein family is otherwise ethnically generic (Gertel 2003, 67). Indeed, names identify their Judaism more than their beliefs and actions. The Inspector's surname along with the maiden name of his deceased wife suggests that Hollywood passed on the archetypal inter-marriage for a Jewish lead character. Yet, even with the family's consternation in response to some anti-Semitic slurs in the first of the three films, "there isn't too much that is really Jewish about *Family of Cops* in any meaningful or noticeable way" (Gertel 2003 67). The movie injects some Jewish elements, including a *yarmulke* (skull-cap)-wearing doctor, an Orthodox Rabbi walk-on, and a child's peculiar reference to a *mezuzah* (an encased prayer on parchment that hangs on the doorpost of a Jewish home), but these painfully forced insertions contribute neither to the Jewish identity of Fein nor to any of the family's Jewish cops.

More recently, the Jewish actor Richard Belzer played a Jewish officer on television, but, although his character had moments in a specific episode that could be characterized as Jewish, the program only minimally investigates his Jewish identity. Belzer played John Munch in both *Homicide: Life on the Streets* (1993–9) and *Law & Order: Special Victims Unit* (1999–2014); but, notwithstanding Munch's long-running crossover character, his "complicated relationship to his religion has been sparingly explored" (Thurm 2013). Munch's Jewishness was only significantly addressed in a single episode of *Homicide* entitled *Kaddish* (the name of the prayer recited by Jewish mourners) about the death of a childhood Jewish friend (Thurm 2013). Arguably, the episode explores his Jewish identity, but does so primarily through his desire to distance himself from it. His remark to the non-Jewish medical examiner that she knows more about Judaism than he does and his disparaging joke that "the only thing Judaism and I have in common is we both don't like to work on Saturdays" (Thurm 2013) allow any further examination of his Judaism to be eclipsed. Granted, audiences eventually see Munch put on a *yarmulke* and enter the *shiva* house (the house of mourning), which he resists throughout the episode, but it is precisely at this point when the episode concludes.

The Jewishness of Mandy Patinkin's Saul Berenson, a CIA officer and integral character on *Homeland* (2011–present), is also inconspicuous, despite the fact that the show is a remake of an Israeli series (*Prisoners of War*) written by the proud, self-identified Jew, Gideon Raff (Gluck 2013). Character Saul Berenson, "looking and sounding like every rumpled Jewish intellectual we've ever seen in the movies" (Harris 2012), recites the *Kaddish* after a deadly terrorist bombing in the Season Two finale; yet, the series rarely reveals crucial aspects of his Jewish identity. Perhaps not coincidentally, Saul Berenson, as with John Munch, primarily conveys his ethnicity as it pertains to the Jewish rituals of death rather than those of life; this association isolates the characters' Jewishness as situational and infrequent, and suggests that it, too, is a fatality.

Predictably, given the uncommon historical and popular associations between the Jews and police, there has been little in the way of meaningful scholarship on this connection. While there are some relevant available news stories through the commercial press, there are a mere handful of books devoted to Jews in police work. These include: *Rookie Cop: Deep Undercover in the Jewish Defense League* (2000) by Richard Rosenthal, a memoir about Rosenthal's assignment with the NYPD to penetrate the JDL in the early 1970s; *Police Ethics and the Jewish Tradition* (2003) *by Stephen Passamaneck,* a scholarly presentation of ethical issues within the context of policing, set against the backdrop of Jewish legal and moral values; and *Jews in Blue: The Jewish American Experience in Law Enforcement* (2006) by Jack Kitaeff, a brief Biblical and historical account of policing, and a compendium of American Jews who have occupied high-ranking positions in law enforcement. Fictionalized Jewish detectives have been examined in the scholarly book by Lawrence Roth, *Inspecting Jews: American Jewish Detective Stories* (2004), and, although primarily a literary study, its clever title reveals the book's attentiveness to the connective issues of Jewish identity and law enforcement central to the other works.

Contemporary Cultural Context

The NYPD's Shomrim Society, a still-thriving police association, continues to function as a crucial connection between the police and Jewish concerns. The Shomrim Society consists of approximately three thousand active and retired male and female NYPD officers of assorted ranks, all of whom are volunteers and pay a nominal membership fee (NYPD Shomrim Society 2015). The organization requires that their members be Jewish, a criterion that, if falling into question, is determined by its spiritual director (Stuart Gang, pers. asso.). In addition to establishing community, social, and educational events that serve Jewish officers and their communities, the Shomrim Society provides its members a network of support and advice from other Jewish personnel within the police, and actively promotes the police as a viable employer for the Jewish community. In New York City, about two thousand of 34,500 officers are identified as Jewish (5.8%) (Gang pers. asso.), a small percentage, given that Jews account for about 13% (just over one million) of the city's population of about eight million. (NYPD 2015; Kestenbaum 2015; Kravitz 2013). In addition, the Shomrim Society offers members the option of purchasing burial rights for themselves and their families in one of two Shomrim-only areas in Jewish cemeteries in Long Island and Queen's (McPhee 2003); members are buried in accordance with Jewish law and their tombstones are inscribed with badge numbers alongside the Hebrew text (McPhee 2003). The fact that Shomrim Societies exist in many of the larger police departments throughout the United States indicates the necessity for Jewish police officers across America to bond with each other and maintain their Jewish distinctiveness.

In London, England, a corresponding organization called the Jewish Police Association (JPA) was established in 2001, and claims more than two hundred members (Jewish Police Association 2013). With a similar mandate as the NYPD Shomrim Society, the JPA recognizes that Jewish police officers as a minority in the Metropolitan Police Service (MPS) could feel alienated within the department and desire the camaraderie of fellow Jewish members. For this reason, as with the Shomrim Societies in the United States, the JPA hosts a number of educational, social, and fundraising events that bring Jewish police officers together, and also connect them with the larger Jewish communities. The JPA is also pro-active in the recruitment of Jewish officers. In 2009, National Improvement Policing Agency (NIPA) Chief Inspector Richard Padwell asserted that relative to the London Jewish population (173,580), there should be 865 (0.5%) Jewish police officers in London, and, in fact, there are only about 150 (.09%) (Symons 2009). The Jewish Police Association acknowledges that this low number is at least partly attributable to the fact that many prospective and existent officers, particularly Orthodox Jews, are viewing policing as inconsistent with their religious practices.

A major concern for some officers in the MPS is whether *yarmulkes* are permitted to be worn by on-duty police. The JPA addresses this issue on their website by depicting an illustration of a *yarmulke* beside a police cap, accompanied by the caption "can you wear both?" (Jewish Police Association 2015), an image that also begs the larger question about the compatibility of being Jewish and an officer for whom a standardized uniform is both compulsory based on standard operating policy as well as tethered to the police's dominant iconography in the arts, media, and popular imagination. The MPS now deems the *yarmulke* worn beneath the cap an "authorized piece of police dress" (Jewish Police Association 2015; Parascandola, Lysiak, and Siemaszko 2012). Hopeful that this reform (and the MPS's approval of beards, which are another sign of religious conviction for male Jews) will attract greater numbers of observant recruits in London (and elsewhere), the JPA sees it as a significant sign of Jewish inclusion (Goldwater pers. asso.; Jewish Police Association 2015).

Some Orthodox officers in other jurisdictions, however, have confronted some resistance regarding their head coverings and beards. Perhaps the most renowned case is that of Detective Steve Riback, who, as a nine-year veteran of the Las Vegas Metropolitan Police Department (LVMPD) in 2007, sued his department for not allowing him to wear a *yarmulke* and beard or, as he also requested, any hat or cap, while at his desk (Thevenot 2007). With lawyers from the American Civil Liberties Union of Nevada, Riback claimed that, as a result of not adhering to Orthodox Jewish custom, he was experiencing "irreparable harm to his emotional and spiritual well-being, and his constitutional rights" (Thevenot 2007). Riback explained that when he worked in the department's vice squad in which he donned a cap and beard as part of his undercover "uniform," he was able to adhere to his Orthodox code of dress, but since being reassigned to an administrative position, he was no longer permitted to do so (Thevenot 2007). In defending the Department, the LVMPD's general counsel stated that "we are a para-military organization, and we remain religion-neutral" (Thevenot 2007); yet, Riback contested this claim, citing that the department permitted on-duty officers to wear International Fellowship of Christian Police Officers pins of an open Bible (Thevenot 2007).

In 2009, the Department was found to have violated Riback's First Amendment right of religious freedom, and the parties settled out of court (Goldman 2009). Riback received $350,000 and permission to wear a baseball cap and short beard, at least until he transfers, a move which would require a new request for religious accommodation (Goldman 2009). Identifying himself as the "The Kosher Cop" on his website of the same name, Riback summarizes the impact of his department's institutional discrimination. He states that throughout his career on the LVMPD, he "has faced many life-threatening situations"; however, none have been as significant as "the decision to become an observant Jew" (The Kosher Cop 2015).

In June 2012, Hasidic NYPD recruit Fishel Litzman, was a month away from receiving his shield when he was summarily fired for not shaving off his beard, despite the fact that *yarmulkes* were permissible (Parascandola, Lysiak, and Siemaszko 2012). The NYPD did not offer a specific reason for the termination, only that Litzman was informed at the outset that the beard would have to be removed (although he even contested this claim) (Parascandola, Lysiak, and Siemaszko 2012). Reasons might have included the safety concerns connected with the gas masks worn during counterterrorism police-training, masks that have to fit directly onto the skin for them to be properly sealed (Parascandola, Lysiak, and Siemaszko 2012). His lawyer argued, however, that many religious Israeli officers have beards, and the gas masks are not an issue, and he ultimately accused the NYPD of religious discrimination (Parascandola, Lysiak, and Siemaszko 2012). The NYPD responded by asserting that they do make allowances for beards based on religious or medical reasons, but insisted that they be no more than one millimeter in length (Parascandola, Lysiak, and Siemaszko 2012). For Litzman, who contended that, as a Hasidic Jew, he was forbidden to cut or shave his beard, the length requirement was irrelevant (Parascandola, Lysiak, and Siemaszko 2012). Litzman, who always wanted to be a cop, has stated that "I will not waver in my firm belief that I can be a successful member of the NYPD and an Orthodox Chasidic [Hasidic] Jew at the same time. I believe that my love of God and my love of the NYPD can co-exist" (Parascandola, Lysiak, and Siemaszko 2012). Notably, eleven years after Sikh rookie Amric Singh Rathour successfully sued the NYPD for firing him for wearing a turban and beard (Parascandola, Lysiak, and Siemaszko 2012), Litzman was vindicated in 2013 when Federal Judge Harold Baer supported his Constitutional rights, underscoring the religious freedom of the approximately twenty-five other Orthodox Jewish officers on the NYPD (Nolan and Parascandola 2013).

Another area of concern for some Jewish police officers is not working on Jewish holidays and *Shabbat* (the Sabbath, which lasts from Friday sundown to Saturday sundown). This issue emerged in 1970s New York when Lou Weisner, consultant for the NYPD recruitment program, initiated weekday police testing so religious Jews would not be excluded from taking the test, typically scheduled on Saturdays (Kitaeff 2006, 9). The NYPD now excuses their religious Jewish officers from working after dusk on Fridays, on Saturdays, and on Jewish holidays (Parascandola, Lysiak, and Siemaszko 2012). To receive accommodation with the least institutional resistance, the JPA encourages all Jewish officers who require time off for religious reasons to plan ahead (Jewish Police Association 2013; Symons 2009). Sergeant Joel Witriol of Brooklyn, for example, now the highest-ranking Hasid in NYPD history, pre-arranged upon his 2014 promotion to have his Sabbath observance accommodated in his new position ("Police Officer Becomes Highest-Ranking Hasid in NYPD History" 2014). That said, the JPA admits that, even when officers provide sufficient notice, accommodating Jewish holidays "is a difficult and contentious issue" (Jewish Police Association 2013; Symons 2009). In 2011, Michael Loebenberg, a Jewish Sergeant in Stamford Hill, England, explained that, despite official concessions for Jewish holidays, it is still a complex issue, as fellow non-Jewish officers can get resentful: "things could get difficult for police officers who don't want to work on *Shabbat* in terms of integrating with teams. Everyone would rather be home with their families on a Saturday, so officers find themselves affected by the attitudes of their colleagues" (Rosen 2011). The Sergeant did not elaborate on how these attitudes got manifested, but they potentially contradict his earlier statement that "there is a perception that large bodies like the police service have an element of anti-Semitism within them but I've never experienced it" (Rosen 2011). Even without receiving work concessions for *Shabbat*, however, some

Orthodox officers can justify working on Friday nights and Saturdays by applying the Biblical principle of *Pikiach Nefesh*: "breaking *Shabbat* to save a life" (Rosen 2011), an obligation that covers an array of threatening circumstances, even when there is no immediate danger to another person.

Nevertheless, the JPA Chairman has asserted that if police departments are going to recruit Orthodox police officers, their holy days and Sabbath observance must be honoured (Symons 2009). Most departments inherently understand the concept of taking off occasional holy days, given the Christian parallels of Christmas and Easter; however, as Loebenberg noted, the Orthodox Jewish requirement of booking off at least one day a week, on a weekend no less, can cause some departmental friction. Yet, while even the most assimilated Jews take off the annual holidays of *Rosh Hashanah* and *Yom Kippur*, they will typically work on the Sabbath, rendering the weekly "problem" moot for most departments.

Adhering to kosher dietary regulations is an additional worry for some prospective and existing officers. Orthodox detective Steve Riback of the LVMPD, reported that, on a daily basis, his unit ate at non-kosher restaurants, prompting him to initiate a request to bring his own food to work (Nehorai 2015). This appeal, he recounted, "subsequently set off a flurry of issues. They said that whatever my sergeant said, I had to do. Without question" (Nehorai 2015). Although Riback was eventually permitted to bring in his own meals, this incident made him realize that being Jewish in the LVMPD could get more challenging with his increasing level of observance (Nehorai 2015). In England, the JPA has arranged that Jewish police officers can bring and store their own food, and, with notice, kosher food also can be brought in for catered events (Jewish Police Association 2013). NPIA Chief Inspector Padwell stated in 2009 that "in terms of kosher food," it has seen "great strides in making the police a more open environment" (Symons 2009). Perhaps this point is best illustrated in New York where Karen Tandy, Chief Administrator of the American Drug Enforcement Agency (DEA) from 2003–07, and Jewish, made a number of changes at the DEA cafeteria to ensure Jewish inclusivity: she banned ham and pork from the cafeteria menu (Kitaeff 2006, 61).

One of the most concerning issues for Jewish officers, all of whom must rely on their colleagues for physical and emotional backing, is pre-meditated, malicious anti-Semitism from within police organizations. As recently as 2014, for example, an NYPD officer of six years, David Attali, claimed that fellow officers "vandalized his locker with anti-Semitic messages, called him a 'dirty Jew', and greeted him with 'Heil Hitler' salutes and hostile text messages" ("Ex-Cop Sues NYPD for Anti-Semitic Harassment" 2015), one with a photograph of Adolf Hitler (Marzulli 2015). Even after he reported and offered evidence of the incidents to the NYPD Office of Equal Employment Opportunity, he was not granted the transfer he requested (Marzulli 2015); "stressed by the harassment," he quit his job just a few months later ("Ex-Cop Sues NYPD for Anti-Semitic Harassment" 2015). Attali sued the city of New York, the five officers he accused, and four supervisors for not relocating him (Marzulli 2015). Retired officer Pete Herley, formerly of the Torrance Police Department of Southern California, traced the pattern of his own department's anti-Semitism: "harmless" Jewish jokes; vandalism of his personal property; and the denial of a promotion, all of which prompted him to leave his position (Pine 2011).

In 2011, Orthodox Jewish officer Steve Harris, a 21-year veteran with the Special Weapons and Tactics (SWAT) team of the Bay Area's Richmond Police Department, admitted that his Judaism can make him feel "isolated" because the few other Jewish officers in his department "[prefer to keep] totally undercover [as Jews]" (Pine 2011). According to Harris, their concealment is attributable to the fact that "they don't want to suffer from anti-Semitism" from within their own department, abuse which, as an observant Jew, he himself has experienced (Pine 2011). Unlike some other concerns of Jewish police officers, however, anti-Semitism is not exclusive to observant Jews, and may be directed at any Jew who possesses a "Jewish appearance" or "behaviour," regardless of his/her level of religiosity. Thus, although not all Jewish officers feel a need to assert their Jewish affiliation, that these officers felt compelled to conceal it exposes an insidious brand of "anti-Semitism by omission," one that likely exists in other North American departments.

Generally, however, police organizations have become increasingly sensitive to issues of anti-Semitism, an awareness demonstrated by their burgeoning programs to promote Jewish inclusivity within police agencies and prevent anti-Semitic acts against citizens. Karen Tandy, for example, had "Jesus" omitted from all official DEA ceremonies and services to avoid the alienation of Jewish police, and Toronto 32 Division authorized the installation of a large outdoor menorah to represent its Jewish police and the relatively large Jewish community it serves, a gesture which, according to Sergeant Lawrence Sager of the Toronto Police Service (TPS), is a North American precedent (Kitaeff 2006, 61; Shefa 2013, B31–2). In terms of law enforcement, the JPA offers training sessions for all officers in the London area who are posted at the bus stops in Orthodox Jewish neighbourhoods, transitory areas that are frequent sites of anti-Semitic attacks ("Bus Safety Initiative" 2010). In Amsterdam, Dutch police are deploying "decoy Jews": they clothe law-enforcers in Jewish religious dress to nab attackers, and equate this strategy with their "decoy prostitutes" "decoy gays" or "decoy grannies" operations (Waterfield 2010). The most extensive anti-Semitism prevention programs are the annual Pre-High Holy Days and Pre-Passover security briefings made by the NYPD to audiences of hundreds of people, including police officers, religious leaders, and community members, to apprise them of potential international and domestic threats to Jewish communities and institutions (NYPD 2009; NYPD 2011).

Even with some significant inroads in recent years in accommodating religious dress, holy days, kosher diets, and anti-Semitism prevention, police departments are still having difficulty recruiting Jewish officers. In the TPS, for instance, located in the Canadian city with the highest Jewish population (approximately 200,000 people, or about 3.3% of Toronto's population, and over half of Canada's Jewish residents), only about fifty of seven thousand police officers are Jewish (0.7%) (The Centre for Israel and Jewish Affairs 2015; Shefa 2014). To try and remedy this problem of recruitment in London, the JPA has initiated within the past few years a specific and unique recruitment strategy in which their goal is to acquire one new officer from every London synagogue (Jewish Police Association 2015). An aggressive recruitment campaign like this one suggests that the police themselves recognize that institutional exclusion and anti-Semitism have been contributing factors of low Jewish enlistment. Ethnic and racial discrimination by the police generally is still a highly-relevant social concern, as evidenced by numerous riots and demonstrations following recent allegations of excessive force against Blacks in the United States. Combine this concern with the low Jewish population, and the fact that, culturally, as discussed, policing is not typically encouraged within North American Jewry, and it is clear that Jewish citizens are not as represented by their own people as much as other groups are. This Jewish under-representation is unsatisfactory, given that, according to Britain's Police Minister Vernon Coker, "our police should reflect the communities they police" (Symons 2009).

In the meantime, to address the lack of Jewish presence in police departments, concerned Jews have established alternative law enforcement agencies to meet the particular needs of Jewish communities. Before the JPA was founded in Britain in 2001, the Community Service Trust (CST) was already established in 1994, and meeting with British police to help protect Britain's Jewish citizens from anti-Semitic attacks (Community Service Trust, pers. asso.). As part of its mandate, the CST offers security recommendations and instruction for Jewish organizations, and safeguards more than six hundred Jewish edifices and one thousand Jewish community events each year, all at no charge (Community Service Trust 2015). The CST has a close working relationship with police, and even produced a practical guide for police officers entering Jewish homes or facilities (Community Service Trust 2015); the "Police Officer's Guide to Judaism" provides information and advice about

Jewish customs that enables officers of all religious groups to interact effectively and respectfully with London's observant Jewish citizens (Community Service Trust 2010).

In March of 2012, *The Canadian Jewish News* reported that Toronto was to be the site of a pilot project for a similar organization organized by the Centre for Israel and Jewish Affairs (CIJA) called the Community Security Network (CSN), which would monitor the city's Jewish area known as the Bathurst Corridor (Bathurst Street from just south of Lawrence Avenue to Highway 7) (Levy-Ajzenkopf 2012). The volunteers were to train under Doron Horowitz, a former Israel Defense Forces soldier, and the National Security Chief of CIJA (Levy-Ajzenkopf 2012). A CSN volunteer could represent any religious or organizational association, as long as he/she, according to Horowitz, "is Jewish, cares, is capable, and is a rational thinker" (Levy-Ajzenkopf 2012). By specifying a "rational thinker," Horowitz reinforced the notion that this group had no vigilante aspirations, noting it would be closely partnered with the TPS (Levy-Ajzenkopf 2012).

Another "police alternative" is the Shomrim Community Patrol (known as Shomrim). Not to be confused with the Shomrim Society of police officers, this organization is a licensed, international collection of independently-formed neighbourhood-watch groups, most of which have been founded since the 1970s. They exist in many densely-populated Ultra-Orthodox Jewish areas, including New York, Brooklyn, Baltimore, Philadelphia, Montreal, and Stamford Hill in London, England, and consist of ultra-Orthodox Jewish civilians from diverse professions who protect Jews (and gentiles, they claim) in their own neighbourhoods from all types of crimes (Arutz Sheva TV 2011). Less dramatic is the regular assistance they offer people facing daily dilemmas, such as needing a boost or being locked out of their cars (Arutz Sheva TV 2011). Typically, volunteers are married men over the age of eighteen, as they are deemed responsible enough to hold this esteemed community position (Hughes 2010). The Shomrim are unarmed and do not have the authority to make arrests, yet they may track and detain suspects using non-contact methods (Hughes 2010). They carry two-way radios and high-powered binoculars, wear identifying jackets (sometimes over bullet-proof vests), and often drive Shomrim-identified vehicles with a siren (Kilgannon 2010). With continuous and effective surveillance, quick response times, and "insider" status, the organization receives thousands of calls per week, offering physical and emotional security to its communities, who are as familiar with the Shomrim phone number as they are with "9-1-1" (Hughes 2010).

Although the Shomrim groups are typically trained by local police, and often serve as a liaison between their ultra-Orthodox communities and law enforcement, their relationship with police is fraught with tension (Hughes 2010). The Shomrim generally feel that the police lack knowledge about Jewish customs and language, and should therefore only protect their Jewish communities at a distance. As a result, Shomrim believe that the police target them as a vigilante group and thus a social menace (Hughes 2010). The police's major trepidation about the Shomrim is that they are frequently the first emergency-response team called by the ultra-Orthodox communities, a practice which can jeopardize police investigations (Kilgannon 2011). The police's concern is not without merit: in a notable kidnapping-murder case in Borough Park in 2011 (when eight-year-old Leiby Kletzky was abducted by Levi Aron as the boy walked home from his day-camp), former NYPD Police Commissioner, Raymond Kelly, reported an approximate two-and-a-half hour time lapse between the notification of the Shomrim and police (Kilgannon 2011). In many ultra-Orthodox communities, the police remain uninformed regarding intra-community crime, as police-reporting is tantamount to committing the serious religious offence of *Mesirah*, the turning in of a fellow Jew to secular authorities (Rivera and Otterman 2012).

The unease between the Shomrim and police is exacerbated by a number of additional factors that undercut police authority. Most basic is the fact that some of the Shomrim cloth badges resemble those of their local police, implying comparable authoritative rank. In addition, the "non-profit" Shomrim receive generous financial provisions from elected officials seemingly to guarantee political support from ultra-Orthodox Jews, a mutually satisfying arrangement that keeps police marginalized ("Shomrim Shanda" 2011). Finally, Jewish news websites, such as *CrownHeights.info*, and other Jewish media, post online videos of the NYPD "bumbling" cases in the Shomrim-patrolled communities, an approach akin to public shaming (2011; Arutz Sheva TV 2011). At its best, the Shomrim and police work together to fulfill their unified goal of protecting civilians; at its worst, the organizations undermine each other's motivations, efforts, and status.

Rather than going to the police, or even the Shomrim at times, ultra-Orthodox citizens are encouraged to report crimes to their Rabbis in order for these community leaders to determine the merits of the complaints (Rivera and Otterman 2012). As a result, some Rabbis have been under much scrutiny recently for how they are using their influential *Beth Din* (Rabbinic Court) to usurp the role of the police (Newman 2010). In 2010, for example, the *Beth Din* of Crown Heights, Brooklyn, nerve-centre of the Chabad-Lubavitch Hasidic movement, ordered, in addition to other "binding" decrees, that "all police relations are to be conducted only by the designated representative [a Rabbi] of the Crown Heights Jewish Community Council and by no other person" (Newman 2010). Such a provision, the religious leaders argue, is intended to protect their traditional ways, to prevent police interference in local crimes which could serve to divide a community, to avoid the possibility of airing false accusations (by not engaging in *Mesirah*), to preserve a suspect's eligibility for marriage or his/her marital status, and to elude negative media attention targeting Orthodox Judaism (Rivera and Otterman 2012; Lungen 2015, 50). Critics of this decree, however, some of whom are within the community, see it as serving to maintain Rabbinic control, safeguarding offenders, and facilitating future criminal acts. This issue has been particularly contentious in cases of sexual crimes against children (Rivera and Otterman 2012); ironically, as it is deemed the most egregious crime, it is the most protected (Rivera and Otterman 2012).

Crime victims and their families who have contravened their Rabbis and reported to the police have often been targets of community ostracism: they have been expelled from religious schools and synagogues, shunned by fellow Jews, and have had their businesses destroyed (Rivera and Otterman 2012). In one case of 2010, Mordechai Jungreis, the father of a mentally disabled teenage boy who was molested in a *mikvah* (ritual bath) in Brooklyn, disobeyed the order of the *Beth Din*, eventually cooperated with police, and was the subject of intimidation by neighbours and Rabbinic authorities (Rivera and Otterman 2012). Jungreis had first consulted many community Rabbis, but none of them wanted to officially report such a horrific case (Rivera and Otterman 2012). He eventually found a Rabbi who advised him to take his son to a non-Jewish psychologist who would then be obliged to call the police; the responsibility, therefore, of accusing a Jew of a criminal offence would not have to fall on another Jew (Rivera and Otterman 2012).

The *Beth Din* of Crown Heights eventually declared in 2011 that the law of *Mesirah* was not applicable to child abuse cases (but was still acceptable for other crimes). The document received majority support, but did not obtain unanimous backing, a result suggestive of the ultra-Orthodox community's ongoing resistance to police reporting (Rivera and Otterman 2012). Arguably, the Jewish prohibition of *Chillul Hashem*, committing a transgression that, in turn, defiles God's name, is not only applicable to the perpetrators, but also to their silent and complicit protectors.

Jewish Issues of Prisoners

Historical Cultural Context

Historically, the rate of criminality has been relatively low among North American Jews, experiencing only one surge at the turn-of the-twentieth-century.

This new and alarming phenomenon was essentially a product of immigration (Weissman Joselit 1983, 11) when, in their new land, Jews experienced a sense of displacement, pronounced economic hardship, and widespread anti-Semitism, all of which prompted "Jewish combativeness" (Norwood 2009, 176). Norwood also cites the Dreyfus Affair (1894–1906) in France as a pivotal contemporary event which prompted American Jews "to demand justice," thus inspiring "Jewish combativeness" (2009, 176). In the urban centres of the United States and Canada, this phenomenon generally took the form of theft and gambling, tending not to highlight "offences against the person, against property with or without violence, and against sexual morals" (Weissman Joselit 1983, 9; Norwood 2009, 174–76; Halpern 2015, 100 and 221 n. 58).

Across North America, social reformers were attempting to deal with the correlated increase of Jewish immigration and criminality. In Canada, with the Jewish population jumping from 2,443 to 16,401 between 1881 and 1906, various organizations were established in Montreal and Toronto to deal with the intensified problem of Jewish crime (Rosenberg 1993, 10 in Tulchinsky 1992, 154 and 176). In America, between 1880 and 1920, more than two million Eastern European Jews immigrated to the United States (Sorkin 1992, xv and 1), and, as such, New York City, where the majority of American Jews resided, was of dire concern for social reformers (Weissman Joselit 1983, 5). The Lexow Committee, formed to investigate the local government's criminal activity, released a report in 1894 which bleakly described "the existence of a sizable Jewish criminal element on Manhattan's Lower East Side" (Weissman Joselit 1983, 5). By 1897, social activist and lawyer Frank Moss scathingly noted in his book *The American Metropolis* that the Eastern European Jews on the Lower East Side were "addicted to vice" and were "the worst element in the entire make-up of New York life" (Moss 1897, vol.3, chap. 9 in Weissman Joselit 1983, 6). With Jewish criminality on the rise, the social problem would only worsen with the huge numbers of Jewish immigrants arriving in America until the 1920s.

New York Rabbis felt a need to establish in 1891 the Jewish Prisoners Association (JPA), which primarily ministered to the spiritual fulfillment of Jewish inmates in hopes of imbuing them with moral decency (and countering the endeavours of Christian missionaries) (Weissman Joselit, 1983, 7; Hirschfield 2015). The JPA's desire to provide support for criminals is endorsed by the *Talmud*, which declares that criminals, just like all persons, are made in God's image, and are thus bestowed with an endless potential for goodness (Bokser 1951, 106–07). Accordingly, "even he who had endangered social security in the commission of crime has not forfeited his inherent worth as a person" nor "lost his link to the human brotherhood" (Bokser

1951, 106–07). Despite the gravity of the crime by a law breaker, then, a criminal had to be treated humanely.

Notwithstanding the JPA's noble pursuit, the organization suffered financial difficulty, partly due to "New York's collective reluctance to admit to the existence of Jewish criminality" (Weissman Joselit 1983, 7–8). Fortunately, in 1893, New York, German-Jewish businessman Jacob H. Schiff and Rabbi Gustav Gottheil, of the illustrious Temple Emanu-El on the Upper East Side in Manhattan, joined forces and financed the JPA, restructuring it as the Society to Aid the Jewish Prisoner (SAJP) (Weissman Joselit, 1983, 8). With two hundred members, most of whom were from the wealthy German Jewish community in which both men were immersed, the organization was focused on "rehabilitating Jewish prisoners" (Weissman Joselit 1983, 8). It was not until 1904, however, with SAJP's establishment of the Hawthorne School, the first entirely Jewish jail in the United States, that "uptown Jews finally overcame their deep-seated reluctance to acknowledge publicly that Jewish criminality was a very real social problem" (AH 1897; First Annual Report, SAJP 1896, 5 in Weissman Joselit 1983, 9).

Only with the passing of a few more years did the Eastern European immigrants join the German Jews in their efforts (Weissman Joselit 1983, 10). Despite the prevalence of criminals on the Lower East Side, where most Jewish immigrants resided, the Eastern European community had not overtly acknowledged until 1912 "Jewish crime as a serious social problem" (Weissman Joselit 1983, 10). Moved by the fear of immorality allegations, of an anti-Semitic backlash, and of impending restrictions on American immigration policies, Jewish immigrants came to perceive the delinquency among them as extremely troubling; indeed, it was in virtually "every sizable Jewish urban community" and "threatened their stake in American society" (Weissman Joselit 1983, 10). With their ultimate goal of overcoming their abject poverty, the Eastern European immigrant community finally collaborated with the wealthier uptown Jews to try and solve the "dimensions of Jewish criminality" (Weissman Joselit 1983, 9–10), a pursuit epitomized by the establishment of the Bureau of Social Morals (Feingold 1992, 48).

After the 1920s and the period of intense Jewish immigration, Jewish crime was no longer a social concern in New York or other Jewish centres (Weissman Joselit 1983, 11). With Jewish acculturation, professional and financial success, relocation to middle-class neighborhoods, and waning anti-Semitism, "the number of Jewish criminals declined markedly" (Weissman Joselit 1983, 11). In the New York State prison population, for example, the number of Jewish men dropped from 14% in 1921 to 7% in the 1930s, and the number of Jewish women lowered from 20% to 4% by 1940 (Weissman

Joselit 1983, 158). (The percentage of incarcerated women was higher than that of men likely due to the fact that women were more readily charged with prostitution or vagrancy for walking city streets alone, and that some homeless women purposely committed crimes, as jails were warmer during the cold months, and likely safer, than city streets. (Poutanen 199, 29–47)). A similar drop was apparent in the conviction/incarceration of Jewish juveniles (Weissman Joselit 1983, 158). Despite some infamous Jewish gangsters active from the 1920s to the 1940s (such as Meyer Lansky (1902–83), Bugsy Siegel (1906–1947) and members of Detroit's Purple Gang), and unlike Italian mobsters, Jewish crime lords did not encourage their children to marry underworld figures or to carry on the gangster tradition (Halpern 2013).

By the outset of World War II, "in both absolute and relative terms, Jewish criminality had ceased to be a Jewish social problem" and "had become an enterprise increasingly divorced from its Jewish context" (Weissman Joselit 1983, 11). In a 1940 study conducted on Jewish prisoners in Ohio, author Lee J. Levinger stated that its result "agrees with several others" that "the total percentage of Jewish prisoners is very low" and "the Jews show a smaller tendency toward recidivism than the prison population as a whole" (Levinger 1940, 212).

The crime wave between the 1880s and 1920s was later regarded by Jews as an anomaly, one that was antithetical to their Biblical status as "The Chosen People" and their particular "ethical and spiritual values" (Weissman Joselit 1983, 168–69; Norwood 2009, 179). Jewish theology referencing the notion that "from all the nations that are on the face of the earth" the Jewish people are God's "treasured people" (*Book of Deuteronomy*, Chapter 14 in Jewish Virtual Library 2015), reinforced the idea that Jewish criminality was not inherently "Jewish" at all. In 1940, Levinger, who was also a Rabbi, went so far as to conclude that "the external factors working on Jews and non-Jews are the same; only the internal influences of Judaism and family loyalty remain to keep them somewhat more law-abiding than the American people as a whole" (Levinger 1940, 212). These Biblical and moralistic notions, which, however construed, have been part of a Jewish sensibility, help explain why, regardless of the small demographic of Jewish prisoners, it was not until 1986 that B'nai B'rith International assembled a number of groups and individuals from Canada, the United States, and Israel to initiate the Coalition for Jewish Prisoner Services (CJPS).

Historical Cultural Treatments

The marginal number of Jewish criminals and prisoners is reflected in their minimal representation in film and television; however, when they *have* appeared, their Jewish identity, unlike media images of assimilated Jewish cops, has often been overt. This trend is rooted in the fact that, with the notable exception of the feature film *Once Upon a Time in America* (1984), the crimes have largely occurred within ultra-Orthodox Jewish communities, and typically against fellow Jews, two factors which make Jewish belief and ritual a core aspect of the characters. Jewishly-observant figures make for particularly "entertaining" criminals because of the seemingly inherent paradox of religious law-breakers. Moreover, their immediately recognizable "old-world" "costume" belies subtlety, and can be a significant source of either drama or humour. Yet, precisely for all of these reasons, depictions of religious Jewish criminals are typically highly degrading (aside from their apparent misconduct). Even in the context of the light-hearted 1970s–80s sitcom *Barney Miller*, "the Hasidim [as criminals] came across as violent, hot-headed and fool-hardy savages" who had "no standards," and who authorized "whatever ethics or beliefs one chooses at the moment" (Gertel 2003, 4), thereby "justifying" whatever crimes they commit. Thus, although the Jewish identity of these ultra-Orthodox criminals may be instantly discerned, it is rendered as ridiculous—for reasons that have little to do with its potentially comedic context.

The film *A Stranger Among Us* (1992) also includes core characters who are unfavourably presented in the context of ultra-Orthodoxy. The drama involves a non-Jewish homicide detective (Melanie Griffith), who investigates a murder of a diamond-cutter in the Hasidic community of New York, and ultimately discovers that a young ultra-Orthodox woman named Mara (Tracy Pollan), within the same community, is an accessory to the murder. The movie "justifies" the crime by revealing some sanctimonious dialogue, attitudes, and plot points: Mara joined the community as a *Baal Teshuva*, a repentant sinner, whose secularism in her former life is presented as an obvious explanation for her crime; Mara is the Rebbe's adopted daughter, and thus has not inherited the Hasidim's "superior genes" of morality; and Mara is "only" an accessory to the murder—committed, of course, by someone "worse" from her unsavoury past who led the Jewish girl astray. The self-righteous characters can "explain away" the murder because it was abetted by someone in their community who was never really "one of them": the "stranger" in the movie's title, then, not only refers to Griffith's character, but to Pollan's as well, for she is branded as the anomaly in their otherwise ethical (and naïve) ultra-Orthodox world.

Similarly, an episode of the television crime drama *Blue Bloods* (2013) profiles a murder in the Hasidic community of New York in which the incident is presented as "defensible" by an ultra-Orthodox Jew. In this episode, frivolously called "Men in Black," a title which references the popular 1997 science-fiction comedic film of the same name, the pious Asher Lefko (Darren Goldstein) kills Levi, (Yuval Boim), one of the Rebbe's sons, for being unfaithful to his wife Rivka (Melissa Errico), the woman with whom Asher is in love. "Justifications" for the Jewish criminality surface when Asher takes the life of his victim for defying the holy commandment of marital fidelity. Furthermore, Levi's affair is proven to have been with a gentile woman—a tall, slim, blond no less, whose lifestyle and appearance stands in opposition to the episode's virtuous Jewish women. All are transgressions "worthy" of retribution, and, ultimately, "warranted" by the tempting "*shiksah*."

The media's characterization of Jewish criminals as ultra-Orthodox is no doubt rooted in liberal Jewish Hollywood's general contempt for religious Judaism. Historically, it served as an obstacle to social acceptance, upward mobility, and financial success. As such, ultra-Orthodox criminals are characters selected to reveal the doubly "deviant" behaviours of committing crimes and prioritizing religious rituals, both of which can be mocked and punished within the secular world of "entertainment."

Although writings about Jewish ethics have existed for centuries, scholarly books specifically addressing Jews as criminals and prisoners did not emerge until the late twentieth-century, primarily in the realm of Jewish social history. These publications include: *The Rise and Fall of the Jewish Gangster* (1980) by Albert Fried, *Our Gang: Jewish Crime and the New York Jewish Community, 1900–40* (1983) by Jenna Weissman Joselit, *Tough Jews: Fathers, Sons, and Gangster Dreams* (1998) by Rich Cohen, *A Murder in Lemberg: Politics, Religion, and Violence in Modern Jewish History* (2007) by Michael Stanislawski, *Jewish Pirates of the Caribbean* (2008) by Edward Kritzler, and *Alice in Shandehland: Scandal and Scorn in the Edelson/Horwitz Murder Case* (2015) by Monda Halpern. According to Halpern, this fascination with [Jewish] deviance may be attributable to several themes related to contemporary North American Jewish identity: Jews feel integrated, accepted, and comfortable enough to reveal their uglier side; liberal and increasingly secular Jews are uncomfortable with the notion of Jews as a 'chosen people,' so seek to demonstrate their fallibility and corruption; Jews want to rehabilitate their image as victims; or, simply exasperated with persistent emphasis on the Holocaust and the Middle East, they want to learn about more 'entertaining' aspects of their history (2015, 4–5).

Books on Jewish criminality are growing in popularity because the topic itself is still undeniably viewed as a novelty. The title of the book *Confronting Scandal: How Jews Can Respond when Jews do Bad Things* (2010), suggests that, even given the paucity of crimes among Jews, or because of it, shock and moral indignation at their bad behaviour still exists and even requires specific coping strategies (See Brown 2010).

Contemporary Cultural Context

Today, the relatively low number of Jews incarcerated in North America raises questions about how Jewish identity is accommodated within prison walls, as, for all intents and purposes, the penal system is not inherently designed to cater to religious and cultural minorities. With only about 28,500 out of 1.9 million inmates in America who are Jewish and just under 180 out of 22,125 in Canada (Aleph Institute 2015; Kramer 2015, 8), Jewish prisoners are a small and "non-visible" minority, whose Jewish identity can go unnoticed by prison administration and fellow inmates. Although this inconspicuousness may be deemed advantageous within the hostile environment of prison, it does not enable incarcerated Jews to form an influential community akin to the culturally-based gangs who command attention from prison officials and who provide a social and protective network for their members. One Jewish inmate in an American prison describes this feeling of alienation:

> During the 13 months after my arrest, I never met another Jew. After I was sentenced and transferred to a prison of 1,600 inmates, scared and bewildered, I questioned whether I would ever find a community of Jews. Inmates with swastikas tattoos on their shaved heads roamed around every corner; anti-Semitic jokes were casual talk in the dining hall; and exclusively Christian literature was strewn on counter tops and tables. ("Prison Yiddishkeit" 2015)

Although some penal institutions and Jewish outreach organizations attempt to provide Jewish inmates with ritual items, relevant books, and the opportunity to engage in study sessions and prayer ("Prison Yiddishkeit" 2015), the issue of accommodating observant Jewish convicts is complex. Given the combination of today's increased cultural sensitivity and decreased financial resources for specific accommodations and security, the often-competing needs of the small population of Jewish prisoners and the prisons in which they are housed can create ongoing conflicts in which there is no clear winner.

At the most basic level, a major problem associated with incarcerated Jewish criminals is how they are identified as Jews. This issue is evident, for instance, in the variety of descriptors that can accompany statistical accounts: the Aleph Institute (AI), a Florida-based prisoner outreach organization, states that in the United States about 1.5% prisoners "are" Jewish (Aleph Institute 2015), but Correctional Service Canada noted in 2014 that in Canada 0.8% of inmates "identify themselves" as Jewish (Kramer 2015, 8). Furthermore, notwithstanding this distinction in terminology, neither statistic reveals how the Jewishness of prisoners is specifically defined or determined. Messianic Jews, for example, identify themselves as Jewish, but, because of their belief in Christ as the Messiah, they are perceived as Christians by all mainstream Jewish factions; indeed, opposing the participation of Messianic Jews in a Jewish prayer group in a Colorado correctional facility, some of its Jewish prisoners refused to attend the program (de Yoanna and Langeland 2004).

Even with the issue of Messianic Jews aside, the ambiguity of Jewish identification has enabled thousands of non-Jewish prisoners in penal institutions to assume a Jewish identity. Chaplain Gary Friedman of Jewish Prisoner Services International (JPSI), an outreach organization in Seattle, Washington, has been vocal in recent years about this matter: the high number of gentile inmates lying about their religion, states Friedman, "is a major problem," and is a phenomenon prevalent across the United States penal system (Zeveloff 2012). He has noted that the issue is integral to Jewish doctrine, but it is also crucial for the pragmatic reasons of prison security and economics, and thus has enormous ramifications in the context of institutional governance (Howland Jr. 2006).

Jewish identification among prisoners is motivated primarily by their desire to access kosher meals intended for observant inmates. Kosher (Hebrew for "fit") means that the food adheres to the specific regulations of *kashrut* (Jewish dietary law), and requires that the selection and slaughtering of animals, and the ingredients, preparation, and serving of all foods, must pass the inspection of a *Mashgiach (Supervisor)*, often a Rabbi. Although the number of prisons in the United States offering kosher meals may vary slightly depending on the specific year under discussion, according to Friedman about forty-two states supply kosher-meal programs and they are "being taken advantage of almost everyday" (Sims 2012). He estimates that approximately twenty thousand inmates in American penal institutions "are falsely claiming to be Jewish just to get a kosher diet" (Sims 2012). In Washington State alone, where Friedman's organization is based, 654 prisoners receive kosher meals, although fewer than twenty are actually Jewish (Sims 2012). In Florida, state prison representatives verbalized concern in 2014 about the marked increase in prisoners, "many of them gentiles," who have expressed a desire to eat kosher meals (Alvarez 2014). Of course, for authentically-Jewish observant convicts, keeping kosher is not simply a personal preference, but a commandment of Jewish law.

Prisoners prefer kosher food for a variety of reasons. Some inmates say that it tastes better and is more nutritious than standard prison fare, and that it is safer to eat because it is inspected and packaged (Zeveloff 2012).

In addition, more than regular meals, kosher meals can garner goods and opportunities on the inside: the virtually tamper-proof packaging makes them practical to transmit through the prison black-market system, and a desired commodity in exchange for prison money, cigarettes, drugs, and other contraband (Howland Jr. 2006; Zeveloff 2012). In fact, in Florida, about 250 prisoners were initially registered to receive kosher food, "but once the other inmates spied the individually boxed lunches" well over triple that number "expressed a sudden interest in keeping kosher" (Alvarez 2014). Ironically, some Neo-Nazi inmates also claim to be Jewish, not only to receive kosher food, but for the opportunity to congregate at the fixed times and locations at which the kosher meals are served; this arrangement places them at the centre of the Jewish prison population (however sparse) for the purpose of retaliation and violence (Howland Jr. 2006). In many prisons, the inmates who receive kosher food are all housed in the same unit, making them a convenient collective target for Neo-Nazis (Howland Jr. 2006).

In the United States, the trend of non-Jews registering for kosher meals in prisons has amounted to millions of dollars. Friedman estimates that well over forty million dollars a year is spent on supplying kosher food to non-Jewish inmates (Sims 2012). Food that is kosher is more expensive than non-kosher fare because "in order to produce kosher food, greater care, supervision, and manpower is required" at all stages of food manufacturing (Ask the Rabbi 2015). These phases necessitate specialized and sometimes more costly ingredients and production, and the hiring and ongoing use of a *Mashgiach*. Also, the demand for kosher food is significantly less than the mainstream market, which contributes to the expense: un-kosher products produced in bulk can be made for much less. In addition, kosher meat involves the hiring of *Shochetim* (Slaughterers) and other specialty salaried-workers, in order for it to adhere to the specific criteria of Jewish dietary law. These inspections are stricter than government regulations, and animals that do not meet kosher standards cause financial losses. All of these expenses, then, are absorbed into the pricing of kosher foods (Ask the Rabbi 2015).

For prisons, kosher meals can cost, on average, almost four times more than the standard food, an expense compelling institutions to scramble for solutions (Alvarez 2014). In California, for example, kosher meals can be as high as eight dollars per day, rather than three dollars per day for fixed meals, and, in Florida, the price of kosher food can total seven dollars per day as compared with $1.54 for regular food (Zeveloff 2012; Alvarez 2014). In Denver, Colorado, where Jewish prisoners won in 2000 their first court case to receive kosher food, the Department of Corrections (DOC) attempted to minimize its increased food costs by compelling inmates to partially subsidize their meals with a monthly payment of ninety dollars (de Yoanna and Langeland 2004). That same year, U.S. District Judge Lewis Babcock ordered that the DOC had to abolish this financial arrangement, which violated the Constitution (de Yoanna and Langeland 2004). The expense of kosher (and to a lesser extent halal) foods have compelled some prison officials to end their religious dietary programs altogether, providing those inmates an economically-viable vegan alternative (Zeveloff 2012): "there's nothing that says an inmate has a right to eat meat" said the Colorado Assistant Attorney General in 2004 (de Yoanna and Langeland 2004). In the end, because most American prisons exist on the state level, amounting to more than fifty departments of corrections across the United States, a variety of approaches exist regarding how to address the issue of costly kosher meals (Zeveloff 2012), none of which seem to be the ideal solution.

Of course, this so-called solution of omitting meat does not speak to other dietary problems for observant Jewish inmates. It addresses neither the special food preparation nor packaging necessary for other foods to be deemed kosher nor the denial of meat's benefits to authentically Jewish inmates, issues not lost on a handful of Orthodox Jews who have sued their respective facilities for not accommodating their religious rights. (Zeveloff 2012). In fact, in addition to the right of religious freedom supported by the Constitution's First Amendment, the *Protection of Religious Exercise in Land Use and by Institutionalized Persons* (42 U.S. Code Chapter 21C), enacted in 2000, supports the point that all prisoners have the right to kosher food if they claim a "sincere" Jewish belief, regardless of this term's ambiguity or their actual religion (a point to be discussed later) (Zeveloff 2012). But, according to Joseph Barnett, Custody Branch Commander of Clark County Jail, Vancouver, Washington, "if an inmate is exhibiting behaviors inconsistent with their stated beliefs, then there can be an administrative hearing and it [the kosher program] can be taken away" (Hidle 2013). Barnett adds that there are at least a couple of these hearings per week (Hidle 2013), no doubt a welcome opportunity to potentially reduce the steep food costs.

Two other reasons why some prisoners claim to be Jewish are conjugal visitation rights and the desire for conversion (Howland Jr. 2006). Friedman argues that because Jewish law states that a husband is obligated to fulfill his wife's sexual needs, some male prisoners who are being deprived of conjugal visitations are assuming a Jewish identity and arguing that their religious freedom is being denied them, a claim Friedman labels as manipulative (Howland Jr. 2006). As well, a small minority of non-Jewish prisoners appropriate a Jewish identity in the genuine hopes of eventually undergoing a Rabbinic-sanctioned conversion while incarcerated. Nevertheless, Friedman believes that a legitimate conversion from within prison walls is virtually impossible (Howland Jr. 2006). Rabbi Menachem Matusof, Chabad leader of Alberta, Canada handles this conundrum by waiting to address the conversion question until after the interested prisoners are released; his suspicions about their sincerity, however, are revealed in his observation that "once they're out, they no longer have interest" (Kramer 2015, 26).

With so many federal cutbacks to programs that accommodate religious practice, imprisoned Jews, for two essential reasons, are in a particularly perilous position of losing their services: first, the tiny population of authentically Jewish prisoners does not seem to warrant specific accommodation. In Canada, for example, government support of pastoral programs for non-Christian groups has been threatened because the low number of Jewish prisoners (and some other minority groups) only requires part-time chaplains, whom the cuts are targeting (Levy-Ajzenkopg 2012, 21). Second, as discussed, non-Jews claiming to be Jewish are availing themselves of expensive Jewish programs, increasing the "Jewish" prison population and the likelihood that some accommodations for Jewish inmates could be cancelled. Simply put, costly religious "privileges" for Jewish prisoners are jeopardized by a demographic that is considered either too small or too large to warrant the expense.

In most North American correctional facilities, the Jewish identity of inmates is determined by nothing more than how they wish to be identified. Prisoners simply fill out general forms declaring their religion, such as Kansas Department of Corrections' "Religious Affiliation Information" and "Change of Religion Request," and the state accepts that declaration at face value (See Kansas Department of Corrections 2015; Howland Jr. 2006). This practice is based on the First Amendment of the American Constitution which states that all people need only have a "sincerely held belief" in their religion of choice (ACLU National Prison Project 2005). This definition, however, is vague and ultimately difficult to discern, as evidenced by the American Civil Liberties Union's (ACLU) explanatory document regarding the First Amendment for inmates. It informs prisoners that "just because you have not believed something your entire life, or because you have violated your beliefs in the past, does not automatically mean that a court will find that you are insincere" (ACLU National Prison Project 2005). But the ACLU then states that courts determine a "sincere" belief by looking at the extended duration and consistency of that belief. Cementing this mixed message, the ACLU adds that, "if you recently converted … you will probably have a hard time convincing a court that you are sincere" (ACLU Prison Project 2005). That, beyond prison walls, conversion is generally regarded as a decisive act of religious commitment complicates the issue further. If these thorny criteria are any indication, it is not surprising that penal institutions have grappled with how to identify their "sincerely" Jewish inmates. Very telling is that the state of New York does nothing proactive to address the issue of prisoner Jewish identification, underscoring the futility of an alternative solution (Alvarez 2014).

Michigan Corrections devised its own approach to "the Jewish identity question." When it began serving kosher food in the 1990s, an unexpectedly high number of prisoners identified themselves as Jewish (Howland Jr. 2006). So, in 1998, in an attempt to reduce expenses, Michigan began a screening interview process: inmates were obliged to submit a written statement about their Jewish beliefs, why they required kosher food, and verbally answer a series of questions about basic Jewish practice (Howland Jr. 2006). Although answers were obtainable in any prison library, Michigan Corrections reported that the number of "Jewish" prisoners was reduced significantly (Howland Jr. 2006). Yet, some prisoner advocates claimed that the interview process was unfair because religious sincerity is difficult to articulate and measure at the best of times, and prisoners who had difficulty expressing themselves, either in a written or oral format, could have been forfeited their religious preference (Howland Jr. 2006). By the same token, for those who would have done well in the interview, Chaplain Friedman would have been dismissive of their results, noting that "knowledge does not equal sincerity" (Alvarez 2014).

Rabbi Lon Moskowitz, the Chaplain at California Men's Colony in San Luis Obispo, California, took a different tactic. He requested that self-proclaimed Jewish prisoners who desired kosher food follow the basic tenets of Judaism for six months before being granted the special meals (Zeveloff 2012). But many human rights activists condemned this form of commitment "testing" (Alvarez 2014), implicitly understanding that, with prison proving to be a hostile environment at the best of times, religious practice behind bars can be an additional challenge that many prisoners could not meet, and should not be construed as religious disingenuousness.

Given the subjectivity associated with quantifying prisoners' "sincerely held belief," Chaplain Friedman wants penal institutions to rely exclusively on the fixed and tangible regulations of Jewish law for assessing prisoners' Jewish affiliation, and uses this measure for Jewish Prisoner Services International (Howland Jr. 2006). Although the organization does not overtly identify itself as ultra-Orthodox, its dependence on Jewish law combined with its traditionally-attired clergy suggest the organization's religious propensity. Its "Inmate Information" form requests that prisoners "please voluntarily provide" detailed evidence of their Jewish lineage or official conversion, and to sign the form declaring that JPSI reserves the right to "determine" if they are "considered Jewish by Jewish religious law standards" (Jewish Prisoner Services International 2010). Without providing the requested information or if their Jewishness is in question, prisoners, as the form states, "will not be eligible to receive religious materials, visitation, or other services from the Jewish community." (Jewish Prisoner Services International 2010). With Friedman's reliance on Jewish law, the ambiguity of Jewish identity is ostensibly removed, providing an expedient way to weed out fraudulent "Jews."

Jewish prisoner-outreach organization the Aleph Institute appears undaunted by the Jewish identity issue so crucial to JPSI. According to the AI's own goals, it tries "to assist all, regardless of their religious observance, affiliation, background or lack of one," and also provides educational programs and social services for non-Jews (Aleph Institute 2015) (although the AI's Rabbi Menachem M. Katz does draw the line at kosher meals (Alvarez 2014)). Skeptics could view this position as the AI's desire to appeal to as many people as possible, with the hope of exposing the susceptible population to the organization's Lubavitch influence. As stated on its website, the AI certainly recognizes that inmates could be "vulnerable to … overt [Christian] proselytizing," but its credo that it helps those who "reach out to us" (Aleph Institute 2015) allows the AI to successfully dodge accusations of this Jewish taboo.

Predictably, Friedman's strict religious standards have generally been met with either indifference or disapproval. Correctional facilities tend not to care about how an inmate is religiously defined ideologically, only that the institutions abide by the Constitution, and efficiently manage practical security and economic concerns that religious practice can precipitate (ACLU National Prison Project 2005). In addition, although JPSI claims to respect "the standards of all mainstream branches of Judaism" (Jewish Prisoner Services International 2015), many liberal streams of Judaism do not condone the rigid Jewish laws promoted by Friedman, which, by definition, counter the principles of less religious factions (Alvarez 2014). While it is true that "all mainstream branches [of Judaism] are in agreement that mere self-declaration" does not make someone Jewish (Jewish Prisoner Services International 2015), the ideological differences within Judaism alone regarding who is Jewish are the source of much discord. Finally, because the First Amendment permits all citizens, even those who are incarcerated, to freely believe and practice whatever religion they choose, some non-Jewish prisoners have named Friedman in multiple lawsuits, contesting his application of criteria altogether (Howland Jr. 2006; Zeveloff 2012).

Yet, Chaplain Friedman believes that the Constitution has been violated in penal institutions, not because it impedes on prisoners' rights, but because it, not Jewish law, is determining the parameters of Judaism (Howland Jr. 2006). To prove his point, he cites the case of one of Washington's most notorious murderers, Roland Pitre Jr.: the now sixty-two-year-old was born Catholic and has never undergone a formal conversion to Judaism, but, in 2001, he sued Freidman and the state of Washington for denying him his legal right to live as a Jew (Howland Jr. 2006). The following year, the State settled the suit with Pitre, permitting him to pray as a Jew, receive kosher meals, and avail himself of other Jewish services until his sentence concludes in 2054 (Howland Jr. 2006). In fact, on the prisoner pen-pal website Prison Inmates.com, Pitre describes himself as "an observant Jewish man who eats kosher as much as possible ..." (2015). Problematic for Friedman is the fact that Pitre leads Friday night Sabbath services as an "observant Jew" and reads aloud from the *Torah* to service participants, a practice that, according to Jewish law, is prohibited to gentiles (Howland Jr. 2006). Moreover, Friedman contends that the inmate's flagrant disregard of this significant Jewish dictate is proof that he is "blatantly insincere," and is thus defying the Constitution's parameters of religious freedom (Howland Jr. 2006). For Friedman and other observant Jews, then, the Constitutional rights of non-Jewish prisoners to worship as Jews, be they sincere or not, have trumped the Jewish laws themselves.

Conclusion

Jewish police and prisoners are certainly on opposite sides of the law, but both groups are subjected to the intrinsic secularism and conformity of paramilitaristic institutions. Although genuine efforts have been made on the part of many police agencies and penal institutions to acknowledge and accommodate the religious needs of Jewish police and prisoners, respectively, these efforts have consistently been challenged within the institutions to which the groups belong. Paradoxically, because both populations are small in number, their religious needs would seem simple to accommodate, but it is precisely because of their minority status and otherness that their particular religious requirements can be easy, and sometimes necessary, to overlook.

Some Jewish police officers have been able to maintain their rituals with the concessions granted, but their religiosity has often come at a price. Resistance from fellow officers and overt anti-Semitism are institutional realities, and the very ideology of police departments, generally, can subvert religious accommodations. As the Jewish Police Association notes, "Whilst the Met

[Metropolitan Police Service] tries to adapt to personal circumstances wherever possible, the operational needs of the organization always comes first." (Jewish Police Association 2013). For these reasons and the historical factors examined, Jewish police officers are still at a premium, and Orthodox communities are frequently relying on alternative Jewish security organizations and Rabbis for protection.

For Jewish prisoners, and those who claim to be, many penal institutions have attempted to facilitate Jewish practices; yet, with the low number of Jewish inmates since the 1930s, potential security issues, and financial limitations, caused partly by fraudulent claims of Jewish identity, prisons can easily justify terminating at least some of these accommodations. When Indiana Department of Correction ended their kosher (and halal) meals in 2009 due to the prohibitive cost, for example, a staff member noted that "we got to the point of almost having to choose between correctional officers or special food" (Zeveloff 2012). Although a court has since ruled that Indiana had to resume their kosher services, the reality is that not all states engage in this practice, leaving some prisoners, whether "authentically" Jewish or not, demanding Jewish services that are "rightfully" theirs (Oster 2011; Sims 2012; Jews in Prison 2015). But, the law states that, while prisoners have the unequivocal right to believe what they want, they do not always have a Constitutional right to engage in or withdraw from actions based on their religious principles; for instance, some ritual objects deemed potential threats to security have been forbidden by prison administrations: ultimately, "a prisoner's right to exercise his or her religion is balanced against the government's interests" (de Yoanna and Langeland 2004; ACLU National Prison Project 2005).

Despite Western society's proud claim to multiculturalism (albeit limited and selective), and the American Constitution's First Amendment, law enforcement and penal organizations cannot entirely adhere to society's emphasis on individualism. After all, the homogeneity of police officers helps to cement their authority, while the uniformity of prisoners serves to reinforce their deference. Certainly, the rights of the individual are vital; however, they must always be tempered with vigilance for the common good. It is the preservation of this precarious balance that serves and protects us all.

Note

1. The title "A *Yiddishe* Cop" is a pun on the traditional Jewish expression a "*Yiddishe kop*," whose literal translation is a "Jewish head," more broadly meaning a "Jewish way of thinking." For providing me with some valuable information, I sincerely thank Michael Arntfield of Western University and formerly of the London Police Service;

Dave Goarley of the London Police Service and past coordinator of its "Citizen Academy"; and Stuart Gang, retired Lieutenant of the NYPD and active member of its Shomrim Society.

References

Books

Bokser, Ben Zion. 1951. *The Wisdom of the Talmud.* http://www.sacred-texts.com/jud/wott/wott07.htm.

Cohen, Rich. 1998. *Tough Jews: Fathers, Sons, and Gangster Dreams.* New York: Simon & Schuster.

Feingold, Henry L. 1992. *A Time for Searching: Entering the Mainstream, 1920–1945.* Baltimore: The Johns Hopkins University Press.

Gabler, Neal, Frank Rich, and Joyce Antler. 2000. *Television's Changing Image of American Jews.* New York: The American Jewish Committee; Los Angeles: The Norman Lear Center. http://www.bjpa.org/Publications/downloadFile.cfm?FileID=13572.

Gertel, Elliot B. 2003. *Over the Top Judaism: Precedents and Trends in the Depiction of Jewish Beliefs and Observances in Film and Television.* Lanham: University Press of America.

Halpern, Monda. 2015. *Alice in Shandehland: Scandal and Scorn in the Edelson/Horwitz Murder Case.* Montreal and Kingston: McGill-Queen's University Press.

Kitaeff, Jack. 2006. *Jews in Blue: The Jewish American Experience in Law Enforcement.* Amherst: Cambria Press.

Lesher, Michael. 2014. *Sexual Abuse, Shonda and Concealment in Orthodox Jewish Communities* Jefferson: Mcfarland & Co.

Niedrhoffer, Arthur. 1967. *Behind the Shield: The Police in Urban Society.* New York: Doubleday and Company.

Passamaneck, Stephen M. 2003. *Police Ethics and the Jewish Tradition.* Springfield: Charles C. Thomas.

Rosenthal, Richard. 2003. *Rookie Cop: Deep Undercover in the Jewish Defense League.* Wellfleet: Leapfrog Press.

Sorkin, Gerald. 1992. *A Time for Building: The Third Migration, 1880–1920.* Baltimore: The Johns Hopkins University Press.

Tulchinsky, Gerald. 1992. *Taking Root: The Origins of the Canadian Jewish Community.* Toronto: Lester Publishing.

Weissman Joselit, Jenna. 1983. *Our Gang: Jewish Crime and the New York Jewish Community, 1900–1940.* Bloomington: Indiana University Press.

Zurawick, David. 2003. *The Jews of Prime Time.* Lebanon, NH: Brandeis University Press.

Articles in Books

Poutanen, Mary Anne. 1999. "The Homeless, the Whore, the Drunkard, and the Disorderly: Contours of Female Vagrancy in the Montreal Courts, 1810–1842." In

Gendered Pasts: Historical Essays in Femininity and Masculinity in Canada, eds. Kathryn McPherson, Cecilia Morgan, and Nancy M. Forestell, 29–47. Don Mills: Oxford University Press.

Articles in Journals

Levinger, Lee J. 1940. "A Note on Jewish Prisoners in Ohio." *Jewish Social Studies*, 2, 2: 209–11. http://www.jstor.org.proxy1.lib.uwo.ca/stable/4464328?seq=3#page_scan_tab_contents.

Norwood, Stephen H. 2009. "'American Jewish Muscle': Forging a New Masculinity in the Streets and in the Ring, 1890–1940." *Modern Judaism*, 29, 2: 167–193.

Articles in Newspapers

Alvarez, Lizette. 2014. "You Don't Have to be Jewish to Love a Kosher Prison Meal." *The New York Times*, January 20. http://www.nytimes.com/2014/01/21/us/you-that's-have-to-be-jewish-to-love-a-kosher-prison-meal.html?_r=0.

"Bus Safety Initiative." 2010. *The Jewish Chronicle*, June 17. http://www.thejc.com/community/community-life/33154/bus-safety-initiative.

de Yoanna, Michael and Terje Langeland. 2004. "Barred from Faith: Inmates in Colorado Prisons Face an Uphill Battle when it comes to Practicing their Religion." *Colorado Springs Independent*, December 9. http://www.csindy.com/coloradosprings/barred-from-faith/Content?oid=1126391.

Geer Thevenot, Carri. 2007. "Jewish Detective Sues Police." *Las Vegas Review-Journal*, August 30. http://www.reviewjournal.com/news/jewish-detective-sues-police.

Goldman, Abigail. 2009. "Metro Approves $350,000 Settlement in Cap, Beard Case." *Las Vegas Sun*, January 26. http://lasvegassun.com/news/2009/jan/26/metro-approves-350000-settlement-cap-beard-case/.

Harris, Matthew. 2012. "Kaddish in Homeland on the Hoover." *The Jewish Chronicle Online*, July 4. http://www.thejc.com/blogs/matthewharris/kaddish-homeland-hoover.

Hidle, Erik. 2013. "Are Clark County Jail Meal Requests Kosher?" *The Columbian*, January 20. http://www.columbian.com/news/2013/jan/20/are-jail-meal-requests-kosher/.

Hirschfield, Robert. 2015. "Essay: A Jewish Oasis Behind Walls of Stone." *The Canadian Jewish News*, July 3. http://www.cjnews.com/news/essay-jewish-oasis-behind-walls-stone/.

Hopper, Tristan and Roberto Rocha. 2015. "Metro Toronto Population Blasts Above Six Million According to Stats Can. Montreal at Four Million." *National Post*, February 11. http://news.nationalpost.com/toronto/metro-toronto-population-blasts-above-six-million-according-to-stats-can-montreal-at-four-million.

Howland Jr., George. 2006. "The 'Jewish' Con." *Seattle Weekly*, March 1. http://www.seattleweekly.com/2006–03–01/news/the-jewish-con/.

Hughes, Mark. 2010. "Justice on London's Streets, the Jewish Way." *The Independent*, January 4. http://www.independent.co.uk/news/uk/crime/justice-on-londons-streets-the-jewish-way-1857591.html.

Jewish Telegraphic Agency. 2015. "Ex-Cop Sues NYPD for Anti-Semitic Harassment." *The Times of Israel*, January 21. http://www.times of Israel.com/ex-cop-sues-nypd-for-anti-semitic-harassment/.

Kestenbaum, Sam. 2015. "Inside the Heads, Hearts and Yarmulkes of Jewish Cops." *Forward*, January 18. http://forward.com/news/212852/inside-the-heads-hearts-and-yarmulkes-of-jewish-co/.

Kilgannon, Corey. 2011. "For Hasidim, Call for Help isn't to 911." *The New York Times*, July 15. http://cityroom.blogs.nytimes.com/2011/07/15/in-hasidic-areas-first-call-for-help-isnt-to-911/?_r=0.

———. 2010. "In Protecting Hasidic Neighborhoods, Squads Patrol without Guns or Badges." *The New York Times*, September 3. http://www.nytimes.com/2010/09/04/nyregion/04patrol.html.

Kramer, Lauren. 2015. "Jews in Jail." *The Canadian Jewish News*, April 8: 1, 8, 25–6.

Kravitz, Derek. 2013. "New York City Area's Jewish Population Rises: Two Groups, Non-observant, Orthodox, Fuel Growth." *The Wall Street Journal*, October 1. http://www.wsj.com/articles/SB10001424052702304373104579109671933282670.

Levy-Ajzenkopf, Andy. 2012. "CIJA Setting up a Community Security Network." *The Canadian Jewish News*, March 12. http://www.cjnews.com/canada/cija-setting-community-security-force.

———. 2012. "Ottawa Defends Cuts to Part-Time Chaplains." *The Canadian Jewish News*, October 18: 21.

Lungen, Paul. 2015. "Manny Waks: Film Blows Whistle on Yeshiva Sex Abuse." *The Canadian Jewish News*, May 14: 50.

Marzulli, John. 2015. "Exclusive: In Lawsuit, Former NYPD Officer Says He was Subjected to Anti-Semitic Attacks at World Trade Center Police Command." *New York Daily News*, January 21. http://www.nydailynews.com/new-york/ex-nypd-made-life-living-heil-article-1.2086167.

Mcphee, Michele. 2003. "Jewish Cops' Final Reward: Fallen Finest Buried Side by Side Thanks to Shomrim Society." *New York Daily News*, July 13. http://www.nydailynews.com/archives/news/jewish-cops-final-reward-fallen-finest-buried-side-side-thanks-shomrim-society-article-1.524972.

Moses, Eliot. 2013. "A Melaveh Malkah To Benefit Rockaway Shomrim." *5 Towns Jewish Times*, January 17. http://5tjt.com/a-melaveh-malkah-to-benefit-rockaway-shomrim/.

Newman, Andy. 2010. "Debate Start on Crown Heights Rabbis' Gag Order." *The New York Times*, December 10. http://cityroom.blogs.nytimes.com/2010/12/10/rabbis-in-crown-heights-issue-gag-order/?_r=0.

Nolan, Caitlin and Rocco Parascandola. 2013. "Fishel Litzman, Hasidic NYPD Recruit, Suffered Religious Discrimination Over Beard: Judge." *New York Daily News*, November 16. http://www.nydailynews.com/new-york/hasidic-nypd-recruit-victim-bias-judge-article-1.1518890.

Oster, Marcy. 2011. "Appeals Court Upholds Kosher Meals for Indiana Prisoners." *JTA*, May 10. http://www.jta.org/category/news-opinion/the-telegraph.

Parascandola, Rocco, Matthew Lysiak, and Corky Siemaszko. 2012. "Hasidic NYPD Recruit fired Over Beard." *New York Daily News*, June 9. http://www.nydailynews.com/new-york/assove-nypd-recruit-fired-beard-article-1.1092499.

Pine, Dan. 2011. "Protect and Observe: Jewish Cops find Camaraderie, Support in Local Shomrim Chapter." *Jweekly.com*, June 2. http://www.jweekly.com/article/full/61916/protect-and-observe-jewish-cops-find-camaraderie-support-in-local-shomrim-c/.

"Police Officer Becomes Highest-Ranking Hasid in NYPD History." 2014. *Forward*, September 7. http://forward.com/news/breaking-news/205287/police-officer-becomes-highest-ranking-hasid-in-ny/.

Rivera, Ray and Sharon Otterman. 2012. "For Ultra-Orthodox Abuse Cases, Prosecutor has Different Rules," *The New York Times*, May 10. http://www.nytimes.com/2012/05/11/nyregion/for-ultra-orthodox-in-child-sex-abuse-cases-prosecutor-has-different-rules.html?_r=0.

———. 2012. "Ultra-Orthodox Shun Their Own for Reporting Child Sexual Abuse." *New York Times*, May 9. http://www.nytimes.com/2012/05/10/nyregion/ultra-orthodox-jews-shun-their-own-for-reporting-child-sexual-abuse.html?pagewanted=all&_r=0.

Rosen, Robyn. 2011. "Life on the Beat with the Hill Street Jews." *The Jewish Chronicle Online*, June 23. http://www.thejc.com/community/community-life/50734/life-beat-hill-street-jews.

Shefa, Sheri. 2013. "Toronto 32 Division Now has its own Menorah." *The Canadian Jewish News*, November 28: B31–2.

———. 2014. "Why are So Few Jews in Law Enforcement?" *The Canadian Jewish News*, May 27. http://www.cjnews.com/news/why-are-so-few-jews-law-enforcement.

"Shomrim Shanda." 2011. *New York Post*, August 7. http://nypost.com/2011/08/07/shomrim-shanda/.

Symons, Leon. 2009. "Shalom, Shalom, Shalom: Coker Wants Jewish Cops," *The Jewish Chronicle Online*, March 12. http://www.thejc.com/news/uk-news/shalom-shalom-shalom-coker-wants-jewish-cops.

Waterfield, Bruno. 2010. "Dutch Police use 'Decoy Jews' to Stop Anti-Semitic Attacks." *The Telegraph*, June 22. http://www.telegraph.co.uk/news/worldnews/europe/netherlands/7846704/Dutch-police-use-decoy-Jews-to-stop-anti-Semitic-attacks.html.

Zeveloff, Naomi. 2012. "Not Just Jews Eat Kosher Food in Prison: Millions Spent on Special Meals for Non-Jewish Inmates." *Forward*, April 30. http://forward.com/news/155363/not-just-jews-eat-kosher-food-in-prison/.

Articles in Popular Magazines

Ghosh, Palash. 2014. "Barney Miller: Forty Years Later, The Most Intelligent, Literate US Sitcom Ever." *International Business Times*, February 19. http://www.ibtimes.com/barney-miller-forty-years-later-most-intelligent-literate-us-sitcom-ever-1556406.

"Prison Yiddishkeit." 2015/5776. *Voices of Conservative/Masorti Judaism*. Vol. 9, No. 1: 18–19, 54.

Sims, Torrey. 2012. "Unkosher: A Lie That's Costing Prisons Millions." *Correctional News*, May 16. http://www.correctionalnews.com/articles/2012/05/16/unkosher-lie-that's-costing-prisons-millions.

Thurm, Eric. 2013. "Network Jews: Police Detective John Munch on "Law & Order: SVU'." *Tablet Magazine*, January 29. http://jewcy.com/jewish-arts-and-culture/network-jews-police-detective-john-munch-on-law-order-svu.

Blogs

"California—Prisons' Kosher Meals Need Rural Rabbis." 2011. *Vos Iz Neias?*, June 12. http://www.vosizneias.com/85264/2011/06/12/assovera-prisonse28099-kosher-meals-need-rural-rabbis/.

E-Mails

Arntfield, Michael. 2014. E-mail correspondence with author, May 29.

Community Service Trust. 2015. E-mail correspondence with author, May 18.

Gang, Stuart. 2012. E-mail correspondence with author, June 21.

———. 2012. E-mail correspondence with author, July 8.

———. 2015. E-mail correspondence with author, May 13.

———. 2015. E-mail correspondence with author, June 1.

Goarley, Dave. 2015. E-mail correspondence with author, May 8.

Goldwater, Nicholas. 2015. E-mail correspondence with author, September 10.

Forms

Jewish Prisoner Services International. 2010. "Inmate Information." http://jpsi.org/wp-content/uploads/2011/10/JPSI-Prisoner-Info-Form.pdf.

Kansas Department of Corrections. 2015. "Change of Religion Request." Attachment B. https://www.doc.ks.gov/kdoc-policies/AdultIMPP/chapter-10/10110.pdf.

———. 2015. "Religious Affiliation Information." Attachment. https://www.doc.ks.gov/kdoc-policies/AdultIMPP/chapter-10/10110.pdf.

Shomrim Society. 2015. "Membership Application." http://www.nypdshomrim.org/shomrimsocietyapplication.pdf.

Handbooks

Community Service Trust. 2010. "A Police Officer's Guide to Judaism," 5th edition. https://cst.org.uk/data/file/b/e/Police-Officers-guide-to-Judaism.1425054129.pdf.

Lectures

Halpern, Monda. 2013. "Jewish Character to Criminality." Lecture. *The Jewish Immigrant Experience in North America, 1880–1945* (HIST 3807E). The University of Western Ontario, London, Ontario. November 6.

Pamphlets

Jewish Police Association. 2013. "Promoting Knowledge and Understanding." http://www.jewishpoliceassociation.co.uk/site/wpcontent/uploads/2013/09/JPA_2009_v3_1.pdf.

Press Releases

NYPD. 2011. "New York City Police Department Holds Annual Pre-Passover Briefing." April 15. http://www.nyc.gov/html/nypd/html/pr/pr_2011_04_15_passover_briefing.shtml.

NYPD. 2009. "NYPD Holds Security Briefing Ahead of High Holy Days." September 14. http://www.nyc.gov/html/nypd/html/pr/pr_2009_ph22.shtml.

Videos

YouTube. 2014. "Homicide Life on the Street 5 17 Kaddish—(Full Episodes)." https://www.youtube.com/watch?v=oUaBaSODKng.

YouTube. N/A. "Melanie Griffith (A Stranger Among Us) Full Movie." https://www.youtube.com/watch?v=_cH2yoOa3TU.

YouTube. 2011. "Who You Gonna Call? The Shomrim," Arutz Sheva TV. December 1. https://www.youtube.com/watch?v=TNdd5hRLr4o.

Websites

ACLU National Prison Project. 2005. "Know Your Rights: Freedom of Religion." https://www.aclu.org/files/images/asset_upload_file78_25744.pdf.

Aleph Institute. 2015. "About Us." http://aleph-institute.org/about-us.html.

———. 2015. "Religious Freedom Advocacy." http://aleph-institute.org/religious-freedom-advocacy.html.

Ask the Rabbi. 2015. "Kosher Costs." http://ohr.edu/ask_db/ask_main.php/262/Q2/.

Community Service Trust. 2015. "About CST." https://cst.org.uk/about-cst.

———. 2015. "Police Partnership." https://cst.org.uk/about-cst/police-partnership.

Gluck, Robert. 2013. "'Homeland' Writer's Work Shaped by Jewish Heritage, IDF Service." *Jns.org*. July 22. http://www.jns.org/latest-articles/2013/7/22/homeland-creators-work-shaped-by-jewish-heritage-idf-service#.VX2aGeWD7IU=.

IMDb. "The Choice": "Homeland." Season 2, Episode 12, 2012. http://www.imdb.com/title/tt2408794/.

———. "Family of Cops." 1995. http://www.imdb.com/title/tt0113024/; "Breach of Faith: A Family of Cops II." 1997. http://www.imdb.com/title/tt0118770/; "Family of Cops III: Under Suspicion." 1999. http://www.imdb.com/title/tt0184456/.

———. "Kaddish": "Homicide: Life on the Street." Season 5, Episode17, 1997. http://www.imdb.com/title/tt0604388/?ref_=ttep_ep17.
———. "Men in Black:" "Blue Bloods." Season 3, Episode 14, 2013. http://www.imdb.com/title/tt2662128/.
———. "A Stranger Among Us." 1992. http://www.imdb.com/title/tt0105483/.
Jewish Police Association. 2015. "Join the Police." http://wwwjewishpoliceassociation.co.uk/site/join-the-police/.
———. 2015. "Resources." http://www.jewishpoliceassociation.co.uk/site/resources/.
Jewish Prisoner Services International. 2015. "About JPSI." http://jpsi.org/about/.
Jewish Virtual Library. 2015. "Judaism: 'The Chosen People'." https://www.jewishvirtuallibrary.org/jsource/Judaism/chosen_people.html
———. 2015. "Vital Statistics: Latest Population Statistics for Israel." https://www.jewishvirtuallibrary.org/jsource/Society_&_Culture/newpop.html.
The Kosher Cop. 2015. "Home." http://www.koshercop.com/Home_Page.html.
London Police Service. 2015. "Community": "London Police Citizen Academy." http://www.police.london.ca/d.aspx?s=/Community/Citizen_Academy.htm.
Nehorai, Elad. 2015. "Kosher Cop: Las Vegas Undercover Officer Fights for his Religious Rights." Chabad.org. http://www.chabad.org/library/article_cdo/aid/806266/jewish/Kosher-Cop.htm.
NYPD. 2015. "FAQ: Police Administration." http://www.nyc.gov/html/nypd/html/faq/faq.shtml.
NYPD Shomrim Society. 2015. "Shomrim Society Membership Application." http://www.nypdshomrim.org/shomrimsocietyapplication.pdf.
———. 2015. "What is Shomrim?" http://www.nypdshomrim.org/shomrim.html.
Prisoninmates.com. 2015. "Roland Pitre." http://www.prisoninmates.com/RolandPitre287574.

8. *Killing for Slender Man: The Emergence of an Electronic Gospel*

LEE MELLOR, VIVEK VENKATESH, JASON WALLIN & TIEJA THOMAS

Introduction

This chapter looks at the rise of the mythical Slender Man, a malevolent twenty-first century entity believed to exist only on the Internet. This includes a critical overview of its credited role in an attempted murder by stabbing committed on May 31, 2014 by two twelve-year-old girls who claimed the crime marked an attempt to gain the favour of this same entity. Assuming a representational approach to the analysis of monsters and monstrosity, it is conventionally speculated that Slender Man functions as a microcosm of social anxiety, fear, and uncertainty while straddling digital and analog spaces. To paraphrase Nina Auerbach (1995), each age produces the monster it needs.

Reflecting the social complexities of their time, monsters coalesce and dramatize such socio-cultural concerns as those related to profound changes in ecological, socio-economic, and technological systems (Levina & Bui, 2013). Thus, we might conceptualize every demon, deity, demigod, and uncanny creature as a means of resolving a particular set of cultural problematics through which it becomes "real" as a dramatization and encounter with actual existential conditions. As it is in many popular and archaic monster narratives, the social uncertainties manifest in the monster are overcome by resolving (curing, subsuming, annihilating, etc.) the creature as an index of uncertainty (Wood, 1986). Herein, Slender Man as the uncanny monster assumes a particular psycho-social significance, for it is both a figure of social transgression and means by which the social order might be righted. In such a way, the monster is inherently schizophrenic, operating as a vehicle for the perversion of social orthodoxy and integral figure through which social normality might be maintained. Extending this general theory of monster studies to the specific case of Slender Man, we advance three general lines of complementary analysis.

First, we will attend to the specific origins of Slender Man with emphasis on its singularity as a monster of the twenty-first century. Second, we will utilize both a representational and ontological approach to examining the Slender Man mythos to speculate on its function as both an index of transgression and vehicle for grappling with the contemporary social order and the challenges it advances for understanding identity, subjectivity, and belief. Third, having examined a series of disparate online accounts comparable to gospels, including fake documentary footage, stories, memes, and computer games, we argue that the genesis and nature of the Slender Man mythos closely mirrors those of antiquity, including paganism, polytheism, and other so-called "new" religions.

In terms of method, we invoke the model of literary criminology as we employ inductive content analysis, corpus-assisted critical discourse analysis and representational methods to analyze the Slender Man stabbings and compare them to crimes motivated by other mythical beings who have been widely accepted as "real," despite a similar lack of scientific proof and a blind adherence to unverified literary accounts. In doing so, we propose that literature which purports to be non-fiction, featuring all-powerful supernatural entities or deities, creates a *delusional interpretive framework* in some readers which may invoke irrational violence or the tolerance of violence. Such delusions are only recognized as such when the literature has not yet reached a level of widespread societal acceptance, leading psychiatrists and some members of the public alike to classify crimes like the Slender Man stabbings as motivated by mental illness, while assigning a missionary and/or political motive to the murders committed by the Yigal Amir (Judaism), Reverend Paul Hill (Christianity) or Osama Bin Laden (Islam). It is argued that delusion derived from literature and/or oral storytelling is the common denominator in all of these acts of violence, and that the Diagnostic and Statistical Manual of Mental Disorders—5th Edition's (DSM-5) definition of delusion is inconsistent and unscientific. In the latter instance, this is because the manual's conception of reality is not based on empirical validation, but rather on an *argumentum ad numeram* logical fallacy. It is therefore unethical to use the DSM-5's criteria to diagnose delusion in a criminal case until this problem surrounding the nature of delusion is resolved. Three possible solutions are proposed and discussed in the conclusion to this chapter.

Killing for Slender Man

On Saturday, May 31, 2014, twelve-year-olds Morgan Geyser and Anissa Weier lured their slumber party friend Payton Leutner into the forests of

Waukesha, Washington where they stabbed her a total of nineteen times. Leaving her for dead, Morgan and Anissa began walking along Interstate 94 in the direction of Nicolet National Forest, some 318 miles away. Within hours, they were located by police and arrested. Leutner had managed to stagger to the road, where a cyclist found her bleeding and alerted the police. Under interrogation, Geyser and Weier placed the blame for the attack on each other. The girls confessed to having conspired to sacrifice Payton to an entity known as "Slender Man," a fourteen[1] foot humanoid entity with a featureless face and tendrils.

Convinced that the digital myth wrought from an online meme was real, Geyser and Weier decided to become homicidal "proxies" of Slender Man, believing that this would prevent him from murdering their families. They also believed that after they had sacrificed Payton Leutner, Slender Man would appear and take them to live in his mansion in Nicolet National Forest.

In the fall of 2014, psychiatrist Dr. Kenneth Casimir diagnosed Morgan Geyser with an early-onset form of schizophrenia at the Winnebago Mental Health Institute. She has reportedly received no treatment and has expressed her wish not to take anti-psychotic medication as it might make her "friends"—described as Slender Man, a girl named Maggie, and several characters from the Harry Potter novels—go away (Vielmetti, July 3, 2015). It is important to note that not all people with delusions are schizophrenic, nor are all schizophrenics delusional (American Psychiatric Association, 2013). Psychologist Anthony Jureky found that Anissa Weier's main issues were struggling for social acceptance and coming to terms with her parents' recent divorce (Vielmetti, May 26, 2015). He felt that Anissa had helped to participate in the attempted murder not only so that she would not lose her good friend Morgan Geyser, but also to prove that Slender Man was real and to prevent him from killing her family. On Wednesday March 11, 2015, Judge Michael Bohren eventually ruled that both girls should be tried in an adult court on charges of attempted murder. As of the the date of this writing, the criminal proceedings have been primarily concerned with appeals to move it to a juvenile court.

The Manufacture and Function of Slender Man

Myriad accounts of the Slender Man myth cite as its germinal origin a June 10, 2009 posting on the Internet comedy and meme forum *Something Awful*, an entry authored by Eric Knudsen, also known as Victor Surge (Tomberry, n.d.). In response to a forum thread querying *Something Awful* users to submit images of paranormal subject matter, Surge posted two monochromatic photographs stylized as found objects. Recessed in the background of two ostensibly commonplace photographs of children, Surge grafted a faceless, obscured and inhumanly gaunt yet giant figure. Accompanying the images, Surge included two anecdotes similarly stylized as found text, each evoking a sense of impending doom linked to the presence of the alien horror.

The original images of Slender Man authored by Surge were born from a series of weird fiction and horror influences including H. P. Lovecraft, Stephen King, William S. Burroughs, and Zack Parsons (Tomberry n.d.). Bearing obvious fidelity to this horrific genealogy, Surge incorporates as Slender Man's major characteristics the Cthulhian alienness of Lovecraft's eldritch bestiary, the amorphous and featureless doom of King's (1980 short story) "The Mist," and the hallucinatory paranoia of Burroughs, of whom Slender Man's apparel seems an ostensible although uncorroborated homage. The found text accompanying Surge's original Slender Man images retread these key antecedents in fantasy horror, in particular the Lovecraft canon. Inscribed in the bourgeois images of happiness, innocence, and unawareness presented in the foreground of Surge's original Slender Man photographs is an obscure and violent horror that mocks human life in a pantomime—one that steals away all manner of metaphysical certainty (Surge, n.d.). In Lovecraftian fashion, the stylized found text accompanying Surge's images assert that to fathom the Slender Man is to court one's doom.

While Surge's original online forum posts are popularly regarded as the origin of the Slender Man mythos, the sampled composition of Slender Man's genealogy is ostensibly more diffuse, sharing unsubstantiated reference with the sixteenth-century German folk monster *Die Großmann* (The Tall Man), Goethe's *Erlking*, and the Scottish dark fairy *Fear Dubh* (The Black Man) (Tolbert, 2013). Such diverse genealogical references reflect an aesthetic and spiritual confluence between Slender Man and the general composition of the *boogeyman* as it appears throughout varied cultures and ages.

Despite the ubiquity of the boogeyman archetype as something of a pan-Western icon of horror having taken on varied forms over the generations, there remains a surprising lack of scholarship on the origins of the legend. Kjus's (2014) research has revealed that more than 15 different mythical beings existed in Norwegian folklore during the first half of the twentieth-century—creatures or entities specifically intended to frighten children, or uncanny composites of more secular dangers the young were taught to fear. Each of these creatures possessed what we refer to as a "don't function": a kind of social control (Innes, 2003) rooted in fable which is intended to prevent children from harming themselves (eg. drowning in a river) or irritating adults (eg. staying up late to talk). The punishment attached to this social control is typically that the mythical creature will "get" the children if they disobey, though sometimes the repercussions of violating are more specific—and graphic (see Appendix 2).

As Kjus points out, the use of such mythical creatures to control the behavior of children has all but disappeared in the twenty-first-century. This sea change is owed, he argues, to fluctuating notions of what constitutes moral child-rearing practices, with the threat of abduction and/or violence at the hands of a horrific entity now widely considered to be psychological abuse. This begs the question: If the boogeyman legend was once used to control the behavior of children through fear, why has its return in the form of Slender Man actually been embraced and nurtured by both youth and adults on the Internet in an age when there are proscriptive controls on the use of such narratives for the purposes of social and moral engineering?

Firstly, concerning the use of narratives in conventional religions, McKay (2004) contends that faith is sufficiently explained by religious belief's capacity to allay our terror of the world and of the human condition, with happiness and greater health benefits as a possible result (Newberg, D'Aquili & Rause, 2001). Similarly, it is possible that Slender Man has been embraced by twenty-first century youths because the entity confers a sense of importance and purpose in their day to day lives that is otherwise lacking. Children in Western society are completely excluded from participating in any political, social, or familial act of any consequence, and in turn seek agency and identity by congregating in virtual spaces online. The existence of a boogeyman in their collective imagination provides them with a shared antagonist outside of their peer group whose actions affect life and death—one that exists in the virtual world they prefer to inhabit. This boogeyman also allows them to believe that they are privy to secret and important information of which the majority of adults are unaware, fostering the illusion that they too are key players in the world by dint of carrying this special burden. Therefore, it is unsurprising that, just as adults have abandoned attempts to perpetuate the time-honored boogeyman legend, it is the children who have taken this mantle in their new online playground.

Predictably, this digital playground is said to be Slender Man's realm. With this in mind, a complementary explanation of Slender Man's popularity is that, while the associated folklore references a wide array of cultural *boogeymen* and serves similarly as an index of cultural anxiety and uncertainty, its significance as a monster of the twenty-first century lies in its connection of folk-monster traditions and the open and mutable powers of technology. In the wake of Surge's original Slender Man posts came an unanticipated surfeit of memes building upon, altering, and extending the incomplete mythos sketched out in Surge's *Something Awful* posts. While such interpretive openness allowed for inventive speculation on Slender Man's origins, powers, and motivations, the monster itself remains a creature spawned from the Internet and its capacity for verisimilitude via simulation and viral proliferation (Slenderman235, n.d.). Unlike the Slender Man stories, in the case of other texts discussing monsters, deities, or entities—texts similarly having multiple authors in many cases—disparate tales have been co-opted and revised, often by factions or institutions, through "interpretation" into a single preferred reading—a dominant narrative often cited as official history.

As producers of the Slender Man fan fiction will attest, the socio-cultural significance of the monster is conversely informed by its *lack* of codification (Tolbert, 2013). To exemplify this, Tolbert (2013) cites a 2009 post by *Something Awful* user "Soakie," who writes that "even if we don't believe in the supernatural, even if our rational minds laugh at such an absurdity ... we are cutting [Slender Man] out and sewing him back together. We are stuffing him with nightmares and unspoken fears" (n.p.). Phrased differently, the Slender Man mythos is unique for the extent to which it has been created and curated by cultural producers and, further, for the ways in which it has become a mutable fantasy resource for a wide range of online participants contributing and consuming the fiction.

In addition to Slender Man's adoption as an open resource for the expression of fear and anxiety, the believability of the mythos of the creature extends concomitantly from its interface with the potentials of new media. Extending from the stylized quality of Surge's original found photographs and texts, contributors to the Slender Man mythos draw upon what Scholes (1967) called the "fabulative" power of technologies which are socio-culturally linked to verisimilitude. In the wake of Surge's original posts, a litany of found photos, videos, and testimonial encounters with the Slender Man have similarly emerged online, as if to corroborate the initial account, and often feature as key characteristics underproduced qualities associated with amateur reportage as being the tell-tale mark of authenticity. In other instances, images of Slender Man frequently appear in archival and historical photos as to retroactively project the monster into history.

Herein, the question of whether Slender Man is in fact "real" or not becomes complex insofar as the mythos adopts forms of mediation through which all variety of culturally accepted truths (mainstream news, archival photography, written testimony) irrespective of their actually having been produced. In other words, the Slender Man mythos draws upon conventional and authentic media forms in order to furnish veracity. We argue that the institutionalization of religious narratives is largely responsible for their popularity, perceived credibility, and the fact that the belief in them is considered valid, while equally unsubstantiated stories such as those in the Slender Man mythos remain on the fringes of society, renders belief in the latter as somehow tantamount to insanity.Perhaps this exception rests in the fact that, unlike other entities who are worshipped and feared, and whose back stories and gospels are also assembled in anthologized, piecemeal format, Slender Man reveals a latent paranoia surrounding new media as a force of surveillance. The threat of Slender Man may very well protract a more generalized paranoia that our online activities are not only being monitored—a fear expressed in accused Morgan Geyser's diary which, when searched was found to describe Slender Man as having "no eyes [yet] always watching" (Sanchik, February 17, 2015). Thus, Slender Man becomes, through this conceptualization, a cipher for wider concerns that the digital world will continuously take more than it gives. Thus, Slender Man is not simply a boogeyman of the digital age; rather, within an age of accelerating technological change, Slender Man becomes a boogeyman that *is the digital age*. For every web, a spider.

To venture one further speculation at the interstice of the Slender Man mythos and the digital era, it is crucial that we consider the confluence of Slender Man and the neo-liberalization of the Internet. Such an interpretive gambit not only gives altered relevance to the business attire in which Slender Man is often portrayed, but more significantly, begins to attend to the motivations of the creature itself. For akin to the neo-liberal impulses of the Internet and those advanced marketing algorithms that not only select but anticipate consumer desire, Slender Man fastidiously surveils and consumes (new) life. More specific to the mythos, Slender Man's desire appears frequently linked to the consumption of children's surplus labor, haunting as it does children's play spaces and scenes of children's play. Here, the creature becomes a force oriented not simply to the consumption of children, but to the consumption of creative energies in this way dramatizing the myriad ways in which internet surveillance, crowdsourcing and social media continually capture and capitalize upon the surplus creative energies of their users. As the survival horror video game *Slender: The Eight Pages* (2012) demonstrates, Slender Man is not simply a force of destruction, but more latently, a creature that demands the continual movement and restlessness of its quarry. Stop moving and you die. This scenario constitutes a truth of the digital age in which to maintain our identities and presence necessitates that we must not only be perpetually productive but render such productivity consumable for Others, intended or otherwise. It is herein that the Slender Man mythos marks an encounter with the horrific underside of the digital age wherein the very means by which identity is technologically constituted renders it a consumable resource for inhuman market forces. Slender Man thus emerges as the dominant monstrous Other of the Internet, concomitantly impelling our agitated movement while forewarning the moment of death should such productivity cease.

While sharing affiliation with boogeymen from other cultures and ages, the Slender Man mythos is born from both contemporary horror referents and concerns, foremost amongst which are the challenges faced in an increasingly technological world wherein the very notions of identity, subjectivity, and production undergo radical mutation. It is on this point that Slender Man might ultimately be thought of as an encounter with the resistances and affirmations of contemporary Western society in the wake of technological proliferation into virtually every sphere of life. Slender Man is, it would seem, an allegory of our contemporary society of control in which users and producers are subtly manipulated and impelled to play according to rules that are not their own (Deleuze, 1992). In this vein, Slender Man signals the new truth of the digital era in which we must continually be in motion, on the run, lest we disappear into an irrelevance tantamount to death. These caveats aside however, the Slender Man mythos might also be affirmed as the harbinger of a coming race that is neither expressly technological or human proper, but of a species that might best be dubbed posthuman. That is, Slender Man might be thought as a dramatization of our technological becoming in which both human life and the bourgeoisie desire for a happier time of innocence and nostalgia become doomed to dystopic supersession (Vint, 2013).

To take this speculative ontology of the creature seriously might then entail that belief in the Slender Man is less delusional than it is an engagement with the strangeness of what is already becoming real (Larsen, 2013). To ally oneself with the Slender Man or to desire becoming its passive proxy is to ride a destructive trajectory of our technological reality in which we might not only submit to an alien technological futurity, but repudiate fidelity to human life by peeling away the veneer of contemporary social values and morality to reveal the faceless and brutal horror beneath.

At a cosmological level, it could be argued that religion serves a similar purpose for adults. When one becomes "grown-up," he or she gains access to social, political, and familial agency; yet simultaneously faces the realization that humans inhabit a cruel and destructive reality which is ultimately beyond their control. Here the adult finds themselves once more in a place without agency. As the Slender Man fable provides a sense of importance and agency to the child's world, so does religion to the adult. In choosing whether or not to obey the "don't functions" of religious doctrine, the adult believes that they are controlling their existence (eg. ascending to Heaven or being cast into Hell) in what is, in actuality, a chaotic and objectively meaningless universe. This helps them to reconcile the horror of the *world-without-us* and the *world-in-itself* with our widespread and rather arrogant anthrocentric concept of the *world-for-us* (Thacker, 2011).

Online Discourse on the Slender Man Attack

The bizarre and sensational nature of the attempted sacrifice to Slender Man generated media coverage both nationally and internationally, and with that, naturally spawned a great deal of discussion in online forums. What follows is a mixed-method analysis of these discussions so as to shed light on online users' reactions to the event itself. Using a Corpus-Assisted Critical Discourse Analysis (CACDA) of Slender Man-related Reddit feeds, we have identified dominant themes related to (i) legal aspects of trying children, (ii) issues surrounding mental illness, and (iii) perceptions of reality versus fiction circulated within online communities and regarding the Slender Man phenomenon in specific.

A brief descriptive portrait of each corpus appears below (see Table 1) and the sites from which the data were drawn, frequencies and lexical sets are listed and tabulated in Appendix 1.

Table 1. Description of Corpus Analyzed using CACDA

Documents	13
Tokens (total # of words)[a]	139,303
Types (total # of unique words)[b]	119,830
Sentences	4,205
Language	English

[a]Refers to the cumulative amount of words within a corpus (i.e. total word count).
[b]Refers only to instances of unique word forms within a corpus.

The mixed method analytic technique of CACDA, as described by Thomas (2015) combines quantitatively-oriented traditional corpus linguistic techniques (*cf.* Hunston 2002) with qualitatively-grounded critical discourse analysis (*cf.* Fairclough 2003), thereby enabling dual objectives. First, CACDA utilizes both descriptive and multivariate, nonparametric statistical analysis techniques to describe data in terms of frequency information and associative textual patterns using words as a unit of analysis. Second, using a combination of constructivist grounded theory (Charmaz, 2008), wherein themes are revealed through the interplay of an inductive content analysis of the data with relevant theoretical frameworks, and the aforementioned critical discourse analysis, CACDA enables a qualitative interpretation of the discursive context surrounding statistically significant associations. The quantitative techniques used such as frequency counts and dispersion analysis (identifying plots and word clusters) can reveal the use and dispersion of important concepts within a corpus. This type of analysis helps reveal not only the frequency of particular keywords within a corpus but also a detailed analysis of the context surrounding each instance of the terms, which can expose certain discursive constructions. We rely heavily on collocation analysis to describe the strength of the relationship between two or more words within the corpus being analysed and we do not generalize beyond the sample of online forums collected for the purpose of the study, especially given that the corpus is comparatively small.

An analysis of Reddit feeds using this described method reveals that discussions principally reflect debates as to whether or not Geyser and Weier should stand trial as children or adults. Some commenters were found to be sympathetic to the fact that the crime was committed by juveniles.

Others acknowledged the fact that the alleged perpetrators of the crime were children, but argued that it remained unsafe to allow these girls to live in civilized society. Other comments pointed to the fact that adolescents may not be entirely culpable for their actions, for example, and underscore tension between the belief that 12-year-olds are capable of understanding that murder is not acceptable (in moral terms) and that they may not be entirely able to foretell the consequences of their actions (in developmental terms). Some commenters, however, suggested that the girls were manipulating the judicial system and accorded them with mental acuity befitting those of an adult. Our analysis also demonstrated that commenters brought up the fact that Slender Man is a relatively recent (2009) Internet phenomenon were used to support arguments that the girls either suffer from mental illness or at the very least, were savvy enough to use Slender Man to justify their actions.

For the most part, the corpus reflects an underlying protective discourse; many comments repeatedly highlighted that at 12-years-old, the girls are *children* as defined by statutory law. Common descriptors for the accused included "girls," "children," "kids," and "little." Discussion comments pointed to the fact that should the girls be convicted as adults, they would effectively be removed from society for the rest of their lives, which is perceived by many of the contributors to be a harsh and unnecessary punishment for individuals of that age. A more favorable course of action posited by the contributors would be to treat the girls for their perceived mental illness.

Overwhelmingly, Reddit users drew links between the girls' actions and mental illness, some even linked the action to criminal insanity. In some cases, mental illness was used as a way of justifying the violent nature of the event, while a small sample of comments highlighted that some users' armchair—and recklessly inaccurate—diagnoses of mental illness were actually framing the girls' delusions as aggravating rather than mitigating circumstances. Other comments advocated for forensic mental health care rather than a custodial prison term; however, many of these same threads emphasized the need for the girls to be permanently removed from society—albeit in an appropriate facility that reflects the underlying pathology of the offence.

What if, however, rather than being children who attempted to murder Payton Leutner for Slender Man, Geyser and Weier had been adults motivated to kill for an entity or deity with a firmly entrenched narrative pedigree? Would Reddit users be bringing up the question of their "sanity" with near as much frequency, if at all? After all, empirical proof that such entities exist is equally as lacking for these popular deities as there is for Slender Man. To quote Nietzsche (1886/1989), "Madness is rare in individuals—but in groups, parties, peoples, ages it is the rule" (Aphorism 156). Unsurprising, really, when we only define delusion as madness when it stems from a narrative existing outside popular acceptance.

Reality as Popular Narrative in the Criminal Justice System

The M'Naghten rules of criminal liability in mentally disordered offenders, which were established in 1843 following the trial of Daniel M'Naghten for murder in England, have been subject to a great deal of criticism. One consideration which has not received much attention, though it is of paramount importance, is the notion that an offender may know that a criminal act is illegal, but may also be deluded into believing that there is a greater metaphysical authority whose laws trump those of men. This is our focus here. To quote the Reverend Paul Hill who murdered an abortion doctor and his security guard in Florida:

> "[I] am convinced that the Lord has called me to ***maintain the defensive duties of the Moral Law, as it applies to the unborn*** [emphasis added] … The law of love requires us to similarly defend the unborn, and uphold the duty to do so. The duty the [sic] defend the innocent with the means necessary is an essential aspect

> of *the Moral Law that is found in both the Old and New Testaments* [emphasis added], and has been recognized and implemented throughout history ... *Not only does the Moral Law require the means necessary for defending the innocent, this duty comes directly from God, and cannot be removed by any human government* [emphasis added]. The duty to defend your own or your neighbor's child, thus, is inalienable. *When the government forbids this defense, the people '... must obey God rather than men' (Acts 5:29b)* [emphasis added]". (Hill, 2003)

Naturally, the salience of this delusion in the criminal act will be completely overlooked when witnesses at the offender's trial are required to swear a legal oath on the same piece of literature which sowed the seeds of his or her delusion. Would we fail to perceive this unsettling irony if witnesses at the trial of Mark David Chapman swore to tell the truth upon *The Catcher in the Rye*? Yet Paul Jennings Hill seems to have never been diagnosed as delusional by mental health professionals. Why is it that, despite the fact that both the crimes of Paul Hill and Geyser/Weier were motivated by the perceived threat of punishment by a metaphysical entity, delusion has been frequently attributed to the latter and not the former?

To assess the presence of delusion, modern mental health professionals typically turn to the DSM-5, arguably the most widely used and authoritative resource for clinicians and researchers attempting to determine the existence and nature of mental illness. Since its original publication in 1952, the DSM in its various editions has undergone a number of significant revisions, and has consistently been a source of great controversy. The DSM-5 offers up two contradictory definitions of what constitutes a delusion. In the section on Schizophrenia Spectrum and Other Psychotic Disorders (hitherto referred to as SSOPD), it specifies:

> "Delusions are fixed beliefs that are not amenable to change in light of conflicting evidence. Their content may include a variety of themes (e.g., persecutory, referential, somatic, religious, grandiose) ... Delusions are deemed bizarre if they are clearly implausible and *not understandable to same-culture peers and do not derive from ordinary life experiences ... The distinction between a delusion and a strongly held idea is sometimes difficult to make and depends in part on the degree of conviction with which the belief is held despite clear or reasonable contradictory evidence regarding its veracity* [emphasis added]." (American Psychiatric Association, 2013, 87)

In the glossary of the DSM-5, however, "delusion" is instead defined as:

> "A false belief based on incorrect inference about external reality that is firmly held despite *what almost everyone else believes* [emphasis added] and despite what constitutes incontrovertible and obvious proof or evidence to the contrary. *The belief is not ordinarily accepted by other members of the persons's culture or subculture (i.e., it is not an article of religious faith)* [emphasis added]. When a false

> belief involves a value judgment, it is regarded as a delusion only when the judgment is so extreme as to defy credibility. Delusional conviction can sometimes be inferred from an overvalued idea (in which case the individual has an unreasonable belief or idea but does not hold it as firmly as is the case with a delusion)." (American Psychiatric Association, 2013, 819)

The fact that there is inconsistency among these definitions of the same phenomenon in a medical manual is obviously problematic. The SSOPD definition stipulates that delusions are "fixed beliefs" while the glossary definition refers to them as "false beliefs." A belief that is fixed means that it is immutable but not necessarily false, whereas "false belief" implies that the belief is untrue but not necessarily intransigent.

A secondary problem is that beliefs are considered delusional in the SSOPD definition if they "are not amenable to change in light of conflicting evidence" or are "firmly held … despite what constitutes incontrovertible and obvious proof or evidence to the contrary." This definition assumes that the delusion in question is one for which evidence can be presented to refute. Indeed, it is common for individuals or groups to make outlandish claims about reality supported only by the argument that their claim cannot be proven to be untrue. This position is a classic *argumentum ad ignorantiam*, a logical fallacy in which the "responsibility or burden of proof is shifted to a critic" (Michalos, 1969, 370).

Finally, the specifications that delusions "are firmly held despite what almost everyone else believes and despite what constitutes incontrovertible and obvious proof or evidence to the contrary" and that such a "belief is not ordinarily accepted by other members of the person's culture or subculture (i.e., it is not an article of religious faith)" (American Psychiatric Association, 2013, 819) raises serious doubts as to the DSM-5's scientific validity. Essentially, it marks the enshrining of an *argumentum ad numeram* logical fallacy, or "using the popularity of a premise or proposition as evidence for its truthfulness" (Bennett, 2013, 55) into a manual which will be used to diagnose mental illness in both forensic and clinical settings. This is of no small consequence, as it will determine the course of human lives.

From a purely empirical perspective, one could posit that the existence of gods, ghosts, angels, and demons is equally as empirically unsubstantiated as that of Slender Man—in part why faith in the absence of such evidence is the cornerstone of all organized religions and creeds. Nevertheless, unlike those who attempt to kill for Slender Man "because [they] wanted proof that he existed" (Fieldstadt, 2015), the assassin who killed his prime minister on "orders from God" (Juergensmeyer, 2003, 48), the fundamentalist who murdered an abortionist because doing so would "illumine the world with the blazing brilliance of the glory of God" (Hill, 2003) or the Jihadist who claimed "I'm fighting so I can die a martyr and go to heaven to meet God" (Hadreas, 2007, 122)" is each unlikely to be diagnosed as suffering from a psychotic disorder—sentencing practices in these and other cases have, in fact, suggested just the opposite.

The simple reason is that the Slender Man entity, as conveyed through oral storytelling, films, graphics and Photoshopped images, or online documents, lacks the popular acceptance of other metaphysical beings. Alarmingly, the popularity of stories is actually being used today under the enduring paradigm of the M'Naughten rules by eminent psychiatrists to define the boundaries of what separates reality and surreality, regardless of empirical validation. In discussing his tea pot analogy, Russell (1952/1997) noted the influence of literature in this process, wryly mentioning that if "the existence of such a teapot were affirmed in ancient books ... hesitation to believe in its existence would become a mark of eccentricity and entitle the doubter to the attentions of the psychiatrist in an enlightened age or of the Inquisitor in an earlier time" (Russell, 1952/1997, 548).

The sociologists Mead (1934/1967) and Goffman (1959) have also written extensively on how individuals draw their views of what is normal and expected of them from society itself. When society sanctions and encourages the adoption of a delusional interpretative framework, there are substantial interpersonal benefits for those who accept it including being embraced and validated by a community which offers support on many levels, being deemed a moral or wise person by one's peers, the promise of an improved existence after death, and being considered somebody who possesses the virtue of faith rather than the stigma of mental illness. The DSM-5 highlights the link between poor social functioning and delusional disorder, yet does not seem to consider the fact that these impediments may have less to do with being delusional, and more to do with the social consequences of possessing a delusional narrative that is not *culturally sanctioned*. Seemingly, by the logic of the DSM-5, when assessing somebody's psychiatric state, in the words of Linda Stiles in John Carpenter's Lovecraftian film, *In the Mouth of Madness* "reality is just what we tell each other it is" (Carpenter, 1995).

Stepping out of the constraints of the DSM-5 to explore the nature of delusion, McKay (2004) summarized the research on neuropsychological deficits associated with religious experience. Deafferentiation of the posterior superior parietal lobule (Newberg & Aquili, 2000) has been shown to blur the dichotomy between subject and object creating a sense of unity with the external world. The impression that certain external stimuli can be perceived as having tremendous significance is associated with temporolimbic epileptic seizures (Ramachandran, Hirstein, Armel, Tecoma & Iragui, 1997; Ramachandran & Blakeslee, 1998), and momentary defective interactions between the left and right hemispheres of the brain can create the sense that one is in the presence of an entity (Cook & Persinger, 1997). Relevant to this last example, is that Persinger reportedly claimed that he had "experienced God" (McKay, 2004, 5) for the first time after stimulating his right temporoparietal lobe with an electromagnetic field. It is important to note that Persinger was referring to the fact that he felt another presence in the room, but did not literally interpret this as an objective god.

McKay (2004) refers to people who can have such an experience and do not interpret this as having a religious or supernatural causality as mystical atheists—persons operating without a *delusional interpretive framework*. Quite simply, a *delusional interpretive framework* refers to a typically metaphysical explanatory narrative, containing multiple elements that are unsupported by empirical evidence, and which is used to process and draw conclusions about the nature of reality. When the *delusional interpretive framework* is commonplace, according to the DSM-5 it is not considered delusional at all, rather a simple matter of personal belief. However, when the *delusional interpretive framework* is more individualized it may result in diagnoses of schizotypal personality disorder or psychosis.

Ironically, mainstream religions have often endeavoured to make pagan characters "more real" by incorporating them into their own stories and gospels. Kulik (2013) has described the various ways in which Judaism and Christianity re-imagined satyrs as demons. Recently, Pastor Robin Swope—purportedly a seminary trained exorcist—has declared that Slender Man is an actual demon, disseminating this information through a literary medium: his self-published *Slenderman: From Fiction to Fact* (Swope, 2012). The book acknowledges that the origins of the Slender Man myth began with Victor Surge on the *Something Awful* forum, but then cites a number of messages Swope has received from people who, having read his "Paranormal Pastor" blog, recounting personal run-ins to him with an entity resembling Slender Man. Swope offers these as evidence that Slender Man exists in reality, saying "many of these stories occurred before the Slenderman mythos was created. Some of them were sent or related to me years before the mythos was started by Victor Surge. What shall we make of these?" (Swope, 2012, 131). However, if we are to judge by the dates provided in the book, of the 34 "Real Slenderman Encounters" listed by Swope (2012), the only one to occur before Victor Surge first posted about Slender Man on June 10, 2009, were "notes taken from a missionary meeting at New City Alliance Church[2] in the fall of 1987" (86). By the time the other 33 accounts were written and posted on Swope's blog, the Slender Man mythos had already been established, with images of the entity and reports of his physical and behavioural characteristics easily accessible on the Web.

Even if we are to comply with Swope's appeal not to simply dismiss all of these accounts as fabrications (which they obviously could be), it is important to note that at least four of these accounts (10.5%) were provided by individuals who claimed to have been traumatized or abused as children, which can result in severe psychological trauma. Thirteen others (38%) occurred either admittedly when the reporting party was within a dream, sleeping, having just awoken (hypnopompic hallucinations), or trying to sleep (hypnogagic hallucinations) late at night. This implies that, even if these stories are not fabrications, nearly 50% of them could be attributed to either symptoms resulting from Post Traumatic Stress Disorder, hypnopompic hallucinations, hypnogagic hallucinations, or dreams, including false-awakenings (American Psychiatric Association, 2013).

Taking the above into consideration, it is puzzling why Swopes would lend any credence to these accounts whatsoever. Paradoxically, while claiming that he had received reports of Slender Man before the myth was created, Swope also offers two other explanations: that Slender Man is either a manifestation of "Parapsychodynamis" or is Death personified. We propose that Swope's pre-existing *delusional interpretive system* predisposes him to interpret mysterious phenomena as paranormal/religious/spiritual/supernatural. With unintentional irony, he concludes his book by proposing that faith, prayer, and Jesus-sanctioned commands are the best tools to combat Slender Man.

Conclusion

The Slender Man mythos emerges at the interstice of myriad social anxieties. For this reason, the Slender Man mythos is not dissimilar from a litany of monster and deity fables that seem real for their reflection of actual socio-cultural problems and concerns. In the contemporary moment of accelerating technologies and technological modes of control, the Slender Man takes on particular import. As a monster of the twenty-first century wrought from a digital gospel, the Slender Man mythos becomes an encounter with mutating forces of technology through which the mythos assumes the appearance of truth. Yet, the Slender Man figures as an anxiety of power in the Internet age, where beneath the habitual use of technology insists a malevolent force of surveillance and control operating beyond our perception and intentions.

Finally, it is both unethical and unscientific for a medical manual that is used to diagnose and treat human beings to define delusions based upon the popularity of a given fable. We propose three solutions to this problem in order to maintain logical consistency in future editions of the DSM:

1. *The elimination of "delusion" as a formal psychiatric concept altogether.* The inability to medically identify delusions altogether would likely push juries to be less sympathetic to the defense, as forensic psychologists would be restricted in their abilities to explain the particulars of an offender's psychosis. In a clinical setting, this could also negatively affect the clinician's ability to effectively treat their patient, as many of their harmful actions are rooted in strongly held false beliefs.
2. *The redefinition of "delusion" to include religious and paranormal beliefs.* This solution would mean that the majority of the global population would qualify as delusional. Although logical enquiry seems to indicate that this is actually the case, the audacity of formalizing this truth would result in considerable blow back which, ironically, could decrease the perceived credibility and usage of the DSM significantly. For this reason, it is unfathomable that the American Psychiatric Association would embrace such a self-destructive solution, regardless of scientific logic. Furthermore, the medicalization of all belief which is not empirically verifiable is unnecessarily and disturbingly authoritarian and intolerant of individuality. The liberation of the non-harmful delusional person from the DSM 5's *argumentum ad numeram* is far preferable, and easier to implement.
3. *The redefinition of "delusion" to include religious and paranormal belief, accompanied by the stipulation that, like recent revisions to "paraphilic disorder," a delusion should only be diagnosed and treated when it is currently causing distress or impairment to the individual or results in personal harm, harm to others, or risk of harm to others.*

This is the solution that is the most realistic and tolerant of individuality, though admittedly one that would have major ramifications for both the criminal justice system and mental healthcare. As a result of this revision, violent or potentially violent offenders who are motivated by religious belief would be mandated to receive psychiatric treatment for their delusions in the same manner as those motivated by more esoteric delusional systems.

Appendix 1

Links to Reddit Threads

Thread Number	URL	Number of Comments
1	https://www.reddit.com/r/offbeat/comments/2yylhz/two_wisconsin_girls_accused_of_repeatedly/	426
2	https://www.reddit.com/r/MorbidReality/comments/2yylky/two_wisconsin_girls_accused_of_repeatedly/	91
3	https://www.reddit.com/r/creepy/comments/276btr/two_twelve_year_old_girls_invite_a_third_over_for/	137
4	https://www.reddit.com/r/news/comments/2cf26x/girl_accused_in_slender_man_stabbing_says_she/	91
5	https://www.reddit.com/r/MorbidReality/comments/2ckyg7/girl_accused_in_slender_man_stabbing_says_she/	67
6	https://www.reddit.com/r/MorbidReality/comments/2wcv3p/see_inside_slender_man_stabbing_suspects_notebook/	68
7	https://www.reddit.com/r/news/comments/27sb0r/13yearold_ohio_girl_stabs_mother_in_2nd/	350
8	https://www.reddit.com/r/news/comments/27lybp/i_wanted_to_live_12yearold_wisconsin_girl/	397
9	https://www.reddit.com/r/UpliftingNews/comments/2be3s7/girl_who_got_stabbed_in_slender_man_case_gets/	253
10	https://www.reddit.com/r/news/comments/2yy0wi/wisconsin_judge_orders_2_girls_to_stand_trial_as/	401
11	https://www.reddit.com/r/WTF/comments/275nt0/two_12yr_old_girls_stab_their_friend_19_times_to/	760
12	https://www.reddit.com/r/wisconsin/comments/274in7/waukesha_two_12yearold_girls_are_being_held_on/	131
13	https://www.reddit.com/r/teenagers/comments/277xzj/other_this_just_happened_where_i_live_12_year/	60

Salient Terms Among Top 300 Words

Term	Frequency
girls	335
adult	330
adults	323
children	265
age	262
kids	259
murder	255
mental	230
life	226
girl	197
Slenderman	195
child	188
wrong	182
right	175
kill	173
understand	168
prison	150
crime	142
parents	137
two	135
help	133
believe	128
Society	122
Real	121
Thought	117
Probably	115
Actually	114
Killing	112
Mean	111
Little	106
Olds	104
Good	103
Young	102
Friend	101
Stabbing	101

Term	Frequency
Doing	100
Got	100
World	100
Off	100
Bad	100
Kid	100
Read	99
Mentally	96
Internet	90
consequences	88
victim	88
crazy	97
slenderman	86
actions	86
stabbed	86
juvenile	84
Slender	84
stab	83
blame	79
death	77
brain	73
jail	73
game	72
punishment	72
developed	68
attempted	67
justice	62
Man	60
stupid	56
normal	55
human	55
illness	54
die	54
problem	51
games	50

Term	Frequency
police	49
legal	49
white	49
school	49
issues	49
trial	49
family	47
judge	47
gun	46
reality	46
attack	46
violent	42
rehabilitation	42
slender	41
serious	41
stories	40
insanity	40
creepy	39
criminal	39
Twelve	39
Crimes	39
behaviour	39
Insane	38
Killed	37
development	36
Black	36
Friends	36
Therapy	35
understanding	34
Capacity	33
Excuse	33
Horrible	33
Evil	32
Decisions	32
Imagine	32

Term	Frequency
Psychiatric	32
Planned	31
Online	30
Mother	30
Plan	30
Problems	29
Knife	29
Responsible	29
Believed	29
Dumb	29
Weird	29
Fault	28
Committed	28
Terrible	28
Character	28
Violence	27
Head	27
Kids	26
Teenagers	26
premeditated	26
Emotional	26
Blood	26
Monsters	26
Dangerous	26
Knowing	25
Hate	24
Juveniles	24
Empathy	24
Parent	24
fictional	23
play	23
fantasy	23
Horror	23
Dead	23

Lexical Sets

Term	Freq.
girls	335
girl	197
Girl	8
children	265
child	188
Children	12
childhood	9
Child	8
childish	5
kids	259
kid	100
Kids	26

Term	Freq.
mental	230
mentally	96
Mental	9
mentality	6

Term	Freq.
really	227
real	121
reality	46
realize	24
realistic	8
Really	6

Term	Freq.
believe	128
believed	29
belief	12
believing	10
beliefs	7
believes	7

Term	Freq.
Slenderman	195
slenderman	86
Slender	84
slender	41

Appendix 2. Kjus's Creatures

Name	Form	"Don't" Function (Social Controls)
Busen (bogeyman)	Non-descript	Be "trollete" ('not behaving as people')
Cellar goats	(same)	Not eat your food
Cellar man	Non-descript	Be "trollete" ('not behaving as people')
Christmas goats	(same)	Wear new clothes before Christmas
Grølen	Non-descript	Not listen; disobey orders to come inside
Julereia	Non-descript	Misbehave
Kåvokjerringa	Giantess in a stone boat	Make too much noise
Kveldvart	Non-descript	Make noise in the evening
Lensmannen	The sheriff	Be a bad child; tell lies
Nøkken	Water ogre	Go down to the river
Øllenikken	Non-descript	Go close to the well
Sami	The 'mountain Finn'	Go out after dark
Svartemannen	The black man	Stay awake
The fox	Fox with two tails	Be bad

Notes

1. Weier described him as being anywhere from fourteen to sixty feet tall.
2. A search of the Internet has revealed various "New City" churches in Canada and the United States. There is an Alliance church called the "Risen King Alliance Church" in New City, New York. The authors have been unable to locate a New City Alliance Church at the time of this writing.

References

American Psychiatric Association. *Diagnostic and statistical manual of mental disorders* (5th ed.). Washington, DC: Author, 2013.

Athens, Lonnie. *Violent Criminal Acts and Actors Revisited.* Urbana, Chicago & Springfield: University of Illinois Press, 1997.

Auerbach, Nina. *Our vampires, ourselves.* Chicago, IL: University of Chicago Press, 1995.

Baker, Paul, Costas Gabrielatos, and Tony McEnery. "Sketching Muslims: A corpus driven analysis of representations around the word 'Muslim' in the British press 1998–2009." *Applied Linguistics 34*(3): 255–278. doi: 10.1093/applin/ams048.

Bennett, Bo. *Logically Fallacious: The Ultimate Collection of Over 300 Logical Fallacies (Academic Edition).* Sudbury, Massachusetts: Archie Boy Holdings LLC, 2015.

Charmaz, Kathy, "Constructing Grounded Theory: A Practical Guide Through Qualitative Analysis". Thousand Oaks, California: Sage, 2006.

Chess, S, Newsom, E. *Folklore, Horror Stories, and the Slender Man: The Development of an Internet Mythology.* New York: Palgrave Macmillan, 2014.

Cook, CM & Persinger, MA. Experimental induction of the "sensed presence" in normal subjects and an exceptional subject. Perceptual and Motor Skills 85 (1997): 683–693.

Create Paranormal Images, "Create Paranormal Images," Something A*wful Forms,* accessed August 2, 2015, http://forums.somethingawful.com/showthread.php?threadid=3150591&userid=0&perpage=40&pagenumber=39

DarkHarvest00. "Dark Harvest I, II, and III" Youtube playlists. August 4, 2015 https://www.youtube.com/user/DarkHarvest00/playlists.

Dawkins, Richard. *The God Delusion.* Boston, New York: Houghton Mifflin Company, 2006.

Deleuze, Gilles. "Postscript on societies of control," *October* 50, no. 2: 3–7.

Fairclough, Norman. *Analysing discourse: Textual analysis for social research.* New York, NY: Routledge, 2003.

Fieldstadt, Mikaela. 'Slender Man' Stabbing Suspects Blamed Each Other in Interrogations. February 22, 2015. Accessed on September 25, 2015 at http://www.nbcnews.com/storyline/slender-man-stabbing/slender-man-stabbing-suspectsblamed-each-other-interrogations-n310176

Genealogy of Religion: Explorations in Evolution, Anthropology, and History. http://genealogyreligion.net/tag/slender-man

Goffman, Erving. *The Presentation of Self in Everyday Life.* New York: Anchor Books, 1959.

Hadreas, Peter. *A Phenomenology of Love and Hate.* Aldershot: Ashgate Publishing, 2007.

Hill, Paul. *Mix My Blood With the Blood of the Unborn.* 2003. Retrieved from http://www.armyofgod.com/PHillBookForward.html

Hunston, Susan. *Corpora in applied linguistics.* New York, NY: Cambridge University Press, 2002.

Innes, Martin. *Understanding Social Control: Crime and Social Order in Late Modernity.* Open University Press, 2003.

In the Mouth of Madness. Directed by John Carpenter. United States: New Line Cinema, 1995.

Juergensmeyer, Mark. *Terror in the Mind of God: The Global Rise of Religious Violence.* Los Angeles: University of California Press, 2003.

Kidd, D & Barnes, R. *The Root of All Evil.* United Kingdom: eyedoubleyousee, 2006.

King, Stephen. *The Mist.* New York: Viking Press, 1980.

Kjus, Audun. "The Boogeyman and the Primitive Mind: On the Concept of Pre-History in Folk Horror." Paper presented at "A Fiend in the Furrows Conference on Folk Horror", Belfast, Northern Ireland, presented September 19, 2014.

Kulik, Alexander. How the Devil Got His Hooves and Horns: The Origin of the Motif and the Implied Demonology of 3 Baruch. *Numen: International Review for the History of Religions.* Vol. 60 Issue 2/3 (2013), 195–229.

Larsen, Lars Bang, "Zombies of immaterial labor: The modern monster and the death of death", *e-flux 15*, Retrieved from http://www.e-flux.com/journal/zombies-of-immaterial-labor-the-modern-monster-and-the-death-of-death/on April 17, 2010.

Levina, Marina & Bui, Diem-My. "Introduction: Toward a comprehensive monster theory in the 21st century", In *Monster Culture in the 21st century: A reader*, edited by Marina Levina & Diem-My Bui, 1–14. New York, NY: Bloomsbury, 2013.

McKay, Ryan. Hallucinating God? The Cognitive Neuropsychiatry of Religious Belief and Experience. *Evolution and Cognition, 10*(1)(2004): 114–25.

Mead, George Herbert. *Mind, Self, & Society from the Standpoint of a Social Behaviorist.* Charles W. Morris (Ed.). Chicago: University of Chicago Press, 1934/1967.

Michalos, Alex. *Principles of Logic.* Englewood Cliffs: Prentice-Hall, 1969.

Newberg, A. B., d'Aquili, E. G. The neuropsychology of religious and spiritual experience. *Journal of Consciousness Studies 7*(2000): 251–266.

Newberg, Andrew, d'Aquili, Eugene & Rause, Vince. *Why God won't go away: Brain science and the biology of belief.* New York: Ballantine Books, 2001.

Nietzsche, Friedrich. *Beyond Good and Evil.* Vintage, 1886/1989.

Parsec Productions, "Slender: The eight pages." Video game published by ParsecProductions, 2012.

Ramachandran, Vilaynur. S. & Blakeslee, Sandra. *Phantoms in the brain: Human nature and the architecture of the mind.* Fourth Estate: London, 1998.

Ramachandran, V. S., Hirstein, W. S., Armel, K. C., Tecoma, E. & Iragui, V. The neural basis of religious experience. Society for Neuroscience 23 (1997): 1316.

Russell, Bertrand. Is There a God?. *The Collected Papers of Bertrand Russell, Vol. II: Last Philosophical Testament, 1943–68*. John Slater & Peter Köllner (Eds.) London: Routledge. 1952/1997.

Rychlý, Pavel. 2008. "A lexicographer-friendly association score". In *Proceedings of recent advances in Slavonic national language processing,* edited by Petr. Sojka and Aleš Horák, 6–9. Masaryk University, Brno. 2008.

Sanchik, M. Slender Man stabbing case: Court learns what private investigator found in Morgan Geyser's bedroom. February 17, 2015. Accessed on September 25, 2015 at http://fox6now.com/2015/02/17/preliminary-hearing-for-girls-in-slenderman-plot-enters-second-day/.

Sanchik, M. Testimony wraps up in hearing for Anissa Weier, charged in "Slenderman" stabbing. May 27, 2015. Accessed on September 25, 2015 at http://fox6now.com/2015/05/27/hearing-resumes-for-anissa-weier-charged-in-slenderman-stabbing/.

Slenderman235. "Interview with Victor Surge, creator of Slender Man," Slenderman235 Wordpress, retrieved on August 4, 2015, https://slenderman235.wordpress.com/2011/10/20/interview-with-victor-surge-creator-of-slender-man/.

Surge, Victor. "Let the Children". Accessed August 2, 2015, http://victor-surge.deviantart.com/art/Let-the-children-142884978.

Surge, Victor. "Stirling City". Accessed August 2, 2015, http://victor-surge.deviantart.com/art/Stirling-City-142885082.

Swope, Robin. *Slenderman: From Fiction to Fact.* Opengate Press, 2012.

Thacker, Eugene. *In the Dust of This Planet.* Alresford, UK: Zero Books, 2011. Kindle edition.

Thomas, Tieja. "Analyzing online discourses of Canadian citizenship: O Canada! True north, strong, and free?" PhD diss., Concordia University: Montreal, Canada, 2015.

Tolbert, Jeffrey A. "The sort of thing that has you covering your mirrors": The case of slender man" *Semiotic Review*, retrieved on August 6, 2015, http://www.semioticreview.com/index.php/thematic-issues/issue-monsters/22-the-sort-of-story-that-has-you-covering-your-mirrors-the-case-of-slender-man.html.

Tomberry. "Slender Man: Part of a series on Creepypasta," retrieved on August 10, 2015, http://knowyourmeme.com/memes/slender-man.

Vielmetti, B. Expert: Slender Man case defendant shows low risk of future crimes. *Milwaukee Wisconsin Journal Sentinel.* May 26, 2015. Accessed on September 25, 2015 at http://www.jsonline.com/news/crime/hearing-begins-on-whether-slender-man-case-belongs-in-juvenile-court-b99507326z1–305047971.html.

Vielmetti, B. Why no help for schizophrenic girl in Slender Man stabbing? *Milwaukee Wisconsin Journal Sentinel.* July 3, 2015. Accessed on September 25, 2015 http://www.jsonline.com/news/crime/why-no-help-for-schizophrenic-girl-in-slender-man-stabbing-b99527566z1–311614861.html.

Vielmetti, B, Kissinger, M. Family history of mental illness revealed in Slender Man case. *Milwaukee Wisconsin Journal Sentinel.* June 17, 2015. Accessed on September 25, 2015athttp://www.jsonline.com/news/crime/critical-hearing-in-slender-man-case-to-begin today-b99520903z1-307851871.html.

Vint, Sherryl. "Abject posthumanism: Neoliberalism, biopolitics, and zombies", In *Monster Culture in the 21st century: A reader*, edited by Marina Levina & Diem-My Bui, 133–146, New York, NY: Bloomsbury, 2013.

Wallin, Jason. "To Die Well: The Death of Death in Curriculum", In *Expanding Curriculum Theory: Dis/positions and Lines of Flight 2nd Edition*, edited by William Reynolds & Julie Webber. New York: Peter Lang, forthcoming.

Wood, Robin. *Hollywood from vietnam to Reagan.* New York: Columbia University Press, 1986.

Wood, Robin. "What lies beneath?", In *Horror film and psychoanalysis: Freud's worst nightmare* xiii–xvii, edited by Stephen Jay Schneider, Cambridge: Cambridge University Press, 2004.

Part IV

Visual Arts & Museum Studies

9. *Crime as Curation: Understanding Crime Through the Lens of the Museum*

VICTORIA BIGLIARDI

Introduction

At its simplest level, removed from all context, the word "curate" refers to the act of selecting, organizing, and presenting any variety of content or information in an informed or meaningful way ("curate", 2010). It is used most commonly in reference to cultural and artistic institutions involved with the creation of exhibits or the preserving of collections. Archivists, librarians, museum directors, and festival planners are all individuals who carry out curatorial duties in their respective professions. The evocation of meaning from the presentation of objects or ideas in a particular manner is a richly systematic process that involves not only a deep understanding of the materials that are to be curated, but also an understanding of how they are to be positioned in relation to each other. In this chapter, I will enmesh traditional notions of curational practice in the context of museum studies with the study of criminal offending and the criminal mind. More specifically, I will do this by presenting and exploring a set of semiotic models that apply this definition of curation to the field of forensics.

Drawing upon foundational concepts of what Danesi (2013) has coined forensic semiotics, it is my aim to connect semiotics as an interpretive tool with the process of forensic investigation through this curatorial lens. My commentary will first examine a proposed relationship between metaphor and crime, including a proposal of a conceptual model for crime scene investigation that explores the overlap of curation, metaphor, and meaning-making among offenders—as well as semioticians who I liken to forensic curators. I will then present the overarching semiotic proposal of this study: crime as curation. Further discussion will consider the intentions and implications of this proposal in a conceptual sense, and will investigate the notion of forensic curation from two oppositional perspectives.

Metaphor and Crime

The term metaphor is generally defined within cognitive linguistics as a figure of speech that makes one concept understandable by likening it to another, more familiar, concept. It refers technically to the mapping between two distinct conceptual fields. These include the *target* domain (the abstract notion we are trying to grasp) and the *source* domain (the concrete concept that, through metaphorical association, allows us to comprehend the abstraction). It can be said, then, that metaphor is our means of understanding the world. As Danesi (2008) writes in *Of Cigarettes, High Heels, and Other Interesting Things,* metaphor allows us "to link an abstraction to something concrete, familiar, experienced" (92). He posits that from a semiotic perspective, metaphor is "semantic glue" that holds all systems of meaning together (91). This basic understanding of metaphor is that of a blank canvas: the mapping relation between these abstract and concrete concepts provides a precise structure that lends well to a variety of disciplines.

The field of forensics, when observed through a semiotic lens, is thus rife with metaphorical signs. Clues left behind at crime scenes are perceived as being connected to the "symbolic and ritual elements" of our culture that we may understand as "metaphors of life" (Danesi, 2013: 133). Forensic semiotics, as an analytical tool, offers a breakdown of some of the metaphorical signs most commonly associated with clues: traces of blood, a corpse, a discarded weapon, fingerprints, and even, in some cases, a signature, personal sign, or other expressive symbol left behind by an offender. A semiotic perspective allows for the extension of these forensic clues into the realm of signification. These traces are then not clues but *signs*—signs, in fact, that are interwoven into a broader context that allows for the interpretation of meaning beyond what is seen at the surface. This type of interpretation can be seen, for example, with blood spatter at a crime scene, which is a violent sign that is in many ways an "[emblem of] the nature of crime itself" with inherent ritual and "symbolic value" (133). Metaphorical applications of forensic tools can be detected with flashlights, fingerprint powders, and other methods of illumination and elucidation, where technologies of varying sophistication bring both figurative and literal clarity to the investigation of a crime. A detective may search a dark crime scene with a flashlight while also seeking to shed light on the truth in the more figurative—or metaphorical—sense, by solving different elements of the crime at hand.

The Curationist Mind

I have preliminarily introduced the notion of curation in this chapter by providing a rather broad definition: the systematic positioning of objects or ideas in relation to each other, so as to evoke a particular meaning. Removed from its typical context of artistic applications, this simple statement becomes relevant to myriad criminal situations. So much of our lives are built around functioning in "curationist" ways—we are hyperaware of our spatial environments, and are conscious of our surroundings in a dialogic way. To focus on one single object or idea at a time is nearly impossible. In our periphery, we are consistently mindful of how the objects around us or the ideas we conceptualize do not exist in isolation, but how they instead work in continuous and uninterrupted relation to one another. We curate our to-do lists, our desks at work, our kitchen cupboards, our thoughts. Every part of our lives, be it physical or psychological, is subject to some form of systematic organization. Our inherent curatorial tendencies result in an endless amount of spatial conversation. Is this surprising? Not at all. The goal of curation to evoke meaning becomes of interest here. The way that some set of things is curated will influence the way that this same set of things is interpreted and understood. The presentation of objects or ideas in a meaningful way has an impact on how we conceptualize it. It is in fact this structure that is of greatest significance with respect to the study of crime.

There is also structural connection here, between the meaning-making of curation and the meaning-making of metaphor. As mentioned before, people use metaphorical reasoning to understand what is unfamiliar to them. The basic structure of metaphor, connecting two things (an abstraction with something concrete), is a model that generates meaning. This meaning is generated at the intersection of these two concepts—the ground of the metaphor, according to I. A. Richards (Danesi, 2008: 97). In essence, we form in our minds a *relation* between the abstract and the concrete. We are actively positioning our experiences of new objects and ideas with our preexisting knowledge and understanding in a conceptual blueprint. We create meaning by curating these experiences in the way that seems most contextually relevant to us. In this sense, I argue that the structure of meaning-making that is derived from metaphorical reasoning bears remarkable similarity to the more tangible structure of meaning-making found with curatorial practice. Similar to how shifting the elements of a metaphor will change its meaning, altering the juxtaposition of objects in a curated space (be they physical or conceptual) will also change the shape of your interpretation and affect the meaning found in the relation between these objects.

This model of the curationist mind—of how we inherently find meaning through objects or ideas positioned in a semantic dialogue—is something very true to semiotic theory. "Signs can never be understood in the absolute, only in relation to other signs," which reveals the "connective propensities of the human brain" (Danesi, 2013, p. 22). It is argued that meaning itself is found within this relational structure. It seems natural to say, then, that the curationist mind is a conceptual lens that allows for a more tangible application of the semiotic mind. To visualize and interpret a series of associative connections in the physical realm of curation is a literal manifestation of the mental processes of metaphor creation and meaning-making that exist in the conceptual realm. I argue here that curation can be a physical extension of metaphorical reasoning. Just as we struggle to articulate our thoughts without the usage of linguistic metaphor, we struggle to understand our real experiences without also considering broader contextual or associative properties.

Crime as Curation

Using this model of the curationist mind, I will here propose an approach to forensic investigation that involves elements of both sign theory and curationist meaning-making—much like in the tradtion of the museum exhibit. An ideal forensic example, one that is implicit and inevitable in every criminal offense, whether ever successfully located by investigators or not, is that of the crime scene—or crime scenes plural in some cases. The crime scene is said to be "a feature of any modern examination of crime" (Bray & Dalton, 2009: 5). They "steal our attention" and "preoccupy the public", truly becoming the "heartland of crime" (5). Given the prevalence of metaphorical signs involved in the evidence and forensic tools used in investigations, the crime scene is interpreted in many ways as a curated space. It is a spatial expression of a criminal act that has occurred in the past, and provides a unique positioning of objects that allows for the reading of a specific meaning. Crime scenes themselves are thus semiotic *texts*, to be analyzed and understood as a presentation of interconnected meanings.

One example of a crime scene text is that of disturbance, as noted in *Signs of Crime*, the treatise that first introduced the idea of forensic semiotics and which is the foundation of this chapter. As described by Danesi (2013), the crime scene, once located by authorities, reveals itself as a collection of signs—broken glass, overturned furniture, blood stains—all of which act in concert as evidence of a violent struggle (134). There are also other less conspicuous signs not readily discernible to the naked eye—latent evidence—that amount to artifacts that require collecting and curating, such as DNA evidence or fingerprints, both of which will confirm the presence of an offender. The investigator, like the offender, subsequently engages not only in curation but also meaning-making, where both of them—criminal and criminalist alike—using a system of signs that defaults to an inner narrative. It is the job of the forensic investigator to collect and interpret all trace evidence at a crime scene in order to figure out how, and perhaps *why*, the crime was committed. So, if crime scene evidence like blood, fingerprints, broken glass, and even the body of a victim are reasoned as metaphorical signs through the interpretation of the forensic investigator, and if all of these signs work together to create a crime scene text, where does curation find its practical application? It is the curationist mind that is able to process and critically interpret these signs in relation to each other, to garner meaning from their particular positioning. It is the application of the conceptual model of metaphors to a physical space: the usage of a metaphorical lens to see meaning-making in a realm that is more than purely conceptual.

Crime scenes bear a quality of inherent curationism, because each trace of evidence is treated not only as a piece of evidence in itself, but as a part of the scene *in relation* with another part of the scene. We understand evidence *A* in relation to evidence *B*—blood spatter on the wall makes the presence of a bloodied knife relevant, just as a bloodied knife makes relevant the blood spatter. This dialogic relationship between trace evidence is what makes crime scenes so interpretable: the semiotic nature of all of these clues mean that each piece of evidence can be conceptually deconstructed and reconstructed over and over again until a picture of real events may begin to develop. As posited in *Signs of Crime*, "all clues at a crime scene are *de facto* signs standing for referents that must be inferred hermeneutically (interpretively and contextually)" (17).

The more complex signs that form texts, like obvious signs of a struggle or intricate and/or exemplary blood spatter patterns, reveal information for a hypothetical recreation of events through their very structure. Less complex signs, despite having their own symbolic or ritual value, are better interpreted through their immediate spatial environments. Is there a connection between this gun and these fingerprints? Does their spatial relationship allow us to infer anything about what happened? Questions such as these are vital to the curatorial process and function as signs-in-*relation* rather than signs-in-*isolation*. The curationist mind, when examining and processing a crime scene, will natutally ask these questions. The inherently curated crime scene tells a story, and the metaphor-oriented conceptual lens of the curationist mind is able to interpret the relationship between the evidence signs in order to reconstruct the events of the crime. This process carries metaphorical value in itself, when considering that evidence presents itself in a concrete form, and that the forensic investigator will in turn interpret the evidence to connect the concrete crime scene signs with an intangible, conceptual vision of what may have happened. This mapping of reality on to imagined reality is figurative in its structure and is again an example of meaning-making arising from associative, metaphorical thought.

The Duality of Forensic Curation

With this notion of forensic curation now presented, I will here deconstruct it into two oppositional applications. On one hand, there is the *literal* source of forensic curation: the criminal. The criminal acts as the curator of the scene of his or her own crime. This curation can be either natural or deliberate. Natural curation occurs at every crime scene, coming from within the method and practice of the criminal. Regardless of whether or not the crime was pre-meditated, there will always be some subconscious level of organization at the scene: the position of the corpse, the way the blood hit the wall, the angle at which a bullet went through a piece of furniture. These spatial organizations occur without modification, but are examples of inherent curationism. Though they may not have been elaborately planned, the physical layout of a crime scene requires the curationist mind for interpretation. The relation between evidence remains capable of evoking a particular narrative or meaning, with or without the calculated or intentional curation of a criminal.

Alternatively, deliberate curation is precisely this type of altered or intentional curation. In forensics, this act is commonly referred to as *staging*, which is defined as the "alteration of a crime scene in order to redirect the investigation" (Schlesinger, Gardenier, Jarvis, & Sheehan-Cook, 2014: 45). A criminal may partake in *Minimal Staging* (no more than one or two alterations, like changing the placement of a gun to frame a homicide as a suicide); *Moderate Staging* (three or four changes made to evidence); or, *Elaborate Staging* (five or more alterations), all of which aim, at some level, to change the way that the crime scene may be interpreted (Schlesinger et al., 2014: 46). The criminal is aware of how a detective or forensic investigator attending the scene may read that same scene, and subsequently makes adjustments to the elements of the scene in order to evince a much different story (perhaps one where they will not be suspected) and thus change the potential—and desired—interpretation. This deliberate staging is quintessentially curational in the tradition of the museum exhibit: the criminal systematically organizes and presents the evidence at their own crime scene to evoke a particular meaning. Their alteration of the elements of the crime scene changes the relation between the elements, which serves to change the interpretation that the forensic investigators will have, and potentially change the outcome of the case. Along with this notion of staging, then, is the notion that crime scenes are not only texts but also *stages*, where criminals perform crimes, tell stories with the hypothetical narrative that arises from the relational positioning of the evidence, and perform their identities by presenting or hiding themselves in a certain manner, such as using signatures, symbols, personal signs, or DNA information.

On the other end of the spectrum, there is the forensic curation that occurs *conceptually* within the detective. Investigators read the crime scene as something that is curated. Approaching a crime scene with the curationist mind, investigators make conceptual connections and associations through observing trace evidence. They understand the presentation of crime scene elements *in relation* to one another, and use this relationship to construct a hypothetical account of what may have occurred. This investigative process is, as stated before, like metaphor creation. The detective is using a spatial understanding of physical evidence to turn metaphorical, iconic signs into indexical signs, signs of crime that work together to point to specific contexts and interpretations. "Detective work is sign-interpretation work" (Danesi, 2013: 17), and with the model of the curationist mind, it allows for the understanding of a naturally or deliberately curated space to generate a set of interpretations that may lead to the solving of a crime.

These two perspectives work together in opposition. As the criminal is the curator of their crime scene, the forensic investigator interprets the scene as something that is curated. Without this dual-function, the forensic process would change entirely. Criminals (particularly those who deliberately alter their evidence), rely on the forensic tradition of interpreting the signs of a crime scene, and of reading the crime scene like a curated text. If the forensic investigator could not derive meaning from the spatial relationships of evidence, the criminal would not curate their crime scene in the first place. Similarly, if no crime scene staging was known to exist, sign-interpretation work for investigators would be significantly less complex, more tried-and-true. Meaning would not need to be evoked, as it would not be hidden in the first place. For this reason, curation is not only inherent to almost all crime investigations—it is also necessary for the maintenance of meaning-making in the crime scene setting.

Conclusion

In this paper, I have proposed a number of semiotic models that address both conceptual methods of forensic investigation and the inherent curated nature of crime, with a specific focus on crime scene examination. Given the prevalence of metaphorical signs in forensic applications, my exploration of the connection between metaphor and crime works to support my proposal that there exists a curationist mind—a metaphorical lens that allows for the conceptual approach of a physical realm. In this proposal, I have revealed similarities between the structure of meaning-making from metaphor and the structure of meaning-making from curatorial practice, and argued that forensic investigators interpret crime scenes as curated texts through associative, metaphorical reasoning. From this, I can support my overarching thesis: crime as curation, or, perhaps that crime *is* curation.

It is clear throughout this study that the principles of curation, especially regarding the making and evocation of meaning, are inherent throughout many aspects of crime. Criminals are seen to physically curate their crime scenes, and detectives conceptually curate their observance of crime scenes to form valuable interpretations. With a semiotic approach, it is evident that these processes are deeply embedded within the structure of crime and of forensic analysis. Through the metaphorical yet analytical lens that I have proposed in this chapter, I believe that the prevalence of curatorial theory and practice in both conceptual interpretations and physical manipulations of crime is of great interest. It could, in fact, pose implications for forensic approaches to crime scene analysis and investigative training in the future, particularly regarding the intersection of forensics with the fields of psychology and semiotics.

References

Bray, R., & Dalton, D. Crime Scenes. *Law Text Culture, 13*(1), 5–12. 2009. Retrieved from http://simplelink.library.utoronto.ca/url.cfm/473822.

Curate. In the *New Oxford American Dictionary*. 2010.

Danesi, M. *Of Cigarettes, High Heels, and Other Interesting Things: An Introduction to Semiotics* (2nd ed.). New York: Palgrave Macmillan. 2008.

Danesi, M. (2013). *Signs of Crime. Introducing Forensic Semiotics*. Berlin, Boston: De Gruyter. 2013.

Schlesinger, L., Gardenier, A., Jarvis, J., & Sheehan-Cook, J. Crime Scene Staging in Homicide. *Journal of Police and Criminal Psychology, 29*(1), 44–51. 2014. Retrieved from http://simplelink.library.utoronto.ca/url.cfm/473819.

10. *Crime and the Canvas: Depicting Criminals and Their Punishments in the Visual Arts, from Antiquity to Present*

Bethany K. Walters & Eric W. Hickey

Introduction

This chapter investigates the various representations of criminal offending, and by extension criminology, as it has existed in Western and near-Western visual arts throughout history, from approximately 3000 BCE to the twenty-first century. Depictions of criminals and their victims, crime, punishment, and law are vast; therefore, only specific examples are discussed here as an introductory primer on this topic. That discussion begins by looking at how art has been used to reinforce social mores, and the relationship between artists and criminals. Examples of specific pieces or exhibits are discussed to illustrate how art has depicted criminological ideals, followed by a discussion of how criminology has also influenced art. The chapter concludes with a few cases illustrating associations between criminals and artists.

Before proceeding, however, it is necessary—given the expansive catalogue of works encompassing various mediums, styles, and traditions available for critical analysis—that some limitations are placed on the definition of the "visual" arts, as well as what constitutes Western and near-Western art for the purposes of this discussion. Developing a suitably comprehensive yet workable definition of both is certainly bound to be problematic and any subsequent list of representative titles contentious. This also means such definitions and an associated list of works must be developed somewhat arbitrarily, a recognizable limitation which in part explains why crime in art remains such a curiously untouched area of scholarship—at least among criminologists and crime historians.

Visual art will be very loosely defined here as a two or three dimensional object created for the primary purpose of visual perception, generally painting or sculpture. Additionally, images chosen for this chapter must also relate to criminology. The majority of images selected for use here have already been the subjects of art history, except for the artwork created by incarcerated offenders; however, these pieces still fit the definition of visual art above. The majority of images selected for inclusion here originated in Western cultures, i.e, Western European Countries and North America, or near-Western cultures, i.e., Egypt and Iraq, as these regions share similar cultural traditions to Western countries. Due to the broad coverage of this chapter, it was not feasible to also include non-Western or Eastern art; a topic which should be explored in future scholarship. The rationale for using this working definition of visual art and Western or near-Western cultures allows for a manageable archive for use in tracing criminology's influence with respect to a broad array of art over thousands of years in a relatively succinct fashion.

Artistic Representations of Criminology in Ancient Art

Artwork from the ancient world, as does contemporary art, tends to mirror the sophisticated and complex social and political structures of early civilizations. Before examining examples from ancient Western and near-Western civilizations, it is important to understand the cultural context in which these works were created. As Bohn and Saslow (2013) note "artworks were made by artists, but their conception was the product of a complex interaction between patron, artists, and society. The patrons who commissioned and paid for a work shaped its formation with their own social, religious, and political views" (7–8). Most of these societies employed a monarchy or imperial system of government, for example, the Roman Empire which lasted from approximately 30 BCE to 476 CE, and Dynastic Egypt generally accepted as existing from 3100 BCE until 350 BCE. The rulers of these lands were seen as living incarnations of deities, which in turn sanctified their divine right to rule. Religion, a vital part of their culture, thus played a central role in all aspects of society, and polytheism—the belief in numerous gods rather than a single higher power or creator—was the dominant system, with the Roman Empire subscribing to polytheism until the reign of Constantine the Great in the fourth century (Elsner 1998, 199). Works depicting ancient laws existed to document events and those same laws, while also acting as a visual reminder to the viewers/subjects of the supreme ruler's right to rule. Additionally, works of antiquity provided a reminder of the very earthly punishments of crimes, whether it be against a person, property, or the state. An early representation of this can be found within the palette of King

Narmer from Ancient Egypt (ca. 3000–2920 BCE) commemorating the unification of upper and lower Egypt (Figure 1). The palette depicts the king slaying an enemy, a warning not only to potential invaders but also his own subjects should they disobey the law of Pharaoh (Kleiner and Mamiya 2006, 43–44). Additionally, the king is depicted similarly to the Egyptian gods, reminding viewers of the kings divine right to rule, and establishing his authority to allot punishment.

Visual representations of crime and punishment are also found in the ancient stele with the Law Code of Hammurabi (Figure 2). A precursor to contemporary criminal statutes found in the British common law system, the stele similarly codified crimes and corresponding punishments in ancient Babylonian society. The stele depicts the sun god Shamash bestowing the Babylonian king, Hammurabi, with the ring and rod which symbolize his divine right to rule (Kleiner and Mamiya 2006, 29). Underneath the image in cuneiform writing is a codex of 282 laws and punishments to which citizens were bound. Most famously, the concept of *lex talionis*, the law of retaliation (an eye for an eye), is outlined within the codex, in addition to other criminal offences and their corresponding punishments, e.g., the punishment for theft was death (Kleiner, and Mamiya 2006, 29).

More subtle images of individual criminals in the art of ancient Rome can be found in the depictions of perhaps the most iconic image of the Roman Empire, the Colosseum, where epic gladiatorial fights between slaves or criminals were staged for the amusement of the ancient Roman people (Editors of Time-Life Books 1997). Many lives and careers inevitably ended in violent death, and as such, images of gladiatorial games, in addition to the Colosseum itself, provided a reminder of this reality while serving as something of an architectural deterrent with respect to criminal offending. For example, the Zliten mosaic, dating to roughly 200 CE, depicts various gladiatorial scenes (Figure 3). One of these representations includes a leopard attacking a condemned prisoner in the gladiatorial arena. These types of images were plentiful throughout the empire and have been found on a variety of different mediums, including frescos, mosaics, oil lamps, and glass, in addition to the creation of statues of gladiators (Elsner 1998).

The concept of *damnatio memoriae*, or the "condemnation of memory" describes the manner in which the visual image, either the name or physical representation of an individual, was physically destroyed, usually after their death (Varner 2004). Ancient Roman art displays evidence of this practice and can be seen when Emperor Caracalla ordered all of the portraits of his brother and co-ruler, Geta, to be defaced or destroyed, after Caracalla murdered him (Varner 2004). In ancient Egypt this practice was especially devastating as

Figure 1. Image of the Palette of King Narmer, ca. 3000–2920 BCE.

Figure 2. Image of the Law Code of Hammurabi, ca. 1780 BCE.

Figure 3. Image of a part of the Zliten mosaic depicting gladiatorial games, ca. 200 CE.

Figure 4. Image of a vessel with the cartouche (name) of Akhenaten erased, ca. 1351–1334 BCE.

this meant part of the deceased's soul, the ren (their name), would cease to exist (Taylor 2001). Perhaps the best-known example of this in ancient Egypt is that of the Pharaoh Akhenaten. Historical records ultimately revealed that Akhenaten declared the formerly polytheistic society a monotheistic one, which predictably was not a decision favored by the people. After his death, his son and predecessor, the famed boy king Tutankhamen, reinstated polytheism as the official religion of Egypt, and as a demonstrable punishment for his father's sins against the other gods, ordered his father's name and image erased from all of Egypt (Brand, 2010).

Akhenaten provided a preview of monotheism which would later become Western Europe's dominant religious system. As the Roman Empire began to decline from its pinnacle between roughly 96–180 CE, the art created within its society evolved to reflect those changes, inspiring newfound styles while continuing to honor traditional artistic elements. This theme of continuality and change (Elsner 1998) lasted through early medieval art, which spanned from approximately 500–1000 CE (Kleiner and Mamiya 2006). Between roughly 100 to 1000 CE, iconography specific to ancient themes were thus reworked to reflect the new religious doctrine of Christianity (Elsner 1998), as a dominant art theme. The realistic tradition captured in Roman art was replaced by a new, two-dimensional regime in painting and sculpture in which depictions appeared within a single plane. This style of art was typical throughout Western Europe during the Middle Ages (roughly 400–1500 CE), and did not stylistically differ until the Renaissance (roughly 1300–1600 CE) when Western art once again begin to adopt realism and incorporate three-dimensional perspective as the dominant style. The subject matter of much of the surviving art during this time was religious, designed to inspire contemplation in the viewer. During this time people were largely illiterate; thus, works of art were intended as education tools for learning the Bible and church teachings (Roberts and Weisberg 1976), although these didactics were more than teaching the history and message of the Bible, as they also represented politics, law, and daily life. This period represents one in which the epistemology of crime—and the aesthetic representations of criminality and deviance—were principally captured in art as the dominant narrative medium.

Artistic Representations of Criminology in Medieval and Renaissance Art, and Beyond

During the Middle Ages, the Renaissance, and the Baroque Era (generally defined as 1600–1750 CE), horrific images depicting wars, the murders of martyred saints, and the crucifixion of Christ were amongst the common images of criminal violence appropriated by the visual arts. Specifically, Christ's crucifixion was one of the most dominant images for thousands of years in Western art (Kleiner and Mamiya 2006). During the time of Christ, crucifixion (beginning around the sixth century BCE and lasting until the fourth century CE) was used as a method of execution for crimes, often reserved, given its inherently cruel design, for slaves and political or religious agitators. As such, Jesus Christ of Nazareth was executed for the crime of treason, a serious offense that carried with it crucifixion as the most barbaric—and public—of punishments. However, in Christianity, the crucifixion symbolizes Christ's transition from human to the divine; therefore, the cross became the dominant symbol of the Christian faith by the sixth century CE (Stott 2006, 27). The image of the cross became a didactic instrument which offered morality lessons via punishment which were meant to inspire contemplation in the viewer of their own morality and mortality; it was an image intended to inspire righteous living—subjects which were expanded upon in images of the Last Judgment.

The concept of the Final Judgment also implied that the ultimate concern during life was the determination of the soul's destination in the afterlife. The theme of the last judgment is famously depicted by Michelangelo di Lodovico Buonarroti Simoni in *The Last Judgment* (Figure 5), located in the Sistine chapel. Images of the last judgment characteristically depict Christ judging the souls of all of humanity and either granting them access to heaven (located on the right/dextra side of Christ) or condemning them to hell (located on the left/sinstra side of Christ). This subject was not limited to being localized to religious buildings, e.g., churches. Rather, the subject of the last judgment was additionally used in secular buildings, not surprisingly, as there was no separation between church and state at that time. Specifically, it was not uncommon in Western Europe to have a fresco of the last judgment on the wall behind the judge's bench in a courtroom or town hall, its being strategically positioned to reflect the heavenly realm on earth (Edgerton 1985).

For instance, Edgerton (1985) reported a painting of *The Last Judgment*, artist unknown, on the wall behind the judge's bench in the courtroom in the city hall on the Domplatz in Amsterdam during the Renaissance. It is similar to other scenes of the last judgment, in which Christ is centered casting judgment on those below. Those deemed worthy of redemption are on the right of Christ while those condemned to hell appear below Christ to his left. Further, the artistic narrative served to replicate the procedures of the actual courtroom. Normally, the judge's bench faced the east wall, the direction of redemption, where the judge determined the innocence or guilt of the accused; mimicking the role of Christ in the Last Judgment. If found guilty the defendant was taken to the left/sinstra of the judge's bench to the secretary's desk to receive sentencing—the same direction damned souls are sent in a last judgment scene. The justice system was analogous to the last judgment and thus linked the secular with the divine (Curtis and Resnik 1987).

In addition to the last judgment as a common image within the Western courtroom, so too is the image of Justice, which still remains a symbol of the criminal justice system. The allegory of Justice can be seen in Ambrogio Lorenzetti's *Allegory of Good Government* (Figure 6). Here the representation of Justizia (Justice) holds her scales, each with a personification kneeling next to a scale: Distributive and Commutative. Commutative is depicted granting gifts of peace and wealth, while Distributive is shown punishing two people by decapitating one and ripping the crown from the head of the other (Edgerton 2003). In Lorenzetti's allegory, execution is portrayed as the most severe form of punishment, reserved for only the most serious crimes, including treason and murder. However, unlike today's rare and private executions conducted behind the closed walls of a prison, public executions were common, often serving as entertainment for family outings (Raymond Paternoster Brame and Bacon, 2008). Thus, the public spectacle of capital punishment took on a certain threefold symbolism. It reinforced civic order, it provided a preview of the last judgment by God to spectators (Edgerton 2003), and it provided a last chance for penance by the condemned (Farago 2014). During the Renaissance in Western Europe there were several methods for execution, depending on the type of crime committed. Usually reserved for the upper class, decapitation was considered an honorable and quick death (Edgerton 2003). There are several works of art documenting these types of decapitations, such as the execution of Mary Queen of Scotts (Figure 7), and the execution of Anne Boylen. Being broken on a wheel, hanged, or drawn and quartered were particularly grotesque and cruel methods of execution reserved for members of the lower classes (Edgerton 2003). Religious crimes, such as witchcraft or heresy, were often punished by being burnt at the stake, as depicted by Francesco Rizi's painting of the *Auto-da-fé*found in the Plaza Mayor, Madrid.

Artists were of course themselves also audience members who witnessed these public executions. This may in part explain the anatomical accuracy of devastated bodies as depicted in the visual arts, such as the severed head of John the Baptist (Edgerton 2003). Additionally, some sketches exist which depict executions of commoners, such as Annibale Carracci's drawing, *A Hanging* (n.d.). The work depicts the hanging of two men, inside a prison

Figure 5. Image of *The Last Judgment* by Michelangelo 1536–1541 CE.

Figure 6. Scene from Allegory of Good and Bad Government by Ambrogio Lorenzetti ca. 1338/9 CE.

with onlookers from outside the prison wall. In the drawing, one of the condemned men is hoisted up on a ladder while his noose is tied. At the same time a priest holds a tavoletta, a small painting of either the Crucifixion or the Passion; both acts were common in practice at executions of that time (Farago 2014). Catholic Brothers from San Giovanni Decollato would visit condemned prisoners, escorting the prisoner to the scaffold and holding the tavoletta for the prisoner to view and contemplate while providing solace as the prisoner died. As Edgerton (2003) also points out, painting and sketching have, since the Middle Ages, been simultaneously used to chronicle executions and at the same time art is used as an instrument in the execution process. Thus, we see in both secular and divine works references to capital punishment.

The bodies of the executed also provided study materials for artists during this period, as the Church allowed for dissection of executed criminals by not only physicians but also artists under the rationale of increasing knowledge of anatomy and physiology, including how the body is represented in art (Edgerton 2003). In some sense, the executed criminal was to become the physiological prototype for entire generations of artists looking to accurately and authentically depict the human form across a variety of mediums. Thus, the criminal physique as a de facto archetype in painting and sketch throughout early Western history, and the implications of this in the study of everything from aesthetics to gender studies to criminology is no doubt a robust but heretofore untapped area of scholarship in the humanities—one that admittedly exceeds the scope of this chapter. Of note, while dissection was typically condemned by the Church, as it was viewed as desecration of God's work, exceptions were made among physicians and artists dissecting executed criminals because it was widely believed that sin dwelled in the flesh. Removing the flesh of those condemned therefore amounted to a final act of penitence (Edgerton 2003). The treatise, *De favrica corporis humani*, by Andreas Vesalius (1543) illustrates knowledge about the body being learned principally through dissection of the condemned (Figure 8). Another example of the concept of removing the flesh as penance for sin is observable in the painting by Gerard David, which was displayed behind the seat of the judges' bench in the town hall in Bruges during the fifteenth century (Edgerton 2003). The painting is said to have depicted the Greek legend of a corrupt judge who was sentenced to be flayed alive, after which his skin was adhered to the judges' chair as a warning for others to avoid corruption. Other similar paintings depicting corrupt judges with severed hands were not uncommon in town halls to remind the triers of fact of their own fallibility (Mundy 1980). Taken together, these images reinforced the idea of sin inhabiting the flesh

Figure 7. Mary Stewart's Execution, drawing, 1613 CE, unknown artist.

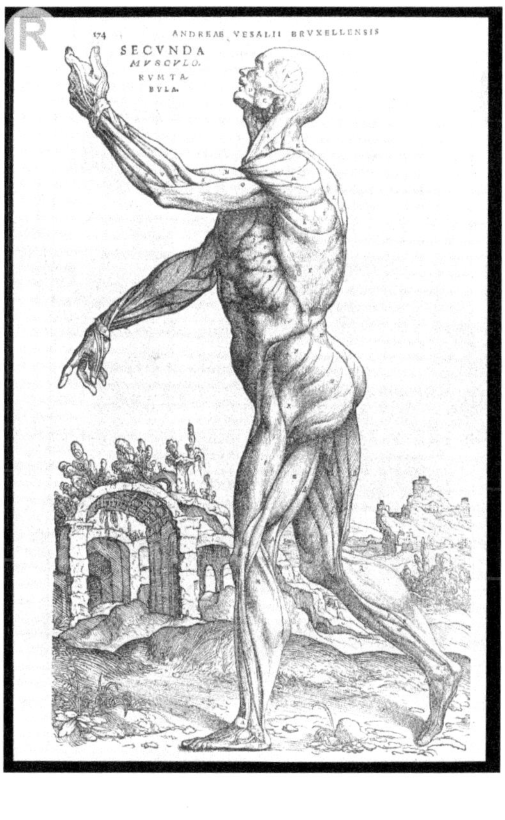

Figure 8. Page from *De favrica corporis humani* illustrating human anatomy in the context of a criminal skinned alive, 1543 CE.

and of both religious and secular punishments which awaited those corrupted individuals.

While religion was a primary subject in most art commissions, some sketches and works directly reflect violence or crime within secular European society. For example, Leonardo Di Vinci's 1493 sketch, *A Man Tricked by Gypsies* depicts a man being pick pocketed, while Titian Vecelli's 1511 fresco, *The Miracle of the Jealous Husband* (Figure 9), depicts a man in the act of murdering his adulterous wife. On a less extreme scale, Michelangelo Merisi da Caravaggio's *The Cardsharps* (Figure 10) and *The Fortune Teller* (Figure 11) both depict hustlers duping their victims. Although these are but a few of the images showcasing criminal activities—both violent and property crimes—they demonstrate the types of offenses common to their respective historical periods. They were offenses common enough, at least, that artists saw fit to document their occurrence.

In the case of non-lethal punishments for what were considered less serious offenses, during the Middle Ages prisons existed primarily to hold those awaiting corporal punishment or torture, with incarceration in itself not being considered a form punishment (Wolfgang 2002). Prior to the fourteenth century in Florence, for instance, sentences of either death or corporeal punishment were largely arbitrary and imposed at the sole discretion of judges. This changed when specific punishments for what were typically non violent offenses resulted in punishments that began to reflect custodial sentences of thirty days or less, at which point prison came to be interpreted as an alternative to torture or other physical punishment (Wolfgang 2002). One of the original prisons in Florence, for example, infamously known as Le Stinche, which held the famous goldsmith Benventuo Cellini for four years as punishment for a sodomy conviction, as well as famed politician and author Niccolo Machiavelli, reflects this paradigm shift, as confirmed by its register of lengthened sentences of inmates received during this same period (Wolfgang 2002). The concept of time and money also came to be intrinsically linked even ahead of European industrialization and the advent of the hourly wage, with the ability to deprive a convict of his time, and thus his ability to earn money, being seen by many of those in power as tantamount to torturing his body (Wolfgang 2002). This shift was similarly expressed in the visual arts, with aesthetic representations of human activities beyond religious worship, including labor and intellectual pursuits, becoming increasingly prevalent, thus harkening in the next era in history.

As the Enlightenment loomed, more secular representations of crime and punishment in the visual arts emerged. For instance, Jacques-Louis David, perhaps best known for his 1754 painting *The Death of Marat* (Figure 12)

Figure 9. Image of Titian's *The Miracle of the Jealous Husband*, 1511 CE.

Figure 10. Image of Caravaggio's *The Cardsharps*, 1594 CE.

Figure 11. Image of Caravaggio's *The Fortune Teller*, 1596–1597 CE.

which, as the title suggests, graphically depicts not only a painted image of an execution, but the artist himself participating in one, albeit indirectly by voting for the execution of King Louis XVI (Farago 2014). As execution methods became more surgically precise and less gory or theatrical over the following centuries—for instance, the guillotine, followed firing squads, the electric chair, the gas chamber, and lethal injection—artists took note and emphasized this technical evolution in their works. Jumping ahead to more contemporary times, photographer Andy Warhol's prints of the electric chair (1963), convey this change to the impersonal and shrouded nature of modern executions (Farago 2014). More recently the works by photographer Amy Elkins display the final words of executed inmates overlaid on to images of their mugshots. Other pictorial representations of actual crimes in contemporary visual arts include Paul Cėzanne's *The Murder* (Figure 13), and Renė Magritte's *L'Assassin Menace* (1926), to name but two.

Contemporary Visual Arts & the Modernization of Criminology in Art

The visual arts have gone on to play an enhanced role in criminology in the last two centuries largely via the work Cesare Lombroso (2013), often seen as the father of positivist criminology with the publication of his seminal treatise, *L'Uomo delinquente* (The Criminal Man) in 1887. At the time of its publication, the text was a comparatively modern, albeit later revealed to be flawed, approach to understanding criminal physiology that was rooted in art. It was also one that recalled the use of criminal cadavers in the Middle Ages as a means of artistically conceptualizing the variability of the human form among artists. Drawing on Albrecht Dürer's sketches of the human form collected in the *Dresden Sketchbook* (1528), Lombroso reproduced many different representations of various criminal types, comparing artistic works dating to antiquity to his own original contemporary sketches, engravings, and photographs of criminals (Dobelbower 2006). This comparative analysis was based largely on his theory of physiognomy—the concept of being able to ascertain personality traits from a person's physical appearance. Lombroso used biological positivism to found the Italian school of criminology, from which it took root as an adjunct of sociology and spawned into its own discipline.

While physiognomy was subsequently determined to be woefully inaccurate as a means of identifying criminality, it lead the way to the beginning of the study of criminology utilizing, at least ostensibly, the scientific method. This included methods of deduction and the incorporation of other sciences—which ushered in criminology's interdisciplinary ethos—such as the

Figure 12. *Death of Marat*, by David, 1793 CE.

Figure 13. *The Murder*, by Paul Cèzanne, 1869/70 CE.

development of mug shots, finger printing, and modern advances in science such as DNA typing. For example, Alphonse Bertillon, a French police officer during the nineteenth-century, developed the practice of systematically photographing criminals—the mugshot (Bertillon 1896). Bertillon illustrated how a new artistic medium, photography, could be helpful to the field of criminology. Additionally, the use of police sketches in helping to positively identify suspects, directly solders artist and criminology together—what today falls under the interdisciplinary umbrella of forensic art. These sketches can be hand drawn, or performed by an officer with the help of a kit—such as Smith & Wesson's once standard Identi-Kit—or can be completed using computer software, in essence turning the law enforcement officer or his or her designate into an artist, for however brief a time.

A broad and discursive subject of analysis and both criminal investigation and forensic examination, art forgery and art crime also directly connects the visual arts to the field of criminology. Whether a given piece is authentic and stolen to be sold on the black market, or a forgery of varying sophistication, art crimes contribute to billions of dollars worth of illicit trade each year. In 2004 the Federal Bureau of Investigation (FBI 2015) created its own art crimes division, expressly for the purpose of interdicting a growing global black market in either forged or illicit art., including paintings, sculptures, writings, antiques, and other rare artifacts. Further litigation still continues over the rightful ownership of art transported during World War II, not only between countries and institutions, but also among private citizens. Such protracted litigation also underscores the intersection between the law and art more broadly. Continuing to look at the direct interaction between crime and art, the next two sections examine the dual roles of specific entities of historical significance as both artists and criminals.

The Visual Artist as Criminal

While much of this chapter has discussed depictions of criminals and punishments in the visual arts, some noteworthy artists were also criminals themselves. The famous Renaissance sculptor and goldsmith, Benvenuto Cellini, for instance, was a serial murderer. He kept a detailed account of his murders in his autobiography: he killed his brother's murderer, and later murdered a rival goldsmith and an innkeeper (Cellini 1902). Additionally, Cellini was charged with crimes of sodomy against both males and females, representing a notable and early documented case of criminal sexual polymorphism well ahead of the associated clinical and forensic literature classified the term and the phenomenon. Likely possessing some psychopathic traits, primarily a lack of remorse for his actions, Cellini managed to eschew criminal punishment due to his reported connections to the Vatican. Today, however, he is primarily remembered for his artworks, and not his crimes.

As perhaps a better known artist-criminal, famed Baroque artist Michelangelo Merisi da Caravaggio committed crimes including battery against both men and women, slander and murder (Langdon 2012). Forced to flee Rome after one of his murders, it was during this time on the run that he painted several famous works, including his defining piece, *David with the Head of Goliath* (1610 CE; Langdon 2012).

The art of Banksy, a British contemporary "street" artist whose art is by definition graffiti, consists of painting and stenciling on public property, such as buildings, walls, and other structures (Figure 14). By definition this type of art is considered graffiti, with criminal mischief being the applicable offense in most Western nations. To date, he has nonetheless retained his anonymity and eluded capture by authorities. While his works were originally considered acts of vandalism, they now are both prized and praised.

The Criminal as Visual Artist

Some criminals have become glorified artists only *after* their crimes became publicized. The works of art, in addition to poems, letters, and even snippets of hair belonging to serial murderers in particular have become popular items in a burgeoning and macabre industry whose assets are generally classified as murderabilia. Some of the most sought after items on related murderabilia websites are the artworks of serial murderer John Wayne Gacy (Figure 15), who was responsible for the sexual assault and murder of thirty-three teenaged boys and young men in the 1970s in Chicago, Illinois (Silverman 2011). Gacy created many paintings and self-portraits as a clown—a reference to his alter ego "Pogo the Clown" while incarcerated awaiting execution.

Following Gacy's execution in 1994 many of his paintings were auctioned and sold for between several hundred and several thousands of dollars; the most expensive painting sold for $9500 (Sale of Chicago Serial Killer's Art Draws Protests 2004). While some of the paintings were deliberately destroyed in a large bonfire attended by some family members of Gacy's victims (Sale of Chicago Serial Killer's Art Draws Protests 2004), others have been displayed in exhibitions (Williams 2011). Most recently, in 2011, the Arts Factory Gallery in Las Vegas exhibited 74 works created by Gacy, after which they were auctioned off for bids ranging between $2000 to $12,000 each. The proceeds from the auction were earmarked for various charitable organizations, as specified by Gacy's art portfolio executor (Williams 2011).

Figure 14. Work by Banksy, generally known as the Skeleton Rower, 2008 CE.

Figure 15. Painting by John Wayne Gacy, n.d.

Other serial murderers who produced art while incarcerated include Henry Lee Lucas and his partner in crime, Ottis Elwood Toole. Lucas was convicted of murdering eleven people, while Toole was convicted of murdering six. Toole was ultimately also identified as the murderer of Adam Walsh, the son of famed *America's Most Wanted* television host, John Walsh, whose mission in helping create the series was to ferret out the killer of his son and other murderers still at large (Neeland 2013). Lucas's art was more technically sophisticated and included landscapes as compared to Toole's which, for the most part, amounted to crude cartoons (Neeland 2013). Similar in style to Toole's artwork, Keith Hunter Jeperson, the so-called "Happy Face Killer" who murdered a total of eight women, also drew crude and puerile cartoon-like images following his arrest and incarceration (Neeland 2013). Richard Ramirez, the "Night Stalker," who was convicted of murdering thirteen people in Satanic-themed home invasion murders in 1980s greater Los Angeles, created works with darker themes, including images of skulls and demons (Rayner 2015). Many other high-profile serial and mass murderers have created artworks that have since become collectable and desirable objects in the subculture of murderabilia. Most recently, a 2014 show in Tokyo featured the drawings and paintings created by 34 men currently awaiting execution on death row (Farago 2014), elevating their works to the status of museum pieces.

Conclusion

This chapter has briefly discussed the complex and often intertwined relationship between criminology and the visual arts within Western and near-Western cultures. Images of varying realism that have been conceived, created, and disseminated throughout history, from antiquity to contemporary times, have consistently demonstrated the complex interactions art has with the criminal world. This includes aesthetic representations of the criminal form as it exists in both life and death, and conceptualizations of the state in meting out punishments up to and including the imposition of death. It would benefit both the field of criminology and of art history to explore how the emerging field of the criminal humanities will help conjoin these traditionally discrete and historically, it would seem, irreconcilable areas of scholarship. Not only would such an interdisciplinary marriage provide a better understanding of history, but also an improved understanding of art, criminals, and crime as inextricably linked over the course of human development, from antiquity to the present.

References

Babette, Bohn, and Saslow, James, M. *A Companion to Renaissance and Baroque Art (Blackwell Companions to Art History)*. West Sussex: John Wiley & Sons, Inc.

Bertillon, Alphonse. 1896. *Signaletic Instructions Including the Theory and Practice of Anthropometrical Identification*. Werner Company. 2013.

Brand, Peter. "Reuse and Restoration." *UCLA Encyclopedia of Egyptology* 1, no. 1. 2010.

Cellini, Benvenuto. *The Life of Benvenuto Cellini*. Charles Scribner's Sons. 1902.

Curtis, Dennis E., and Resnik, Judith. "Images of Justice." *Yale Law Journal:* 1727–72. 1987.

Dobelbower, Nicholas. The Arts and Science of Criminal Man in Fin-De-Siècle France." Paper presented at the Proceedings of the Western Society for French History. 2006.

Edgerton, Samuel Y. *Pictures and Punishment: Art and Criminal Prosecution During the Florentine Renaissance*. Cornell University Press. 1985.

Edgerton, Samuel Y. "When Even Artists Encouraged the Death Penalty," *Law & Literature* 15, no. 2. 2003.

Editors of Time Life Books. *What Life Was Like When Rome Ruled the World: The Roman Empire, 100 BC–AD 200*. Alexandria, VA: Time-Life Books. 1997.

Elsner, Jaś. *Imperial Rome and Christian Triumph*. New York: Oxford University Press. 1998.

Farago, Jason. "Pictures at an Execution: The Condemned in Art." http://www.bbc.com/culture/story/20141014-pictures-at-an-execution. 2014.

Federal Bureau of Investigation. "Art Theft." Accessed May 12, 2015: https://www.fbi.gov/about-us/investigate/vc_majorthefts/arttheft/art-crime-team. 2015.

Kleiner, Fred S., and Mamiya, Christin, J. *Gardner's Art through the Ages: The Western Perspective Vol. 1, 12 edition*. Belmont, CA: Thomson Wadsworth. 2005.

Langdon, Helen. *Caravaggio*. Random House. 2012.

Lombroso, Cesare. *L'uomo Delinquente-Quinta Edizione—1897*. Bompiani. 2013 Reprint.

Mundy, James. "A Preparatory Sketch for Gerard David's Justice of Cambyses Panels in Bruges." *The Burlington Magazine*. 122–25. 1980.

Neeland, Emily. Last modified August 2. "Top Ten Serial Killer Artists" http://blog.privateislandparty.com/top-ten-serial-killer-artists/.

Paternoster, Raymond, Brame, Robert, and Bacon, Sarah. 2008. *The Death Penalty: America's Experience with Capital Punishment*. USA: Oxford University Press. 2013.

Rayner, Karly. Last modified March 4. "This Twisted Artwork by Serial Killers Gives Us a Shocking Peek into the World's Most Evil Minds." 2015. http://moviepilot.com/posts/2015/03/04/this-twisted-artwork-by-serial-killers-gives-us-a-shocking-peek-into-the-world-s-most-evil-minds-2750369.

Resnik, Judith, and Curtis, Dennis E. *Representing Justice: Invention, Controversy, and Rights in City-States and Democratic Courtrooms*. Yale University Press. 2011.

Roberts, K. H., and Weisberg, R. "Medieval Drawing and the Arts of Memory." *Coranto*, 10, 28–42. 1976.

"Sale of Chicago Serial Killer's Art Draws Protests." *St. Petersburg Times.* 2004.

Silverman, Karen Sandlin. "John Wayne Gacy: Defending a Monster." Reed Business Information. New York. 2011.

Stott, John. *The Cross of Christ.* Downers Grove: InterVarsity Press. 2006.

Taylor, John H. *Death and the Afterlife in Ancient Egypt.* University of Chicago Press. 2001.

Varner, Eric R. *Monumenta Graeca Et Romana: Mutilation and Transformation: Damnatio Memoriae and Roman Imperial Portraiture.* Vol. 10: Brill. 2004.

Vesalius, Andreas. *De humani corporis fabrica.* No. 4. Norman Publishing. 1543. [1998 reprint].

Williams, Mary Elizabeth. "What Would You Pay for John Wayne Gacy's Clown Art?" 2011. http://www.salon.com/2011/05/13/ted_kaczynski_john_wayne_gacy_auctions/.

Wolfgang, Marvin E. "Crime and Punishment in Renaissance Florence," in *Crime and Justice at the Millennium,* 365–81: Springer. 2002.

Index

A

AIDS, 65
Aleph Institute (AI), 155, 161
America's Most Wanted (television series), 226
American Civil Liberties Union (ACLU), 159, 161, 163, 169
American Psychiatric Association, 75, 96
Anti-Semitism, 138, 143–146, 150–151, 162
Antisocial Personality Disorder, 90
Antiquity, 172, 207–208, 221, 226
Artwork, 3, 208, 224, 226–227
Artificial Intelligence, 63, 67–70
Atlanta Vampire Alliance, 127
Authenticity, 6, 37–38, 41–42, 44, 49–50, 99–100, 102, 105, 176

B

Bakhtin, Mikhail, 101–102, 105, 113
Banksy, 224–225
Bathory, Erzebet (Elizabeth), 117, 120
Battle rapping, 37, 49–50
Black markets, 157, 223
Boogeyman, 174–175, 177, 193
Borderline Personality Disorder, 62–63, 69–70, 89, 98

C

Capital punishment (see Execution)
Caravaggio, 218, 220, 224, 227
Cecil, William, 17–19, 35
Cellini, 218, 223–224, 227
Chabad, 148, 159, 170
Chapbooks, 33
Charon, Rita, 2, 8
Clues, 1, 200, 203
Communication, 6, 37, 48–51, 53, 57, 61, 126, 128, 132
  Satisfaction, 48
  Studies, 6
Community Security Network (CSN), 147
Community Service Trust (CST), 146, 168–169
Conversion, 17–22, 28–30, 158–159, 161–162
Corpus Assisted Critical Discourse Analysis (CACDA), 172, 179
Corpus linguistics, 6–7
Crime scene(s), 1, 8, 104, 199–200, 202–206
Criminal humanities, 3–6, 8, 11, 226
Criminal investigation & detection, 1–2, 5, 82, 137, 140, 200, 204–206, 223
Criminal mind, 7, 94, 199
Criminal profiling, 7, 82
Criminogenic, 37–38, 43

Criminology, 3, 7–8, 38, 43, 49, 99, 117, 121–123, 127, 130, 132–133, 172, 207–208, 212, 216, 221, 223, 226
Gothic, 117, 121–123, 130, 132–133
Literary (see Literary criminology)
Critical discourse analysis, 172, 179–180
Cultural pathology, 14–15, 21
Cultural studies, 115, 127, 130

D

Damnatio memoriae, 209, 228
Delusion, 76, 128, 172–173, 178, 181–187, 192
Deterrence, 3, 209
Deviance, 5–7, 39, 76, 79, 154, 212
Dexter (television series), 83, 93
Diagnostic & Statistical Manual of Mental Disorders (DSM), 75–76, 90, 96, 128, 132, 172, 192
Diegetic, 101, 103, 108
Documentary, 6–7, 39, 57, 86, 99–102, 103–108, 111–114, 172
Dracula (character), 7, 120–121, 123–125, 131, 133
Dracula (novel), 7, 120–121, 123–124, 132
Dramaturgical theory, 48, 52

E

Early Modern Period, 6, 11–15, 24, 29–30, 34
Elizabethan England, 12–15, 17–19, 21, 26–28, 30, 32
Eminem, 50–51, 58
Execution, 12–14, 17–20, 21–30, 32, 34–36, 106–107, 110–112, 213–214, 216–217, 221, 224, 226–227
Execution of Justice in England, The, 17, 35
Exposition, 102
Expressive/transformative theory of violence, 48–49

F

Film (medium), 2, 5, 47, 73–74, 81–92, 95, 99–104, 106, 108–114, 120–124, 127, 131–133, 139, 152–154, 164, 184
Studies, 6, 71
Foucault, Michel, 20–21, 35
Forensics, 5–8, 62, 67, 73, 77–78, 82–84, 95, 117, 127–130, 181, 183, 187, 199–200, 202–206, 223
Forensic semiotics, 5, 8, 84, 199–200, 202
Forgery, 223
Friday the 13th (film franchise), 82
Friedman, Chaplain Gary, 156–159, 160–162

G

Gacy, John Wayne, 82, 224–225
Game of Thrones (television series), 93–94
Gangsta Rap (see also: Hip Hop music), 6, 37, 41–43, 47–49, 55
Gone Girl (novel & film), 89

H

Halloween (film franchise), 82
Hallucinations, 186
Hammurabi, 209–210
Hasidim, 153
Herman, Amy, 1–2, 4
Herzog, Werner, 105–107, 110–113
Hip Hop music (see also: Gangsta Rap), 6, 37–45, 48–56
Holidays, 143

I

Ice-T (artist), 36, 41–43, 52, 54–55, 57–58
Identity, 15, 17, 20–21, 31–32, 38, 47–48, 50–52, 56, 126–127, 129, 135–136, 138–140, 153–156, 158–161, 163, 172, 175, 178
Immigration, 150–151
Immortal technique, 40, 58

Internet, 5–7, 126, 171, 173, 175–178, 180, 186, 189, 192

J

Jarecki, Andrew, 105, 112
Jay-Z (artist), 50–52, 58
Jewish Police Association (JPA), 141, 143–146, 150–151, 169
Jewish Prisoner Services International (JPSI), 156, 161, 168

K

Kosher, 142, 144, 146, 156–158, 160–163, 165–170
KRS-One (artist), 52, 54–55, 58

L

Last Judgment, The, 213, 215
Latent Semantic Analysis, 65
Literary criminology, 3, 7, 38, 43, 49, 172
Literary studies, 6, 9, 130
Logical fallacy, 172, 183
Los Angeles Police Department (LAPD), 4
Lovecraft, HP, 174, 184
Lyrics, 38, 46, 51–52, 54

M

M'Naghten rules, 181
Meaning-making, 29, 33, 199, 201–206
Medical humanities, 2–3
Medieval, 57, 94, 212
Mesirah, 148–149
Metaphor, 8, 16, 25, 32, 61, 111, 113, 128, 131, 199–206
Metaphysics, 7, 174, 181–182, 184–185
Metonymy, 61
Murder, 1, 6, 13, 15, 24, 27–29, 31–34, 42–43, 47, 55, 61–62, 64, 73, 82, 89, 93–95, 105–106, 108–109, 111, 122, 129–131, 148, 153–154, 162, 171–173, 180–181, 183, 189, 209, 212, 214, 218, 221–226
Murderabilia, 224, 226
Museums, 1, 7–8, 197, 199, 202, 205, 226
Metropolitan Museum of Art (New York), 1–2
Morris, Errol, 112–113
Myth, 7, 51, 73, 82, 90, 117–120, 122, 124, 128, 130, 132, 171–178, 186

N

Narrative, 1–5, 8, 11–15, 18–19, 21–24, 27–34, 82–83, 86, 89, 99–113, 122, 124–125, 131, 171, 175–177, 181, 184–185, 203–205, 212–213
Nashe, Thomas, 6, 11, 13–16, 18, 24, 26–28, 30–31, 33–36
New York Police Department (NYPD), 1–4, 137–138, 140–141, 143, 145–146, 148, 164
Notorious B.I.G. (artist), 44, 50–51, 53–55

O

Orthodox Jews, 139, 141–145, 147–149, 153–155, 160, 163

P

Paganism, 172, 185
Painting, 1–2, 5, 8, 61, 208, 212–214, 216, 218, 221, 223–226
Part-of-Speech Tagger, 65
Peel, Sir Robert, 4
Persecution, 13–16, 21–22, 25–30, 32–34
Phantom community, 44–45, 49, 52–53
Photographs, 144, 174, 176, 221, 223
Police, 1–2, 4, 7, 43–44, 47, 49, 64, 109, 135–140, 142–150, 162–164, 190, 223
Providence, 11, 13, 16, 18, 21, 24, 29–32
Providentialism, 12, 33–34
Psychopathy, 6, 34, 73–95, 128–129, 223
  Checklist, 77–78
  Child, 89–92
  Corporate, 73–74, 86–87
  Criminal, 81–86

Female, 87–89
Primary, 78, 84, 86, 89
Secondary, 79
Psychosis, 75, 185, 187

R

Rabbis, 139, 148–149, 151–152, 156–157, 159–161, 163
Ramsland, Katherine, 126, 128
Reality, 7, 27, 34, 41, 45, 75, 86, 88, 99–103, 105, 117, 119–120, 122, 163, 172, 178–179, 181–185, 188, 190–191, 204, 209
Referents, 178, 203
Religion, 7, 17, 19–20, 40, 46, 128, 135, 139, 142, 156, 158–159, 161, 163, 172, 175, 178–179, 183, 185, 208, 212, 218
Renaissance, 1, 121, 212–214, 223
Renfield Syndrome, 117, 128–129
Representation, 5–6, 8, 12, 14, 20–21, 25, 30, 32, 47, 62, 77, 87, 100, 102, 109, 123–124, 130, 137, 138, 146, 152, 171–172, 207–209, 212, 214, 218, 221, 226
Retributive violence, 13, 29, 31, 33
Revenge, 12, 21, 29–32, 34, 80, 82, 89, 93
Rick Ross, 51, 57, 59
Rome, 11, 13–15, 17, 21–23, 25–27, 33–34, 93, 209, 224

S

Sabbath, 143–144, 162
Sanguinarian, 124
Schizophrenia, 173, 182
School shooters, 64
Self-image, 37, 42–43, 45, 48
Shomrim Community Patrol, 147
Shomrim Society, 138, 140–141, 147, 164
Signs, 76, 107, 112, 200, 202–206
Sketching, 176, 214, 216, 218, 221, 223
Slasher films, 73, 81–83
Slender Man, 7, 171–192
Sociopaths, 32, 34, 75–76, 79, 88, 90–91
Spectators, 31, 99–103, 105–113, 213
Splitting, 6, 61–65, 68
Stele, 209
Stigma, 16, 38, 50–51, 89, 95, 184
Stoker, Bram, 7, 120–121, 123
Strain theory, 38–39
Suicide, 24, 42, 63, 76, 204
Symbolic interactionism, 38

T

Talmud, 136, 150
Television, 5–6, 44, 74, 82–83, 90–95, 99, 101, 109, 121, 138–139, 152–153, 226
Tepes, Vlad, 117, 120
Thurston High School shooting, 64
Trace evidence, 109, 200, 203, 205
True Detective (television series), 93
Tupac Shakur, 44–48

U

Unfortunate Traveller, The, 6, 11–16, 22, 33–34

V

Vampire studies, 7, 125–126
Vampirism, 7, 117, 122–125, 127–131
Clinical, 117, 128–129
Criminal, 117, 130–131
Real, 117, 124–125, 127–128
Victims, 3, 6, 8, 26–28, 41, 47–48, 53, 56, 75, 79, 81–82, 87, 94, 104, 106, 108–110, 120, 123–124, 129, 131, 135, 139, 149, 154, 189, 203, 207, 218, 224
Virginia Tech Massacre, 62, 64

W

Wolf of Wall Street, The (film), 87

Y

Yarmulkes, 141–142

CRIMINAL HUMANITIES & FORENSIC SEMIOTICS

Michael Arntfield and Marcel Danesi
General Editors

This series publishes monographs, anthologies, annotated literary editions, and comparative studies that critically engage the humanities as a locus for the study of criminal offending, criminal investigation, deviance, penology, and deterrence, as well as the epistemology of justice. We are especially interested in submissions with a strong interdisciplinary orientation and which lie at the crossroads of theory and practice. In other words, this series is foremost concerned with using artistic, literary, and multimedia texts, situations, and other products of the strictly non-investigative world as vehicles for exploring long-standing social and procedural issues of interest to both academia and the general public. By engaging a wide readership encompassing both scholars and practitioners, it is the intent of this series to breathe new life into the humanities and cultural studies, not to further alienate or obfuscate the scholarship done in these disciplines. For this reason, collaborations between authors representing academic institutions and those working in both private and public knowledge sectors, including government and specialized areas of law enforcement, are encouraged to collaborate with respect to this project.

The series will publish studies and anthologies that explore the connection between fictional writing, movies, music, traditional electronic media, the Internet, and other domains of popular culture and how they have influenced the perception of crime and criminality. The synergy that exists between real crime (reality) and imagined criminality as manifesting itself through representations in writing and media is the primary focus of the series.

We also welcome submissions that draw on any number of semiotic, linguistic, and comparative literature traditions, particularly those espousing new approaches to these fields and which allow key concepts to be unpacked within the framework of the criminal justice system, the forensic sciences, or other professions or institutions that serve the public interest.

For additional information about this series or for the submission of manuscripts, please contact:

Peter Lang Publishing
Acquisitions Department
29 Broadway, 18th floor
New York, NY 10006

To order other books in this series, please contact our Customer Service Department:
800-770-LANG (within the U.S.)
212-647-7706 (outside the U.S.)
212-647-7707 FAX

Or browse online by series at:
www.peterlang.com

www.ingramcontent.com/pod-product-compliance
Ingram Content Group UK Ltd.
Pitfield, Milton Keynes, MK11 3LW, UK
UKHW020214290926
15470UKWH00001B/178

9 781433 131943